S0-EJS-859

The Shock of Men

THE SHOCK OF MEN

Homosexual Hermeneutics in French Writing

LAWRENCE R. SCHEHR

Stanford University Press, Stanford, California 1995

Stanford University Press
Stanford, California

Printed in the United States of America

CIP data are at the end of the book

Stanford University Press publications are distributed exclusively by Stanford University Press within the United States, Canada, Mexico, and Central America; they are distributed exclusively by Cambridge University Press throughout the rest of the world.

For my brother David

Preface

Until quite recently, the *New York Times* was still referring to a certain kind of person as an "admitted homosexual." Such a phrase is better than "practicing homosexual," for it implies that the individual may have gotten it right after all that practice. Liberals would certainly say that the *New York Times* has made strides in the decade. It uses the word "gay," refers to an individual's "longtime companion" in obituaries, and, in other realms, has finally accepted the title "Ms." One still has to wonder about a world in which the expression "admitted homosexual" has any currency. Certainly the expression "admitted *heterosexual*" is amusing at best. In our confessional culture, one only admits *bad* things: one is an admitted alcoholic, child molester, wife beater, homosexual, or cocaine addict. The function of the speech act of admission is not to reveal what one is. One would then be an admitted heterosexual or gentleman and there would no longer be self-declared feminists or communists. This speech act is an accomplishment of a laicized confessional mode that helps neutralize any possible ramifications of the act.

What have we done when we have said that William Burroughs is an admitted drug user, that Adrienne Rich is an admitted lesbian, that Marcel Proust was privately, but not publicly, an admitted homosexual, or even that some public figure is an "unadmitted" or "closeted" homosexual? To be sure, in some cases, there are questions that are juridical in nature, but my concern here relates to literature. Categories can destroy meaning: seeing the work of Burroughs as being guaranteed by the transcendental signifier of the author's drug addiction, or that of Proust by homosexuality, may be a way of devaluing their writing. The categorization may mean that a special set of rules will eventually be applied to the text, rules not used when the writer is an "admitted heterosexual." The liberal gesture of sweeping all that away does not suffice, since there is clearly a difference between white male heterosexuality and so many other possibilities: white male heterosexuality has the long-standing possibility of imposing its meanings and power, a possibility it denies to others as it fills the space of representation. Yet defining those others from the perspective of white male homosexuality hinders reading and understanding more than it helps.

Feminism has taught us that there are "other" voices that are disfigured or compromised by their relation to the power structure and the signifying system. Feminism has also taught us that this "otherness" is not at all secondary. It is "other" only to the extent that white male heterosexual discourse is also "other." The difference is that white male heterosexual discourse forgets that it too is "other." Feminism has put into question the kinds of repression and disfiguring of discourse that occur through the imposition, or simply the presence, of a certain form of power. It has also expounded upon the differences in form and detail that an "other" discourse might have, unique to itself and as valid as the forms of the dominant discourse.

In this book, I have chosen to concentrate on a group of authors, each quite different from the others, in whose work homosexuality operates as a productive and meaningful force. What has interested me is the way in which each of the authors uses homosexuality as a means of questioning the systems of dominance, power, and semiosis already in place. To a greater or lesser extent, there is an underlying hypothesis, sometimes avowed, sometimes silenced, sometimes turned about: while heterosexuality may be the dominant mode of the world, the figure of its power, and the means of its continuation, it is not inherently "better" than another version of sexuality. The world can be seen through other eyes, interpreted through other figures, or opened up to different possibilities if the mechanics of sexual reproduction are not given transcendental cultural meaning.

During the course of this study I have tried to examine the ways in which textuality and sexuality relate to one another, the various ways in which the signifier "slips" when it is not anchored to a dominant transcendental meaning-system. As we have learned from the literary theory of the past twenty years, considering the text as an immanent object may lead to a reductive formalism that ignores the various ramifications of the subject. Thus I have tried to open up the works in question and move my own comments away from being a rehearsal of the theme of homosexuality in the work of these writers. I have been interested in looking at a wider concept of interpretation that includes an understanding of specific textual hermeneutics and an exploration of how the text produces a theory of textuality that is supposed to explain the specific instance of textuality. In many cases, what I try to show is how a liberation from the constraints of dominant textuality and interpretation can lead to a complex of significations that still observes rules of form and plays within parameters without being constrained to adopt the meanings proffered a priori by the dominant textual system.

Some of the material in the chapters on Camus and Tournier appeared in an earlier form in two articles: "Renaud Camus' Roman Columns," *SubStance* 67 (1992): 111–28; "The Homotext of Tournier's *Les Météores*," *SubStance* 58 (1989): 35–50. I would like to thank the University of Wisconsin Press for its permission to reuse this material.

Unless otherwise indicated, I have done all translating myself while keeping the references to the original text. In this way, despite some sins on the side of awkward, literal translations, scholars have better access to the primary sources.

I am grateful to a large number of people without whose help this book would not have been possible. At the University of South Alabama, the Graduate School and the College of Arts and Sciences provided me with grants to do research on this material. Bernard Quinn has been a dedicated chairperson, looking out for my best interests, arranging for reassigned time, and being supportive in every personal and professional way possible. I would also like to thank Helen Tartar and Peter Kahn of Stanford University Press and my copy editor, Ann Klefstad; they have all worked tirelessly to turn a manuscript into a book. For reading and rereading, for stimulating conversations, for remarks, support, and encouragement, my gratitude goes to the following: George Bauer, Réda Bensmaïa, David Bell, Alain Buisine, Renaud Camus, Elisabeth Cardonne-Arlyck, Lawrence Kritzman, Caryl Lloyd, James Mandrell, Gerald Prince, Mireille Rosello, Charles Stivale, Stephen Whitworth, and especially Jean-François Fourny. Their advice has been cogent, their recommendations have, I hope, borne fruit, and, in every way, their help has been inestimable.

L.R.S.

Contents

Abbreviations

Ag	Camus, *Aguets*
AS	Barthes, *L'Aventure sémiologique*
BL	Barthes, *Le Bruissement de la langue*
BVP	Camus, *Buena Vista Park*
CA	Camus, *Chroniques achriennes*
CC	Barthes, *La Chambre claire*
Cor	Gide, *Corydon*
DZE	Barthes, *Le Degré Zéro de l'écriture*
EpCl	Sedgwick, *Epistemology of the Closet*
EPQ	Camus, *Elégies pour quelques-uns*
ES	Camus, *Esthétique de la solitude*
FA	Camus, *Fendre l'air*
FDA	Barthes, *Fragments d'un discours amoureux*
GMB	Tournier, *Gaspard, Melchior & Balthazar*
Gd'O	Tournier, *La Goutte d'or*
I	Barthes, *Incidents*
JR	Camus, *Journal romain*
JVC	Tournier, *Journal d'un voyage au Canada*
L	Barthes, *Leçon*
"MFN"	Barthes, "Masculin, féminin, neutre"
M	Barthes, *Mythologies*
Mét	Tournier, *Les Météores*
NA	Camus, *Notes achriennes*

NMT Camus, *Notes sur les manières du temps*
Pour Deleuze, *Pourparlers*
PPC Foucault, *Politics, Philosophy, Culture*
Pr Descombes, *Proust*
PT Barthes, *Le Plaisir du texte*
RA Tournier, *Le Roi des aulnes*
RB Barthes, *Roland Barthes*
RF Camus, *Roman furieux*
RR Camus, *Roman roi*
SFL Barthes, *Sade. Fourier. Loyola*
SR Barthes, *Sur Racine*
SS Foucault, *Le Souci de savoir*
T Camus, *Tricks*
Trav Camus and Duparc, *Travers*
VI Tournier, *Le Vagabond immobile*
Vig Camus, *Vigiles*
VLP Tournier, *Vendredi ou les limbes du Pacifique*
VP Tournier, *Le Vent Paraclet*
VS Foucault, *La Volonté de savoir*
VV Tournier, *Le Vol du vampire*

The Shock of Men

But 'midst the crowd, the hum, the shock of men,
To hear, to see, to feel, and to possess,
And roam along, the world's tired denizen,
With none who bless us, none whom we can bless;
Minions of splendour shrinking from distress!

Byron, *Childe Harold's Pilgrimage* (2:26)

Introduction: From Gide to Foucault

Since the eighteenth century, sex has continuously provoked a sort of generalized discursive erethism.

Michel Foucault, *La Volonté de savoir*

In his fragmentary autobiography, Roland Barthes tells of his fondness for amphibologies. Unlike a syllepsis, which is a word that has both a denotative and a figurative meaning, an amphibology is a word with two distinct denotative meanings. One example is the word "function," which means both relation and use. Another is "voice," which refers both to sound production and to grammar (*RB* 76–77). A word that one would have expected to find on Barthes's list is absent: "erethism." The word actually refers to not two things but three: a general irritation or arousal, a specifically sexual desire or arousal, and a discourse of violent exaltation. It is not surprising that the definitions overlap: after the strict medical definition, *Le Petit Robert* defines the literary meaning of the word as "a violent exaltation of a passion; an excessive mental tension." This amphibology "erethism" has phantom doubles in two other amphibologies with which Barthes will eventually deal: "diathesis," which means both medical propensity and the grammatical voice of a verb (active, middle, or passive), and the word "voice" itself.

Erethism: excitement and discourse, excitement of discourse, discourse as excitement. It is as if the violence of erethism forced the edges of these separate realms to blur, as if the very subject fractured definitions. The evidence is certainly there for all to read. For a century and a half, the discourses of sex have been focal points in the social sciences, the life sciences, and the humanities. Even in the times and places we consider sexually repressive, such as Victorian England or reborn Puritan America, the amount of discourse on sexuality is prodigious. The very discourses of sex and those of the repression of sex seem touched by the same erethism as the subject of those discourses: sex.

As is well known, in *La Volonté de savoir* Michel Foucault studies this erethism in his discussion of the received knowledge concerning the "repressive hypothesis," whereby sex is deemed to have been repressed in the Victorian era (*VS* 9–67). Foucault wonders about the very possibility of repression when such a vast quantity of material about sex is being produced. How can there be repression of sex, he asks, when everyone is writing about it? Foucault raises three specific doubts about the validity of the hypothesis according to which the nineteenth century was supposed to have repressed sexuality (*VS* 18). The first is a question as to whether there is historical evidence for the repression of sex in modern times. Then Foucault wonders whether the mechanics of power essentially relate to the order of repression as such, and not to organization, channeling, utility, or control. The third doubt relates to the discourse on repression: Foucault wonders if this discourse is not itself part of the same historic network that it supposedly denounces. Could not the so-called repression really be a figure of the technological organization of human behavior to make it useful? Foucault argues that the result of this so-called repression has been both a solidification and a flourishing of a system of sexual heterogeneity, far from the fully regulated system that repression would otherwise have produced (*VS* 71). In other words, despite its prohibitions, taboos, and channeling of behavior, discursive erethism has led more to diversity than to homogeneity in matters of sex.

According to Foucault, the erethism of the nineteenth century allowed people to talk about sex in all its manifestations. Cloaked in the respectability of scientific discourse, eugenic social science, pedagogy, and even city planning, the various discourses constitute sexualities as objects of discourse within the constituent reality they signify. The existence of sexuality as an object of study within the realm of the human sciences thus constitutes the sexual being behind the "symptomatic" manifestation of some particular sexuality. The discourses of the nineteenth century constitute the homosexual as an individual with the invention of the word "homosexual." So, too, does the "cold bath theory" posit that far from being pure asexual individuals blessed with an inborn morality, young men are sexual beings in a virtually constant state of arousal. Pollution—coincidentally another amphibology—was viewed as a serious problem in this era, because masturbation could no longer be seen as an isolated event: it was perceived as relating to the individual committing the heinous act.

No longer was it possible on a general scale to separate the sin from the sinner. If it was a question of "loving the sinner but hating the sin," it soon became difficult to separate the discourse on the "sin" from the discourse on the "sinner."

One of those discourses will concern us here: the discourse of and about homosexuality. As Richard Mohr shows in *Gay Ideas* (222–23), social and scientific explanatory discourses about homosexuality can be classified in three categories. First, there is a realist argument, which finds "sufficient causes in or from nature to explain the sexual desires of a person for members of his or her own biological or genital sex." Realist discourse thus deals with causes. The second kind of discourse deals with definitions. This is the essentialist argument, which posits some culturally neutral definition of homosexuality that can be objectively applied across cultural and historical lines. Foucault's argument has become emblematic of the third type of discourse, the social construction of homosexuality. Simply put, the social constructionist argument sees the content or meaning of the word "homosexuality" as having been produced by the social structures and formats in which any given individual finds himself or herself.

Foucault's argument about the social construction of homosexuality has now become an obligatory reference in gender studies. As Mohr remarks (238), "The most famous case is the bit from Foucault on homosexuality so frequently used as boilerplate for academic witnessings and pledge takings." Knowing, then, that my reader is fully aware of the argument, I shall just briefly summarize it. Homosexuality is seen as a part of the human condition when the action of homosexual sex is related to the individual behind it and not primarily to a legal or religious code that speaks of actions instead of individuals: "Homosexuality appeared as one of the figures of sexuality when it was turned from the practice of sodomy into a sort of interior androgyny, a hermaphroditism of the soul. The sodomist was a backslider; the homosexual is now a species" (*VS* 59). The nineteenth century invents the homosexual as an individual with a life. The very words "homosexuality" and "homosexual," coined in 1869 by a Hungarian writer, Benkert, signal the individual behind the action, as did the earlier nineteenth-century word "uranist" as well as all the neologisms produced since then. The advantage of the word "homosexual" was that it seemed to have the additional quality of being scientifically neutral, neither euphemistic, derogatory, nor culturally biased. Armed with a new vocabulary, the nineteenth century begins to consider the homosexual as a person with a present, a past, and a future: "The homosexual of the nineteenth century became a character: a past, a history and a childhood, a personality, a life-style; a morphology as well, with a vague anatomy and perhaps a mysterious physiology" (*VS* 59). No longer an isolated action, the homosexual act is indicative of the homosexual who performs that act.

Now the definitional aspect is only one side of the coin. As the reader knows, Foucault's concern is also with the use of these discourses. Along with his argument about the social construction of homosexuality, Foucault continues to oppose the repressive hypothesis about sexuality. So beyond the definition and investigation of homosexuality, there are apologies, explanations, and pleas for understanding that arise simultaneously with the discourses that seek to control. Homosexuality is not subject to repression because the two kinds of discourses, controlling and understanding, are equipotential in the space of discursive praxis. Concomitant with the discourse on perversity is a discourse of liberation, explanation, and justification. From the moment these multiple discourses appear, the discourse of and on homosexuality begins to speak in the name of homosexuality: the discourse of homosexuality tames its own strangeness; it uses the same language as the dominant discourses; it argues for its own "naturalness." Homosexuality may be less frequent than heterosexuality, but it is no less natural: "homosexuality began to talk of itself, to claim its legitimacy or its 'naturalness' and often with the same vocabulary and categories with which it was medically disqualified" (*VS* 132). The reader should not be surprised that one of the consequences of the social constructivist argument is its recourse to "nature": if so many people are talking about homosexuality, it must be part of the natural world. The invention of the homosexual seems suddenly to transcend the immediate social context. As Mohr remarks,

> If the nineteenth-century homosexual is just one sort of homosexual, then we must suppose that Foucault has a definition of "homosexual" that he does not give us but with which he presumes we are operating and that is defined in socially and culturally neutral fashion so that the qualification "nineteenth century" adds something, is significant. (238–39)

Let us leave the question of nature for now—we shall return to it below—to follow Foucault's discussion about repression and about the manipulation of discourses of and about "perverse" sexualities.

For Foucault, there is no repression as such, if repression is considered to be the social equivalent of both *Verdrängung*, the unconscious act of repressing something into the unconscious, and *Unterdrückung*, the conscious act of suppression. According to Foucault, because people are talking about sexuality, it is neither repressed nor suppressed:

> What is said about sex must not be analyzed as the simple surface on which these mechanisms of power are projected. It is in discourse that power and knowledge

> are articulated. And for that very reason, discourse must be seen as a series of discontinuous segments whose tactical function is neither uniform nor stable. More precisely, one should not imagine a world of discourse divided into accepted and rejected discourses or between dominant and dominated discourses, but rather, a multiplicity of discursive elements that can play a role in diverse strategies. (*VS* 132–33)

Foucault uses the term "juridico-discursive" for the domain that forms the relations of power and determines the instruments that allow for its analysis.[1] For him, the relation of discourses fits into a juridico-discursive system. There are five main aspects to these juridico-discursive relations. First, there is a negative relation between power and sex: the former relates to the latter through rejection, exclusion, refusal, and the like. Second, the rule is insistent: power dictates the law of sex to sex. Sex is submitted to a binary logic of the permitted and forbidden or the licit and illicit. Power acts by stating the rule. Third, power participates in a cycle of the forbidden; as far as sex is concerned, the objective of power is for sex to abandon itself. Fourth, there is a logic to censure that takes three forms: it affirms that something is not permitted, it prevents that thing from being said, and it denies that that thing exists. Finally, the whole is united: juridico-discursive power acts at all levels in the same way (*VS* 109–11).

For Foucault, then, though sex is not repressed, its manifestations and its discourses are channeled in various ways in order to maintain and preserve the power structure. The absence of repression *stricto sensu* does not mean that such "perverse" sexualities as homosexuality are not subject to manipulations by various systems of power and by dominant discourses. It is this point in Foucault's argument that has proven so interesting to the proponents of the social constructivist model: homosexuality as such is not repressed, but it is organized, controlled, channeled, made forbidden, submitted to correction, and so on. Most notably, Eve Kosofsky Sedgwick sees the dichotomizing definition of homo/heterosexuality as fundamental for the world of the end of the nineteenth century. Relating definitions and discourse to a power grid, she seems to make an analogy between that double definition and other modes of divisive discourse. These were

> decades in which so many of the other critical nodes of the culture were being, if less suddenly and newly, nonetheless also definitively reshaped. Both the power

1. Among the many readings of this material Judith Butler's stands out. In her excellent book *Gender Trouble* Butler (2–34) comments extensively on Foucault's systems of juridico-discursive power as they relate to the constitution of the feminist subject. Butler's entire book is fundamental to an understanding of the current status of the intersections and overlappings between feminist politics and theory in American intellectual circles.

relations between the genders and the relations of nationalism and imperialism, for instance, were in highly visible crisis. (*EpCl* 2)

If, for Foucault, homosexuality is not repressed, and if, for other social constructivists, the ideas of control and organization have proven far more fruitful than a simple act of repression would have, one cannot deny that the various apologists for homosexuality in the late nineteenth century nonetheless labored under the (mistaken) belief that they were fighting the repression of homosexuality. Following Foucault, though, we can see these writings as manifestations of discursive strategies that recognize the power of the discourse on sexuality as both a product of nonrepression and an instrument that seeks to repress. If *sex* is not repressed in the second half of the nineteenth century, the dominant juridico-discursive mechanism still seeks to silence *certain forms* of sex. Power attempts to silence certain discourses, but in the very manifestation of this power, which is the erethism of discourses on sexuality, the complete suppression of the other discourse is made impossible: the discourse of power cannot exist without the phantom other discourse that it attempts to suppress. For the discourse of power to function, it must maintain the targeted "other" discourse as an object. If the discourse of the other disappears completely, the dominant discourse has no function and thereby loses its dominance.

Various apologies for homosexuality have had currency and influence within the framework allotted to these ghost discourses. Sometimes, backed with the logic of scientific reason in a comparatively liberal or enlightened climate, an author can state simply and directly his or her findings, observations, and recommendations. Yet even within the scientific world, the "love that dare not speak its name" may remain anonymous. Thus the same Hungarian writer who created the neologism "homosexual" —Benkert—took on an anagrammatic pseudonym, Kertbeny, when writing a letter to the Prussian Minister of Justice in support of a right to privacy (Fernandez 62). Perhaps because of this mistaken belief in retribution or repression, apologists for homosexuality looked for a stronger weapon than science. In addition to the enlightened arguments for understanding, which could quite rightfully be seen as the expected product of a scientific age, one finds an argument for acceptance based on nature, to which we now turn.

As we have seen, there is recourse in the Foucauldian history of homosexuality to a natural argument. The sheer quantity of discourse about sexuality, even about "perverse" sexuality, would seem in the long run to normalize the concept by making it familiar. It is a short step from that familiarity to a view maintaining that homosexuality was always (or often) natural, that is, part of nature, and that various perversions in the power structure were what denatured homosexuality. I am not saying that the social constructivist model needs nature, but that a socially constructed nature is one of the consequences of the plethora of discourses. At the same time, the natural argument does not need the support of social constructivism. One could argue for an essentialist history in which sexual relations between two males were always considered by some to be "natural."

One of the spheres in which the natural argument plays an important role is literature. Let us turn to one of the most important literary apologies for homosexuality, André Gide's *Corydon*. Gide published this work in 1911 in a small, privately circulated edition of about twelve or thirteen copies. There was an expanded, definitive edition in 1920, also circulated privately, of about twenty-one copies (Marty, 290; Pollard, 3–10). As late as 1921, Gide's *Journal* (692–94) indicates that he was willing to lend the text to Marcel Proust on the condition that the latter not show it to anyone. The work was published by Gallimard in 1924, presumably in more enlightened times and, significantly, after the publication of Proust's own *Sodome et Gomorrhe*. Still, since then *Corydon* has been more frequently out of print than in.

Corydon is a classic—even an archetypal—apology for homosexuality, and consists of four dialogues. The short first one sets up the parameters for what will follow: it functions to naturalize or normalize the radical subject matter by relating this discourse to the standard approaches of the nineteenth century. Corydon proposes to speak "as a doctor, a naturalist, a moralist, a sociologist, a historian" (*Cor* 28). But along with the characteristic scientific argument comes a radical version of the natural argument. Sexual reproduction and heterosexuality are seen as just one possibility among many: "far from being the only 'natural' act, the act of procreation, in nature, among the most disconcerting profusion, is most often only a fluke [*raccroc*]" (*Cor* 32). Following this assault on normal assumptions about the primacy of procreation, Gide writes a second chapter that consists of a denaturing of nature itself. The argument displaces the neatly encapsulated ideas we have about nature; much as Montaigne had done in the "Apologie de Raymond Sebond," Gide insists that nature is far more varied than we seem to believe. Moreover, such variation is itself perhaps the most "natural" thing about nature, far more "natural," in any case, than the ordinary, domesticated, ordered vision of nature we usually have. The third chapter is written as a segue to the second: the truth of poetry follows the truth of nature. The great minds of literature have realized that natural variation, specifically pederasty, exists, and have depicted it in poetry. In fact, when poetry turns its eyes away from that nature, it is itself denatured: "Bucolic poetry began to be artificial the day that the poet stopped being in love with the shepherd" (*Cor* 98). In the final chapter, along with the continued need to recognize the natural qualities of homosexuality, Gide promotes the hypothesis that homosexuality is most overtly prevalent in periods of high culture.

In its final version, *Corydon* is quite clearly different from works such as *Sodome et Gomorrhe*. I am most interested in this division: one would expect solidarity between Proust and Gide, but they could not be further apart. So before we look a little more closely at Gide's arguments, I should like to bring to the reader's attention a quote from what would seem to be an aside, a footnote to the preface of *Corydon* that dates from late 1922. Gide uses the publication of Proust's work—the opening pages of *Sodome et Gomorrhe*, which appeared in 1921—both as a support and as a target:

> Certain books—those of Proust in particular—have gotten the public used to being outraged and to considering coolly [*de sang-froid*] what it tried to ignore or preferred to ignore at first. Many minds willingly believe that they suppress what they ignore. . . . But, at the same time, I fear that these books have greatly contributed to misleading opinion. The theory of the man-woman . . . that Marcel Proust seems to support may in fact not be false. But it explains and concerns only certain cases of homosexuality, those precisely that I do not deal with in this book: cases of inversion, effeminacy, and sodomy. And I see today that one of the great faults of my book is precisely that I do not deal with them and that they are far more common than I first thought. (*Cor* 8–9)

Gide is making the same argument about suppression and repression to be made seventy years later by Foucault. While Gide clearly does not approve of Proust's depiction of the effeminate homosexual, he nevertheless acknowledges the fact that Proust's novel has—in a short time, I would add—helped normalize such a character. Gide recognizes that there must be a discourse of the other, the minority, for the dominant discourse to remain dominant.

Whereas for Foucault the question of ethics is only incidental to the structuring of discourses by power, for Gide the ethical matter provides an appropriate ground for a textual dynamics. Still, even in the case of Gide, with his double inspiration of classical sources and nineteenth-century science, the ethics are never personal. He seeks rather a global, desubjectified ethical position that will include homosexuality within the realm of the natural. More accurately—and this is where the footnote is the telling clue—Gide will seek to include *some* homosexuality within the realm of the natural. This is not to say that Gide and Foucault have the same position;

Gide's essentialist/realist position is not that of Foucault's social constructivism. Yet, as Mohr notes, where Foucault at times seems to appeal to a transhistorical view of homosexuality, Gide seems to appeal to a socially constructed category for the bad homosexual, the invert, or the effeminate figure.

In almost the same breath, Gide manages both to praise and to criticize Proust. Some of the dynamics of Gide's position obviously relate to a mimetic rivalry with the other author. The rejection of the manuscript of the first volume of the *Recherche*, Gide's belated recognition of its interest, his ultimate regret at having rejected the book, the various criticisms in the diaries of Proust's failure to be publicly homosexual, and this footnote to the preface to *Corydon* all seem to indicate such rivalry on Gide's part. Though Proust was the younger author, he already seemed in 1921–22 to be completing a great, complex novel. In 1922, the only one of Gide's narratives whose complexity even begins to approach that of the *Recherche*—*Les Faux-Monnayeurs*—was still three years away from publication. Proust seemed to be accomplishing something that Gide found elusive: an integration of homosexuality and narrative. Gide knew that he could not very well have a Virgilian shepherd wandering around in his own novel, yet he found no alternative of his own to Charlus that would keep that character's complexity and magnitude. Gide could justify his nobler undertaking with a criticism of Proust, only to follow it belatedly with a compliment and a recognition, be it the recognition of *Du côté de chez Swann* or the rather incredible admission that he forgot to talk about inversion in his defense of homosexuality.

It is impossible to take Gide at his word in this note when he says: "one of the great faults of my book is precisely that I do not deal with them [inverts] and that they are far more common than I first thought." The forgetting of inversion is hardly a plausible apology for a lapsus in the defense. It is hard to believe that Gide has ignored the existence of so-called inverts or that he sees them as merely the marginal sociopathic versions of the good homosexual, in other words, the pederast. And Gide's pederast, as the argument shows, has high culture as the mirror of his truth; the invert has nothing more than a modern, somewhat tawdry scene of seduction in a courtyard. Gide needs a raison d'être, a pedigree, and a precedent for his version of homosexuality. He needs a history, and like Michel Foucault, he finds it in Greece. But whereas Foucault finds a series of discourses that will define the possibilities of sexuality, Gide needs to find a poetic type that will authorize any single instance of behavior. The pederast has a pedigree; the simple invert does not. Gide's apology for homosexuality will thus be founded in part on this act of discrimination, which separates the good pederast with his noble intentions from the bad, marginalized homosexual, the invert like Charlus, who is at best an exaggerated caricature in a novel.

Corydon is by and large the narrative of that pedigree. The history of the good pederast is blessed by nothing less than the aesthetic version of creation coupled with a reference to one of the great homosexuals of history: "a large photograph of Michelangelo's *Creation of Man*" (*Cor* 16). Supported by the genre of philosophical inquiry that is Socratic dialogue and bolstered by poetry with references to Walt Whitman, *Corydon* begins to make an argument for the natural state of homosexuality. This portrayal is far from that of the execrable love *contra naturam* vilified in so many quarters: "I wager that less than twenty years hence, words like 'unnatural,' 'antiphysical,' etc. will no longer be taken seriously. For me, only one thing in the world is not natural: the work of art. Everything else, willy-nilly, belongs to nature" (*Cor* 32). In this world, then, it is a choice between two versions of the good: one is ontologically good because it is a part of nature; the other is aesthetically good because it is a work of art. Gide situates homosexuality in an aestheticized world where culture is the greater good, and where nature provides the support and sustenance for culture.

For Gide, nature provides the classical argument of the apology, but nature itself is put into question: nature may not be natural; it may be only a product of culture. The unlikely source of the argument is Pascal: "I fear that this nature is itself but a first custom, as custom is a second nature" (*Cor* 38). Hence the argument for the natural is grounded in the following logic: the only thing that is not natural is the work of art, but the work of art has its own value system based on aesthetics and thus has merit without needing to be attached to nature. Nature itself may be a cultural product and therefore, we might extrapolate, we can evaluate nature based on cultural criteria. One of the cases Gide offers of the cultural nature of nature is instructive: Gide finds evidence that androcentrism itself, the bulwark of civilization, is itself a product of culture. The fact that an androcentric society claims natural right does not in any way diminish the presumption of the claim. So if androcentrism is not intrinsically natural, can we maintain that heterosexuality is? Male-dominated, heterosexist society is a construction within the realm of the artificial but it is falsely given as natural by the juridico-discursive power system (to use Foucault's terms). In the end, Gide's transhistorical argument seems to be a large-scale social constructivism that takes the entire history of the West as its time frame.

Aside from exposing certain false claims of naturalness, much of the rest of Gide's defense depends on the existence of homosexuality in nature, that is to say, in the animal kingdom. He repeats a familiar gesture of making the human both more and less strange in its diversity, a gesture made by apologists such as Montaigne in the "Apologie de Raymond Sebond," and Sade in dozens of didactic passages. Such an argument runs as follows: human existence and nature are far more manifold than anyone can imagine. Human existence and nature are so varied that any decision as to what is proper and improper is bound to err because all such definitions posit an essentialist definition of the human. But no definition of the human could ever include every variant, and thus every definition is wrong, nonneutral, and exclusionary. Even without aesthetics, Gide would argue, human nature is as varied as is the natural world.

So homosexuality is natural; it is part of the manifold creation. Moreover, it can be demonstrated to have a productive cultural value and can take its rightful place among the possibilities of human existence. The opposition is not between nature and culture, but between the true and the artificial. If the work of art has its own truth that it proceeds to demonstrate and fulfill, it can be categorized as good. From that belief in a good transhistorical aesthetics that replaces the rejected transhistorical definition, Gide is led to an ethical imperative:

> And the day that one decided to write a history of the relation of uranism to the plastic arts, one would not see uranism flourish in periods of decadence, but, on the contrary, in glorious, healthy epochs, those precisely in which art is the most spontaneous and the least close to artifice. (*Cor* 100)

It is a short step from such a statement to an ethico-aesthetic valorization of homosexuality; in a classic rhetorical reversal Gide *inverts* the hierarchy between homosexuality and heterosexuality: "homosexuality in both sexes is more spontaneous and more naive than heterosexuality" (*Cor* 102).

The tenuousness of such remarks is ultimately less interesting than the underlying epistemology that valorizes one position at the expense of another. Gide's epistemology thus repeats standard heterosexist juridico-discursive epistemology and, as the remark on Proust emblematically shows, it depends on a relegation of certain instances—such as that of the invert—to controlled categories. An apology for homosexuality that depends on the argument of the naturalness of homosexuality seeks in general either validation or valorization for the position it is putting forth. In its appeal to a Rousseauistic version of nature, Gide's polemical excess implies a reversal of the standard juridico-discursive act. Yet the identical act of appealing to nature seems to beg the question, especially after Gide himself, quoting Pascal, indicates that the opposition between nature and culture is a false dichotomy.

Let us turn now to the foundations of the problematic of homosexuality shared by Gide and Foucault, in order to continue to develop what I perceive as the common position held in arguments about social construction and about essence. It is only in light of an exploration of that foundation and its implications that we will be able to see a strikingly different position that seems to dominate, *pace* Gide, in modern literature. It may seem odd to see Foucault's position in *La Volonté de savoir* and Gide's in *Corydon* as having been inspired by idealism (Kantian for Foucault, Platonic for Gide). Foucault's every gesture seems to sweep away the transcendental posits that idealism requires.

In Foucault's discussion of sexuality, the appeal to Greece relates to a problem that will appear in full force in the third volume of *Histoire de la sexualité*: the resurgence of the subject. Aside from being the appropriate subject matter for a history of sexuality, "Greece," as a collection of signifiers and discourses, serves to guarantee the idealism of Foucault's discursive praxis, because, after all is said and done, "Greece," the mythic origin of the West, transcends the immediately historical. Greece provides, if not an ahistorical essence, then a transhistorical one that has been around for two and a half millennia, most of recorded history. The argument based in Greece is not, for all that, an appeal to permanent essence; it is, however, an originary case that defines the base of the Western conscious subject. In that, regardless of historical change and juridico-political power structures, the case has some sort of permanence in the history and culture of the Occident.

Both for Gide and for Foucault, Greece is the natural version of culture as well as the locus at which culture begins to fall. Going back to Greece means finding justification at the origin of the division between nature and culture and finding the original spot at which the difference was understandable. Gide's Greek justification is seconded by the pastoral mode of the reference to the bucolic stereotype of Corydon, the personified apologist of noble homosexuality and the figure of the *oaristys*, the amorous idyll described in such poetry. In his work, Gide reaffirms both the naturalness of homosexuality and its appropriateness as the means of reinscribing nature considered to be a product of culture. Within the social constructivist model there is recourse to nature; within the natural model there is recourse to a concept of social construction in which juridico-discursive power is itself perversion. Gide and Foucault are not linked by a similar approach or similar politics but they do agree: Foucault's social constructivist position and Gide's essentialist/realist position are saying the same thing.[2] Let us look more closely at Gide and Foucault together.

Given the realist argument as developed by Gide in *Corydon*, one could clearly imagine its obverse: though part of nature, homosexuality is *contra naturam*, a demonic force, a sign of the devil, the demiurge, or evil incarnate. Before the reader laughs, he or she should remember that such a tack has been used as recently as 1993 in the United States in the arguments against lifting the ban on gays and lesbians in the military. The argument *about* nature always carries the possibility of the argument *against* nature, and it is still part of our world. Now, along those lines, one could say that the view of nature is determined by the discourses of social construction and that there are always remainders of previous discursive systems, aberrations, anomalies, and anachronisms. In other words, the politically correct argument may use the arguments of monstrosity proffered in various guises by the voices of blatant heterocracy to combat that heterocracy.

Perhaps Foucault's position is undercut because the definitions and descriptions of homosexuality he unearths are often aberrant, archaic, or contradictory relative to what science knew then or knows today. Let us take a very simple, well-known example: American antisodomy laws. Aside from the fact that their very existence is anomalous in a postindustrial society, the antisodomy laws still on the books in a number of American states are testimony to an archaism that persists: they focus on the specific actions of, one would assume, an otherwise guiltless individual. In the state of Alabama (to shift the focus from the oft-repeated stories concerning Georgia's sodomy laws), the laws forbidding sodomy and sexual misconduct define the criminal action as any sexual congress between two individuals who are not married to each other, as well as any sexual act, such as oro-genital or bucco-anal contact, other than intercourse between spouses. Since the law is very specific in maintaining the fragmentary nature of the "crime," the discourse about homosexuality at the end of the twentieth century may still have vestiges of the isolated action condemned by antisodomy laws that existed before the "homosexual" was invented as an individual.[3]

2. Despite his critique of the social constructivist position, Richard Mohr agrees with Eve Kosofsky Sedgwick's programmatic list of categories. But note well, Mohr is precisely appealing to gay studies as "a moral vision." Can it be, as Stanley Fish would have it, that "theory has no consequences"? That, for example, Richard Mohr's critique of social constructivism and Eve Kosofsky Sedgwick's highly social constructivist position can have the same result?

3. The irony of the situation is that such laws coexist in the same country with the Castro in San Francisco, Greenwich Village in New York, or the French Quarter in New Orleans, a mere hundred or so miles away from the state of Alabama. Actually the irony goes even

The question then is not about reforming our definitions to purify them. It relates to the merits of the social constructivist and realist arguments. Yes, Foucault is right, but he is especially right about a period, the nineteenth and twentieth centuries, that itself puts stock in the power of discourse. The realist argument is also right, especially in its idea that there is some transhistorical concept of male-male sex, fuzzy around the edges and slowly changing over time. Regardless of the definition, there is some continuity of male-male sexuality that was around long before the "invention of homosexuality." Clearly, homosexuality was not invented in 1867 in Central Europe, only to remain uninvented in Great Britain until a quarter of a century later when the word was used in English for the first time.

Or perhaps the social constructivist and realist arguments are both wrong: it doesn't matter, some would say, for that sort of theory has no consequences. What matters is what is done with the given. Let us imagine that, hypothetically, we find the answer to the dilemma of nature versus nurture. Can anyone really believe that such a discovery would solve the "problem" of homosexuality? If we knew that homosexuality was a natural phenomenon, would we use some twenty-first–century equivalent of ultrasound to weed out future fairies? Or, for that matter, to ease them into the world? If we knew that homosexuality was a product of nurture, would we insist that parents act so as to avoid falling into the bleak inverted triangle of Oedipal disaster?

Where I find Proust, Barthes, Camus, and Tournier more radical, more revolutionary, more insightful, and ultimately more satisfying on this matter than Gide and Foucault, despite all the interest of these latter two, is that the answer does not matter to them. What matters, as I have just said, is what one does with the given. Far more radical than the argument of nature versus nurture is an argument with deontological or hermeneutic consequences. So though they seem to some to be strange bedfellows (so

---

deeper, since the state of Louisiana itself still, as I write, has antisodomy laws. So, depending on the perspective, one could certainly sympathize with Foucault's view that homosexuality is controlled and not repressed: the gay bars that are central to tourism in New Orleans coexist with presumably unenforced antisodomy laws. On another front, the same state of Louisiana has mandatory AIDS education but this cannot occur within the context of a discussion of sex. On the legal question, the isolation of the action also relates to the problem of legal definition, which, it seems to me, in criminal law does not define the individual but the action, whereas at least in certain aspects of civil law, such as contract law, it relates to the individual whose signature guarantees his or her whole being. Hence, in criminal cases, one might assume that the rationale for more serious sentencing given to a recidivist is that he or she can no longer believably just confess the isolated crime, but must put himself or herself on the line.

to speak), Proust joins Sartre in a realization of a condemnation to freedom and joins the early Heidegger in the realization that each human being is thrown into the world. As Proust, Barthes, Camus, and Tournier show, the argument is not about nature versus nurture, not about social construction versus realism or essentialism (a position that finally seems particularly anachronistic in its logical positivism), but about a text that is a search for a meaning, even when no transcendental validity is found. All four authors show us another thing: the real historical search, for those who are interested, is for a *dispositif* that can explain one additional dichotomy: the opposition between social constructivism and realism.

What I am terming this thrownness or this existential condemnation to freedom depends on the constitution of the subject as subject. I am not, for all that, making a claim for the integral nature of the subject or for any transcendental independence of the subject. Rather, I see in the work of these four authors the constitution of the subject, and specifically the homosexual subject, as the work of the text. And I believe the constitution of this subject is done, not *with* the aid of Greece as a background, but *against* a gradual desubjectivization that seems to be the mark of modern and postmodern society.

If, as I have suggested, the work of the four authors I am surveying in this study consists of an examination of the subject, then it behooves us to examine the function of the subject in the work of Gide and Foucault in order to understand that against which these four authors are implicitly or explicitly writing. For Gide, the subject can free himself or herself from the pressures and weight of the structures that inscribe him or her in Western society. The famous scenes of contact between the repressed European male and the free Maghrebin boys in *L'Immoraliste* and *Si le grain ne meurt* attest to this will to freedom. Having shed the skin of the West, the liberated individual is free to be himself or herself, free in his or her *disponibilité*, free to be homosexual. Time after time, the guilt and weight of the West come back, eternally haunting the subject; but freedom is at least posited as a possibly attainable, ideal goal. On the other hand, the function of the subject in Foucault's work is far more problematic, for there is a growing ambiguity that starts in the first volume of *Histoire de la sexualité*. Foucault seems to recognize that the question of sexuality necessitates a revision of his own view of the subject. He can no longer dissolve the subject in a sea of discursive practices. It is to the resurgence of the subject in *Histoire de la sexualité* that I now briefly turn.

The second and third volumes of *Histoire de la sexualité* had not yet been published when Hubert Dreyfus and Paul Rabinow wrote their excellent study of Foucault; thus their examination of the shifts in Foucault's work ends with a study of his concept of bio-power. Still, they already see an ambiguity about the subject of enunciation present in the first volume. As they note, "Where Foucault himself stands, in relation to his descriptions of the repressive hypothesis, is not explicitly clear. He coyly sidesteps the problem of whether he is exempt from the descriptions he is providing" (131–32). Writing at approximately the same time, Karlis Racevskis also accepts the initial dissolution of the subject in Foucault's writing as he follows Foucault through the changes from archaeology to genealogy to bio-power; Bernard Sichère also addresses this matter a few years later (75–147). While concurring with many other critics in his assessment of Foucault's dismissal of the subject, Racevskis finds that the subject in Foucault's work is brought back at a metadiscursive level. For Racevskis, the very dissolution of the subject in Foucault's writing can be glossed with a Lacanian reading of the subject:

> The first apparent purpose is to dissolve the subject, to dismantle the founding notion of a subjective consciousness; then, in the void thus created at the center of discourse, it becomes possible to develop a new kind of awareness that will radically alter our thinking about discourse. It is the absence of the subject or the subject as nonbeing that allows for a new approach, yet paradoxically the question of the subject remains—for the subject is still a presence in discourse, although it is the presence of an absence. Indeed, the dissolution of a conscious subject does not eliminate the subject but produces a shift in perspective: we have oriented thought toward the unconscious subject. From an awareness of the Same we have moved to that of the Other. We have arrived at the dimension of the Symbolic. (30)

Most recently, James Miller (245–84) has proposed that the change in Foucault's concept of the subject relates to his lifelong interest in limit-experiences, which turned into an epiphany in California when Foucault experienced both LSD and San Francisco's extensive gay subculture. While many critics would undoubtedly find Miller's approach schematic or teleological, his idea does have the advantage of relating the resurgence of the subject in Foucault's work to sex itself. One might say that Foucault's discourse on sexuality was enabled by his own radical position on the subject, and that discourse in turn led to a rediscovery of the subject—of desire, if not of enunciation—during his writing of *Histoire de la sexualité*. The clues are certainly there. In an interview entitled "The Minimalist Self," Foucault does not give absolute priority to sexuality as the manifestation of humanness. He does, however, individualize the relation of sexuality to the subject; for once, the object of study is not just a discursive praxis. As he notes: "Sexuality is not *the* secret but it is still a symptom, a manifestation of what is the most secret in our individuality" (*PPC* 11).

In freely granted interviews Foucault seemed to allow himself a liberty, even a verbal erethism, that he withheld in his own ascetic writing. It is as if that freedom itself were somehow, like an individual's sexuality, the metonymy of the subject that would never be directly enunciated. In an interview entitled "An Aesthetics of Existence" Foucault talks about "the *parrhesia* (free speech) of the governed, who can and must question those who govern them" (*PPC* 51). This *parrhesia* makes its way into the concerns of the last volume of *Histoire de la sexualité*. In this last work, Foucault admits his own subjectivity as interpreter, a position he had constantly erased in favor of the safer, more arid position of a nonsubject, an archivist.

John Rajchman draws a parallel between the question of the "individualization of the author" in a text like "What Is an Author?" and the question of the individualization of the "homosexual person" (as opposed to a person who commits certain specified "acts" of a homosexual nature) in the volumes of *Histoire de la sexualité*. Rajchman (32) goes on to say that these "two procedures to 'individualize' intersect in the 'political reality' of the homosexual writer—a matter of obviously specific concern for Foucault." In a similar vein, Mark Poster (54) addresses the constitution of the subject in Foucault's last writings. He sees "Foucault's strategy of dispersing the centered subject among discourses and practices that generate 'technologies of power'" as something that continues in Foucault's writing through the end of the first volume of *Histoire de la sexualité*. But in his commentary on the second and third volumes, Poster makes the following point:

> Foucault isolates sex as the nub of the question [of self-constitution] without, however, giving much attention to that selection. . . . Could it be said that Foucault selected sexual activity as the venue of self-constitution because for him, a gay person, it was a center of his own self-constituting action? (67–68)

Against the general tide of those who posit the return of the subject in these volumes, Gilles Deleuze feels compelled to make a renewed argument about the functions of subjectivity in Foucault's work. Deleuze sees this "rediscovery" or "reintroduction" as an incorrect assessment of what he calls the "subjectivation" of man. Deleuze comments:

> It is idiotic to say that Foucault discovers or reintroduces a hidden subject after having denied it. There is no subject, but a production of subjectivity: subjectivity is to be produced, at the right moment, because there is no subject. (*Pour* 154)

One could thus ask the question at one remove: Why is it that here and now Foucault touches on the production of subjectivity, and engages his text in a more personal matter? Whether one is Nietzschean along with

Deleuze and his reading of Foucault or directly critical, one must recognize that the Foucauldian enterprise that denied the subject as constituted and constituting agent within the realm of discourse does change in the third volume.

Deleuze (109) himself, in his book on Foucault, has pointed out that the second volume of *Histoire de la sexualité*, *L'Usage des plaisirs*, is in several ways a break with Foucault's previous writing; in part this is simply because of the historical distance of its subject matter from the modern era of the seventeenth through nineteenth centuries that had traditionally been Foucault's domain. Second, and most important, it is in this book that Foucault deals with the relation to the self. Finally, there is a break with the double project of *La Volonté de savoir*, which related sexuality to power and knowledge. The discursive erethism of the first volume of *Histoire de la sexualité* changes into a specific, singular erection in the third volume. Talking about the pathology of sexual activity as it is recorded in medical thought of the first and second centuries, Foucault remarks the interest in satyriasis or priapism, which is described as a sexual erethism (*SS* 134–35). Each erection is singular, individual, and resistant to a generalized discursive praxis.

So there is general perception that the question of the subject problematically resurfaces in Foucault's last writing, and this is a position espoused by critics who have otherwise eschewed the notion of subjectivity in Foucault's text. Up to that point, Foucault's reading of homosexuality is representative of the most stringent sort of social constructivism, valorizing the discursive, general, or social approach and dismissing the singular approach as mere literature.

I would say then that Foucault's change of stance is most significant, for it brings to light the consequences of the generalized *positions* on homosexuality that have been part and parcel of *readings* of homosexuality. The generalized form taken by readings of homosexuality has maintained homosexuality in an arena in which questions of ethics, power, dominance, and psychology are always major forces. Certainly, from a deontological point of view, this is not to be rejected. The consequences of this position must translate into a legal concept and then be retranslated into a redistribution of the juridico-discursive norms. In that, the position of a homosexual text is no different from that of any other text labeled as minority by the weight of juridico-discursive opinion and power. But at the same time, each instance of a homosexual text is an individual discourse. Each "homosexual" text must be considered exactly as one would consider a white male heterosexual text.

My thesis is simple: a homosexual text (whatever that is) has exactly the same right to interpret the world as does a text from a dominant, heterosexual discourse. At the individual level, the homosexual text must be allowed to overcome the liberal constraints placed upon it. Liberalism, in the American sense of the word, recognizes a minority voice but often continues to label it as such. The minority text thus necessarily, *nolens volens*, has to comment on the general questions of ethics and power. Certainly a heterosexual text will always comment on power, will always implicitly or explicitly relate it to a juridico-discursive system of ethics. But it would be reductive to insist that this always be the *primary* goal of a heterosexual text. The same criterion should exist for the "homosexual" text: it should have the same rights to go beyond the frame of *Wiederspiegelung* that a dominant discourse has.

The position of the individual subject also implies a different literary history for the homosexual text, one that is not bound in the dialectic engendered by the insistence on the general. If Foucault's insistence on generalized discursive praxes seems revolutionary in his earlier discussions of madness, medicine, or systems of knowledge, his position is far less revolutionary in the realm of the sexual. The truth of homosexuality has been seen as plural and general, different from the truth of heterosexuality, always seen as individual: though we would never dream of categorizing a book or a movie as "heterosexual," most of us have no problem talking about a homosexual movie, book, or art exhibition. In other words, today, we would say that something has "gay subject matter," whereas we would never dream of saying that something has "straight subject matter." The dialectic of sexual discourse has insisted on the level of the general as its *modus operandi*, and has used the apology, even in a scientific guise, as its rhetoric and genre. But the individual homosexual was lost in the apologetics and found himself or herself *discursively* imprisoned in a paltry, bivalent opposition of being in or out of the closet. It was as if every homosexual individual had silently and acceptingly internalized the juridico-discursive opposition imposed on him or her.

Foucault's belated recognition that the sexual subject is as important as the generalized and desubjectivized loci of enunciation of discourse has repercussions in the way we read a "homosexual" text. Specifically, we can no longer maintain the uneven opposition between a heterosexual discourse, seen in every case as a unique and singular instance, and a homosexual discourse, seen in every case as a metonymy of the whole and as the *apologia* for its very existence. Accepting such a division blinds us to seeing the singularity of any instance of homosexuality. We thus repeat, albeit unwillingly, the categorization of the juridico-discursive power system described by Foucault.

I have gone on at some length about the resurgence of the problem of the subject in Foucault's work because of its apparent contradiction of the social constructivist approach he had espoused before. No one should think, however, that this resurrected subject is whole, integral, complete, or *disponible* in a Gidean sense. No, the subject is tentative, fragmented, and split: it is a subject in search of itself. In short, it is like the subject we have already alluded to as the basis for the writing project of Proust, Barthes, Camus, and Tournier. Foucault belatedly discovers what Proust, among others, already knew, and one could retitle the trilogy of the *Histoire de la sexualité* and call it *A la recherche du sujet perdu*.

Foucault's belated discovery, which calls for a reexamination of social constructivism, has not been universally heeded. On this side of the Atlantic, criticism seems to have taken a different tack in the development of gender studies. More faithful to Foucault than Foucault himself, many critics seem to be saying that the social construction is so pervasive that there is no escape. Yet in some of the railing against oppressive systems I seem to read a utopian vision: if there were some escape from social construction, the individual would come out as healthy and whole as the Gidean individual, fully capable of *disponibilité*. Part of that idealism seems to come from the American experience, which seems to be saying something liberating with its metaphor of the closet: open the door and you will be free.

The most well-known version of the social constructivist view of homosexuality in literature can be found in Eve Kosofsky Sedgwick's influential volume *Epistemology of the Closet*. This book shows the imprisonment of a certain Anglo-American mentality in a series of damning binarisms whose deconstruction, according to the author, is necessary. For Sedgwick, the epistemology of the closet consists of "the relations of the known and the unknown, the explicit and the inexplicit around homo/heterosexual definition" (*EpCl* 3). The continued Puritan nature of Anglo-American culture (more and more American, and less and less Anglo-) maintains the "closet" as the uneasy coexistence in the homosexual individual of the singularity of his or her own discourse and the generalized model of homosexuality.

At some perhaps unconscious level, however, Sedgwick realizes that there is a problem: the American model is more parochial than even the garden European variety. She knows that when the closet door is opened and the individual is released from the bonds of social construction, he or she is still not whole. Some would say that there is a gap, wound, or scar at the heart of the psyche. Some would say it is because there is never full release from those bonds, not even for white male heterosexuals, for they too are in a closet, if closet there be. But no one could possibly believe that Gidean freedom will result from the questioning, deconstruction, and ultimate destruction of the canons of social construction.

The author herself seems to see the *peculiarity* of the model, all the while accepting it. For Sedgwick the "epistemology of the closet" is potentially "*peculiarly* revealing" (*EpCl* 3, my emphasis). Further on, she notes that the

> dichotomy heterosexual/homosexual, as it has emerged through the last century of Western discourse, would seem to lend itself *peculiarly* neatly to a set of analytic moves learned from this deconstructive moment in feminist theory. In fact, the dichotomy heterosexual/homosexual fits the deconstructive template much more neatly than male/female itself does, and hence, importantly differently. (*EpCl* 34, my emphasis)

Sedgwick also states that "a deconstructive understanding of these binarisms makes it possible to identify them as sites that are *peculiarly* densely charged with lasting potentials for powerful manipulation" (*EpCl* 10, her emphasis); that "the special volatility of postmodern bodily and technological relations may make such an attempt [to pry 'essentially gay-genocidal nexuses of thought' from 'their historical backing to attach to them newly enabling meanings'] peculiarly liable to tragic misfire" (*EpCl* 41); and that Melville's Claggart in "Billy Budd" has a "nameless peculiarity" (*EpCl* 95). In fact, in what is to me a "peculiarly" appropriate *mise-en-abyme* found in her reading of Wilde, Sedgwick comments on Wilde's own use of two words, "curious" and "subtle," that "trace in *Dorian Gray* the homosexual-homophobic path of simultaneous epistemological heightening and ontological evacuation" (*EpCl* 174). Curiouser and curiouser.

What should one make of all this "peculiarity"? Does it apply to Continental and especially to French models? It is undeniable that certain writers, primarily of the Anglo-American as opposed to the French tradition, still constantly reinvent the epistemology of the closet, but should we automatically extend that paradigm to other traditions? Even if I were writing about Anglo-American literature in this book, I would certainly propose displacing the primacy given to that model of reading. But that is not my aim here. Quite frankly, along with finding the word "peculiarly" most peculiar in this "anti-homophobic" work, I take great exception to Sedgwick's use of the term "Euro-American" (*EpCl* 2, 16, 49, 51, 53, 54, 134). It wrongly assimilates different traditions, different modes of liberation, and different rooms or closets. Sedgwick is not alone in her "peculiar" terminology. In his study of "gay self-representation in American literature" (his subtitle), David Bergman uses the word "Euro-American" in a fashion similar to Sedgwick's as he repeats the arguments of social constructivism:

> Because homosexuality in Euro-American culture is so tied to the dominant culture from which it emerges, and because its terms and values are generated out of the "violent dialectic" with that discourse, it is mistaken to connect the structure of current, western homosexuality with the male-male sexual activity of other times or cultures. The modern Euro-American homosexual views him- or herself in vastly different ways than the Greek pederast or the Melanesian pubescent. Though both progay and antigay forces have linked Euro-American homosexuality to institutional male sex in other cultures—especially the Greeks—such linkage only further distorts and obscures the nature of homosexuality in Europe and North America. (27)

One could ask all sorts of interesting questions of this passage, such as: Is homosexuality in non-Euro-American culture not tied to the dominant culture? Is the nature of homosexuality in Europe and North America the same? Is there thus an essence despite legal, social, and moral questions and if there is an essence, why is it not found in non-Euro-American cultures? But what I want briefly to focus on is the fact that Bergman relies on Erik Erikson's theory of "ego identity"; therein lies, I believe, a clue to one of the many problems with "Euro-American" as a term. (Since I am focusing on the concept of the subject, I shall restrict myself to this one aspect of a much larger problem.) Erikson's theory of ego psychology seems to support the possibility of an "ego identity," be it lost or found. I could not say whether Sedgwick necessarily shares Bergman's Eriksonian view. Rather, Sedgwick and Bergman share a logic that counts in binary oppositions, one symptom of which, in Bergman's case, is a belief in the wholeness and presence of identity as expression in Eriksonian ego psychology.

Completely different, whether at the level of fiction, the essay, or theory, is European discourse, which catches the identity in an ever-changing discourse between individual and history, as Jacques Derrida has so eloquently demonstrated in *L'Autre Cap*. Identity is always part of a dialectic, not merely a dichotomy; identity does not spring from the closet fully clad or fully unclad, as the case may be. And what goes for the structuring of a European identity, even in fiction, can be said *a fortiori* for the unsuturable gaps of Lacanianism or Derrideanism. If the American dream is of wholeness and integration, there is a European sadness at the impossibility of such a dream. And while one could obviously find examples of Europeans who believe in Eriksonian plenitude and examples of dialectical American beliefs, my point, quite simply, is that Proust, Barthes, Camus, and Tournier do not fit this "Euro-American" closet at all.

Perhaps this can best be explained by taking two brief examples from literature. In the genre known as the "French farce" or "bedroom comedy" (as opposed to the safe and vaguely Puritanical "drawing-room comedy") practiced by Feydeau and others, there are no closets. Of course, Parisian bedrooms do not have closets, but this is just an explanation by means of an allegorical example. In these farces, there are rooms leading to other rooms; every once in a while one finds a wardrobe in which the fleeing lover may temporarily hide from a jealous spouse. Aside from this absence of closets, both literal and figurative, the difference between the American situation and the French one can be illustrated with a well-known, though perhaps apocryphal, anecdote told about a potential production of *Tea and Sympathy* in France. The prospective producer is supposed to have said (in a thick French accent, as the story is told), "So the older woman gives herself to the young man to prove he is not a homosexual. So what is the problem of the play?" Questions relate to public and private space, to *pudeur*, to seemly behavior, but no one would ever assume that people are not having sex. For that, ultimately, is what the closet implies: if someone is in the closet, I mean really in the closet, does not the rest of the world assume, if only for a moment before the snide smile or wink of an eye, that he or she is chaste?

Lest my reader think I am condemning (American) gender studies, this is decidedly not the case. Just as I admire Gide's bravery even though, as I have said, I find his position limited, I also admire the bravery it took to first lay out the territory of gender studies in a less than receptive environment. And I would note that as a critical practice, it occurred far earlier on this side of the Atlantic than in Europe. But more and more, there is the recognition that the notion of the social construction of homosexuality and thus the model of the closet are simply not sufficient. Taking clues from a complex, newly invigorated feminism, writers such as Judith Butler, in *Gender Trouble*, and Kaja Silverman, in *Male Subjectivity at the Margins*, are reworking the very questions of opposition and dichotomy that had passed into the realm of received knowledge. For example, Butler sees identity itself as fundamentally subverted. She never forgets, for example, that "the masculine subject only *appears* to originate meanings and thereby to signify" (45). No freedom from the bindings of newly deconstructed dichotomies can help change that appearance into a reality of signifying: freedom will not produce a masculine-feminine collective subject that really signifies.

On the other hand, I continue to have problems with statements such as the following by Diana Fuss, from the introduction to her volume *Inside/Out*, a book of "lesbian theories, gay theories." Fuss starts by saying that the "philosophical opposition between 'heterosexual' and 'homosexual,' like so many other conventional binaries, has always been constructed on the foundations of another related opposition: the couple 'inside' and 'outside'" (1). So far so good. Fuss moves quickly to make the opposition a dialectic:

> Many of the current efforts in lesbian and gay theory, which this volume seeks to showcase, have begun the difficult but urgent textual work necessary to call into question the stability and ineradicability of the hetero/homo hierarchy, suggesting that new (and old) sexual possibilities are no longer thinkable in terms of a simple inside/outside dialectic. (1)

And then, in the beginning of the second paragraph, Fuss flatly states that the "figure inside/outside cannot be easily or ever finally dispensed with" and that "the inside/outside polarity is an indispensable model." You can't have it all ways. I do not deny that there is a hierarchy, that there is an opposition, or that there is a paradigm at work. What good does it do, though, to establish a universal key that will fit every lock? How do we find the specificity of a text? Why do we endlessly imprison ourselves in oppositions that cannot generate any individual instance of textuality? And how can we use the term "dialectic" without realizing that an integral part of the "dialectic" is the move to go beyond it in an *Aufhebung* that goes beyond the insistence of the number two, of binary oppositions, and of shackled couples? When Silverman (386) posits the possibility of Proust's Marcel being a lesbian (an interpretation she does not follow), she is at least freeing the text, the reader, and the systems from the domination of binary, oppositional logic.

In this study, then, I want to underscore the difference between imprisoning binarism, aptly discussed by Sedgwick as the "open secret" and "the closet," and the hermeneutic of interpretation or the use of homosexuality as interpretive and narrative theory, at work in each of the four authors studied in this volume. By helping to open up the field of queer theory with the advantage of a set of French texts, I hope to make a contribution to an invigorated approach to this very complex subject. This is not to say that the French scene has been free of the dyadic. Even the category of what Sedgwick calls the homosocial in *Between Men*, effectively studied by Wayne Koestenbaum in his work on literary collaboration, may or may not be trans-Atlantically translatable. The homosocial seems related to a certain Anglo-American sensibility as an ironic byproduct of Puritanism; and this ambiguous third category itself explodes the opposition: the homosocial is neither heterosexual nor homosexual. The categories of the homosocial, the potentially erotic, and the nonsexual all seem to be *peculiarly* Anglo-American, and comparable scenes in French literature, for example, appear tinged with a gloss that is somewhat more than "potential" if not always actualized.

Certainly when we turn to France, we do see a conservative position that at first looms large. It has consistently emphasized the dyadic within the realm of the homosexual. But the dyad is not the same as that found in the work I have just been discussing. The received literary-historical version of homosexuality in twentieth-century French literature is a striking example of how various kinds of categorization have diminished the possibility of finding the unique, nonmetonymic voice of a number of authors. This version of literary history is a logomachy that pits the brave writers who were more or less openly homosexual against the closet cases. The first group includes Gide; Jean Genet, for whom the apologetic rhetoric extends to the six hundred pages of *Saint-Genet* by Sartre; and, in a more worldly vein, Jean Cocteau. The second group, usually keeping their doors ajar or at least looking through the peephole, includes Proust, Marcel Jouhandeau, and Henri de Montherlant, among others. Proust, of course, is the eternal scapegoat or at least the straw man for those who would seek to "out" him in favor of the braver, more open Gide (Fernandez 47).

But could we not say that something far more important and far more interesting is already at stake in the literariness of homosexuality? Let us briefly think about Proust in this light. One could argue that the novelistic processes used by Proust go beyond the limitations of his own personal view of homosexuality, which he perceived as something to be kept more or less under wraps in the "public" acknowledgment of his "private" life. Now, the relations are extremely complicated among various demarcated categories—official biography, hagiography, textual evidence, and the gradations of difference between public life and private life. Quite simply, a yes-or-no logic does not work, at least in Proust's case. Why does it seem to work elsewhere? Again, because of a certain dichotomy in presentations of homosexuality in Anglo-American spheres, one finds operative models of inquiry there that do not work in all French spheres. Thus, despite the fascinating subject of literary collaboration, a study of which could be most insightful in French as well, I take issue with the following hypothesis used by Koestenbaum:

> Indeed, despite the lovely aura of contraband I attribute to collaboration, I follow a conventional method of close reading which applies biography to text, treats biography as text, and depends on the integrity of the author as more than a social construct or a fiction superimposed on intertextual anarchy. I can describe collaboration as a disruptive act only if I retain a conservative allegiance to singular authority. (9)

Obviously, if one insists on the sanctity of the biographical fact and the close reading of a text as a reflection of the author, one would always choose Gide over Proust. One would, therefore, be contributing to a reinforcement of the dyadic model. But, in the same breath, if we give the text precedence over the liberal gestures of the author—or the lack thereof—another picture may emerge. It could be argued that Proust and Gide are in positions analogous to those occupied by Balzac and Zola, respectively, in Friedrich Engels's famous letter to Margaret Harkness, written in April 1888 (Marx and Engels 6:531–34). Engels writes that Marx preferred Balzac to Zola, despite the conservatism of the former and the liberalism of the latter. To Marx's mind, Balzac used irony as a tool that was far stronger than Zola's political commitment or positivist approach.

It is not so much Proust's irony that contrasts with Gide's earnestness, nor even so much the question of structure in the text, though that does certainly play a role. The closed nature of the *mise-en-abyme* of Gide's texts, including *Les Faux-Monnayeurs*, tends to reinscribe homosexuality as a general theme much more than the open structure of Proust's work does. More important, Gide's text tends toward a bivalency that reproduces the false oppositions on which a certain view of homosexuality has been constructed: nature versus culture, guilt versus innocence or freedom, in versus out of the proverbial closet. Gide's bivalency seems somewhat like the "epistemology of the closet" of Anglo-American tradition. Is it due to the Puritanism of a Protestant upbringing? Perhaps this is a contributing factor, though as we shall see below, Barthes, who shares this Protestant background, does not share the guilt of Puritan ethics. On the other hand, Proust's text is constantly displacing closure along a line of signifiers, along a hermeneutic chain that never closes into a circle. Proust's interpretive strategies are quite literally the saving grace.

By reexamining the question of the interpretation of homosexuality according to the subject and not according to general oppositions, one can unearth a whole history of homosexual writing that is not imprisoned in the dichotomy of being in or out of the closet. The authors I have chosen are all in this category of extramoral homosexual textuality. It should be obvious that I am not concerned with the "homosexuality" as such of the four authors studied, or for that matter, the "homosexuality" of authors I am not considering. Though each reflects some aspects of a generalized discourse, Marcel Proust, Roland Barthes, Renaud Camus, and Michel Tournier all write according to the discourses structured by an individual subject. Each of them sees the oppositions I have discussed as being secondary to the processes of interpretation by and through the subject. To clarify some points, then, in the final part of this introduction, I would like briefly to turn to the relation of interpretation, theory, and narrative. I would especially like to address some basic concepts concerning narrative that may eventually elucidate the position of the "homosexual writing subject." To see how the position of the homosexual writing subject comes into play, it is first necessary to review, albeit briefly, certain general theoretical and critical positions that are at work in realist narrative and its aftermaths.

At a surface level, theory may be considered to be the proposed intrinsic decoding of the work, the kind of alphabet and grammar needed to map out a preliminary reading of a narrative or a set of narratives. This intrinsic position posits or extrapolates accumulated practice, generic norms, and codes and ultimately includes an explanation of its own special status as one of the decoded messages of the text. It posits implicit and explicit readers and writers, generates textual grammars, and offers heuristic devices for understanding. A textual theory is also a means to closure: by explaining, it can reduce the play of meanings to a graspable set. In other words, it can create a theme by positing closure. At the same time, the theoretical construct is a product of the text, as is this posited closure; both need to be examined as part of the text.

Any narrative proposes a method, a path through the text that illuminates some things, highlights others, forces another group to appear as background to what is put forth, and makes yet another set disappear. This method or these methods are multiple: internal or external to the story itself, unified or contradictory, helpful or misleading. The method is external when, often as not, it is separate from the story. The explanation consists of independent acts of enunciation that frame a tale without belonging to the story line. But if the method is outside the story, it is still part of the work in question. Balzac's or Stendhal's instructions to the reader, the independent set of remarks that form the enunciation of the text, have nothing to do with Eugène de Rastignac or Julien Sorel. These characters could live their "lives" wholly ignorant of the authors' theories: Julien Sorel does not need to know how a novel is a mirror pulled along the side of the road. The remarks have everything to do with *Le Père Goriot* or *Le Rouge et le Noir*: whether we accept or reject the remarks as valid interpretations of the characters, themes, situations, or stories, we must nonetheless consider them to be integral parts of the text in question.

Similarly, the ordering of material along a pseudo-historical time line with or without loops or according to a multiple series of acts of enunciation and interpretation informs any critical reading of the text. Stendhal, Balzac, and Flaubert often wrote novels following the first path; Proust chose the latter, as Gérard Genette has shown in *Figures III*, his *tour de force* on the *Recherche*. So a Balzac novel will often follow a historical development, loop back in a flashback to tell the "origins" of the story, problem, or conflict, and then pick up the narrative thread again while maintaining historical verisimilitude. In contrast, Proust moves through past and future interpretations, reminds the reader of events that have already occurred, interprets past events for a third, fourth, or fifth time, and presages future ones in word and deed. To reduce Proust's novel to a historical time line would vitiate the entire enterprise. In fact, Margaret Gray (2–3) has recently criticized Genette for imposing a "notion of temporality" that is "too conventional, too chronological" on the text since, for Genette, "time is broken into discrete units." To see Proust's novel, however, as a series of imbricated interpretations, I shall argue, is exactly the motor we need to understand it.

Each text puts forth some means of enabling the reader to gain entry to the material, a set of theories about what is going on and how it is occurring. These theories are part and parcel of the text, often appearing as figures of rhetoric, subversions of the story, or, for that matter, developments of the story. I would argue that the whole of *Le Côté de Guermantes* is a complex demonstration of life as interpretation, and of novelistic situations as the example, demonstration, and fulfillment of a hermeneutic. But not coincidentally, *Le Côté de Guermantes* is the locus in which the text doubles back on itself in an act of enunciative recursion. Just as there is a loop at the level of the action in *Le Père Goriot* (the story of Goriot's fortune) or *Madame Bovary* (Emma's education), in the *Recherche*, a similar recursiveness occurs at the level of the operant, which, in this case, is not action but interpretation.

Narrative, then, is its own theory. This broad statement is meant neither as a formalist encapsulation of all that narrative may be nor as a reductive statement about the role of theory in narrative. Narrative is *not only* theory but is *always* theory. Even the simplest story has a discursive plane, a means of expression, and thus a contrast between the action and how the action is told. Theory is narrative's own attempt at bridging the gap. Let us consider the case of a simple narrative in which the gap between contents and expression seems to be nonexistent. This is the case in which, to use an oft-quoted expression, the story seems to tell itself. In his famous article on French verb tenses, Emile Benveniste (241) says that "the author [must] remain true to his aim as a historian and proscribe everything foreign to the recounting of the events (discourses, reflections, comparisons). In truth, there is no longer a narrator."[4] We immediately realize that the concept of the self-told story is as much an ideological construct as any other. It implies an immanent relation between signifier and signified and between word and thing; it excludes contrary meanings, dialogism, syllepses, amphibologies, and counter-discourses; it proposes an uncomplicated relation between the individual instance of text and the language as a whole. Moreover, we might conceive of a situation where the understanding of a story is only (and ironically for us) considered to be immediate if it is explained by enunciation and thus "mediated."

This understanding of theory can be applied to a fundamental problem for the study that follows. If signifiers slavishly indicated signifieds, if there were no slippage, no tropes, and no gaps, we would undoubtedly have something other than literature. I doubt that that "something" exists, for the once-posited purity or the semiotic tautology of science or history is an ideological master-trope like any other. In any case, it would not be literature. In literature, signifiers refer elsewhere: to other signifiers, to chains, constellations, or collections of signifiers; to ideas, concepts, and desires; to whole worlds. By positing the question of the relation between narrative and its designs, we are essentially asking to see if we can sketch the lines between text and its object. In this study we are looking at the figures that are formed between textuality and sexuality.

Sexuality is probably the most telling sign of interpretation. Sexuality

4. Benveniste argues as a theoretical linguist; for a literary scholar, the position of a historian is not as transparent as Benveniste might wish. One should consider the tropes of historical writing, that is, the rhetoric intrinsic to any history, a problematic elucidated by Hayden White in *Metahistory*. Moreover, Benveniste's choice of text, Balzac's "Gambara," is doubly unfortunate. Benveniste indicates that there is an "authorial reflection that escapes from the plan of the story [*récit*]" (241n), a note that leads the reader to wonder whether there can ever be a pure *récit*. Second, "Gambara" was a collaborative effort between Balzac and his secretary, Auguste de Belloy, and questions about enunciation must necessarily be asked. Still, even if one could find an example that did not betray itself for this second reason, the supposed transparency of history would always come into play.

is interpretation just as interpretation is simultaneously the transcription of sexuality as well as its own theorization. The advantage of reading through homosexuality is clear: such interpretation puts transcendental signifieds into question and thus, through a recursive process, puts into question the whole process of interpretation. Reading Proust then would become the necessary remedy for confinement in a dyad.

In his study of Hart Crane, Thomas Yingling (35) sees homosexuality coming to the homosexual "as a denaturalized sign, intruded into his life *as a sign*, turned by others from a 'natural expression' into a sign that can henceforth be significant only of his own alienation from his body and from the social fabric woven by the power of others." I have no quarrel with the semiosis of homosexuality, but as I shall argue, this semiosis is often a means of liberating the hermeneutic from the oppression of the ideology-laden referent that comes with its own prepackaged meaning. Certainly this oppression may be true in some cases, but even a basic existentialist reading, to say nothing of a Hegelian dialectic or a deconstructive reading, will turn that oppression into a liberating force in the realm of the textual.

Homosexuality also helps liberate textuality from some of the constraints imposed on any given text by the dominant structures of "white," "male," "heterosexual," "bourgeois" discourse. That these terms are contained in inverted commas, or ironically, in "inverted" commas, is a sign that no text is as fully "white" or "male" or "heterosexual" or "bourgeois" as the dominant figure of discourse would have it be. Any text belonging to the dominant set relies in part on an assumed complicity between the dominant ideology, culture, and sign systems and the individual instance of text. One of the fundamental insights of Derridean deconstruction is that any given text buys into that system and simultaneously undercuts it: a Derridean problematic is thus far different from a position that seeks merely to "deconstruct oppositions." Not inside or outside, heterosexual or homosexual, male or female, but inside *and* outside plus *neither* inside *nor* outside; heterosexual *and* homosexual plus *neither* heterosexual *nor* homosexual; male *and* female plus *neither* male *nor* female. The texts examined here do not build a prison-house of sexuality; in them, homosexuality frees the work from the a priori modes to which it is ascribed: homosexuality is a fulcrum, or a lever, that moves textuality off its mark. In the writing of someone like Barthes, though homosexuality is seldom mentioned, it is tacitly and elegantly used to dislodge systems and structures from their comfortable niches.[5]

5. The discussions in my chapter on Barthes that do not touch on homosexuality should be seen as a reading of that act of leverage. Thus I am also not comfortable with Bernard

The relations among narrative, theory, interpretation, and (homo)sexuality are the focus of this study. I stress that the choice of authors is neither arbitrary nor comprehensive. Others might have served as well, but each of the four authors engages the very questions I have been talking about by providing a metatextual recursivity on interpretation. For Proust, Barthes, Tournier, and Camus, interpretation is always a theme, with the implicit attendant false closure that a theme implies. At any given moment there will be several layers of textuality and textual problematics. This can perhaps be best understood as a series of questions: What gaps are there between the text and its world? What gaps are there between the text and its sexuality? What mechanisms, tropes, modes of understanding, and differences are set forth to bridge these gaps, that is, to theorize them, interpret them, and interpret that very act of theorization? And finally, what status is given in the text to the act of interpretation: what value, import, and weight are placed on a meta-hermeneutics? This global theory will be the text itself.

One must ask a question about the status of theory separate and apart from narrative. In the case of Proust, one can use terms from literary criticism and keep their metadiscursivity pure. In fact, one is almost bound to approach Proust differently from the three other authors in this study: Proust's text presents a technical and formal complexity far greater than that of the other three. Among other factors, both the sheer number of pages and the still-present concern for some form of realist fidelity to the "world described" beg the critic to use some shorthand approach such as Genette's terms. The place that Proust occupies in the canon, the various reinscriptions of his work by critics, and the general horizon of Proustian interpretation all need to be taken into account. Also, Proust stands as a textual father or uncle to the other three writers, who have all, at one point or another, necessarily analyzed Proust to agree with, overcome, or answer him. Thus the methodology of approaching Proust through his critics and through a certain narratology also implies that in the texts of Barthes, Camus, and Tournier this analysis of Proust has already occurred. When Camus or Tournier or Barthes writes, it is, among other things, as a reader of Proust.

The status of theory in the text is not so easy to argue with Roland Barthes (for obvious reasons), or for Renaud Camus and Michel Tournier. If I have chosen Barthes as a text for study akin to that of Proust and

Comment's remark (81) in which he objects to "putting Barthes on the analyst's couch in order better to embalm him under the categories of the Oedipal complex, homosexuality, or who knows what?" Certainly Barthes's homosexuality is worth more than that.

certainly influenced by the *Recherche*, it is not without a recognition of the obvious: more than anyone aside from Jacques Derrida, Barthes is responsible for what we currently understand by "theory." To talk about amphibology in a text by Barthes means to engage the text's own comments on the subject. In a more complicated fashion, one must consider what remains unsaid. For example, Barthes has recourse to the language of Lacanian psychoanalysis. But the imaginary and the symbolic of Barthes are not those of Lacan; and the text—the one you are reading, the one we have read—is engaged in a logomachy with the invisible and oft-unquoted text of the formidable other, a position that includes, at various times, Lacan, Derrida, and Foucault, to name only a few. No one should think that the text of Barthes lacks a nontheoretical dimension or even a dimension that could be called fictional or literary. A similar argument can be made in the case of Tournier, formerly a philosophy student and currently someone who remains on the Parisian intellectual scene, even in his hideaway in Chevreuse, which is geographically and spiritually close to Jean Des Esseintes's fictional hermitage in Fontenay. Tournier is aware of the consequences of theory and even if he does not quote or even directly allude to the Parisian theory mavens, theory itself is palpably there. In fact, as I have argued in an article on Tournier, one can read his novel *La Goutte d'or* as a gloss on the theories of the day. And for Renaud Camus, student of Barthes, quoting Barthes, quoted by Barthes, the case is clear.

Interpreting Proustian Interpretation

No longer write in the "transitive sense," but write a *text* (the word *text* not being a direct object, but what is called an "internal accusative").

Vincent Descombes, *Proust. Philosophie du roman*

And I take comfort from the case of Palamedes, also, who died in circumstances similar to mine.

Xenophon, *Socrates' Defence*

I. Reading Innocence

From the outset, I should state that this chapter will not be an in-depth interpretation of *A la recherche du temps perdu*. Instead, by focusing on the idea and sense of interpretation itself, I am proposing a way of engaging both the work as a whole and parts of the novel in particular. The intertwined figures of interpretation and homosexuality are fundamental subjects of the book, and they provide us with a flexible model for understanding the work. In addition, I shall assume that the reader is familiar enough with the plot and organization of the novel to be spared both summaries of the events and holistic psychological interpretations of the characters. I am also assuming that the reader is acquainted with standard critical approaches to the work. My reading then will take a triple approach: in the first part of the chapter, I shall look at how to interpret a scene depicting homosexuality. In the second part I shall proceed negatively, by looking at the problems of interpreting the famous description of the generation of "men-women" at the beginning of *Sodome et Gomorrhe*—problems produced, as I hope to show, by the recalcitrance of the text itself. Finally, I shall attempt some sort of synthesis between the first two parts by offering an approach to the intertwined figures of interpretation and homosexuality combined with an approach to reading that same description as related to the models of interpretation established in *Le Côté de Guermantes*.

Let us say it bluntly and directly: Marcel Proust's novel *A la recherche du temps perdu* is undoubtedly the most ambitious literary undertaking in which homosexuality is the determining factor for interpretation and for general hermeneutics. Homosexuality is at the heart of the hermeneutics, serves as the posited transcendental origin of meaning, and circumscribes the text. As Monique Wittig has aptly noted in an essay entitled "The Point of View" (in *The Straight Mind*), Proust "made 'homosexual' the axis of categorization from which to universalize" (61). It is not the theme of homosexuality but its patterns, structures, and discourses that serve as heterosexuality would in another work: as a general hermeneutic paradigm and *dispositif*, but also as an un-normative and ab-normal norm, as a bent rule, and as a "queer" plumb line of interpretation. Despite the seemingly resolutely heterosexual nature of "Un Amour de Swann" and the love affair between the narrator and Albertine in *La Prisonnière*, homosexuality sets the pattern, of which heterosexuality is the important but minor variant in this universe. The themes of the novel, including what we might inaccurately call the "theme of homosexuality," all rely on that general homosexual hermeneutic.

Furthermore, I would state that any valid reading of the novel should be able to engage the question of homosexuality.[1] An interpretation that could not successfully deal with the questions relating to homosexuality in the novel cannot be considered effective in explaining the work. I am not saying that everyone has to talk about homosexuality, but that every reading should be able to engage the question. Thus, to take the most banal example, a psychoanalytical reading that departs from or arrives at the Oedipus complex may miss the mark if that alone is the "answer," if the text is somehow perceived as a symptom of the failure to resolve the Oedipal crisis, meaning that homosexuality is seen as secondary to the "normal" world.

Any sophisticated reading of the *Recherche* must also take the recursivity of the novel into account. Every reading needs to engage the structure of Proustian narration that returns over and over to an event and builds layer upon layer of interpretation. The kernel of an event inevitably seems to fade when surrounded by these layers of interpretation: what importance could we really give to the story of a man dipping a small cake into a

1. I would exempt from this categorical statement a work like Genette's *Figures III* whose formalism neither engages the problem at hand nor refuses it. This does not mean, of course, that such a formalist reading would not work with the proposed paradigm. In fact, I think it would be extremely profitable to read Genette's figures of Proustian narration with and against the homosexual paradigm.

cup of herb tea? If, as I am supposing, the novel is about interpretation, we can readily conclude that any given reading tells as much about the critical method used as it does about the text in question. A reading of interpretation elaborates a reflexive hermeneutic about the processes of interpretation involved in explaining the novel. I hope, then, to show two things in this chapter: that the novel is the story of interpretation and that the linchpin of interpretation for Proust is homosexuality. If the work is a story about France during the Third Republic, if its themes are love and jealousy, if its analytics are aesthetic and psychological, it is, insofar as the verb "to be" can be used, a story about homosexual interpretation.

What is this interpretation? What, if anything, is interpreted? All things considered, the events of this long book are few in number; and even fewer are decisive in determining fortunes, changes, and peripeteiae in the plot. The passions of some characters may certainly determine the direction the plot takes: Charles Swann's jealousy concerning Odette, Charlus's passion for Morel, and Marcel's possessive desire for Albertine are all well-known examples. Yet even in this third example, one could plausibly argue that Marcel's jealousy is based on an interpretation of the two other scenarios of jealousy. In other words, it is not so much Marcel's possessive desire for Albertine that determines the direction the novel takes, but the interpretive reading he has given the two previous stories of passion. Or, even more radically, the direction of the plot in this part of the novel is based on the previous interpretation of passion and jealousy written by the narrator.

Equally important in determining the direction of the novel are absences and blanks at the level of action that the text rushes to fill with analysis, commentary, and verbal architecture: the wait for the maternal kiss, the imagined activities of Odette or Albertine, the "unsaid" of social events, the absent lineages, the unmentioned misalliances, or the unreported *bons mots* of the Duchesse de Guermantes. The unrepresented of the novel determines as much of the story as the represented—if not more. Interpretation does not need the excuse of a concrete event to occur. And finally, along these lines, one might consider the rare plot changes in which the author chooses one path over another, a decision that seemingly leads a character in an irreversible direction. At the level of the story, of course, characters irreversibly grow old (*Le Temps retrouvé* being the best example) and die (the grandmother and Swann, for instance). But that irreversibility is not reflected at the level of narrative itself. The structure of the text integrates these events: one of the primary lessons is that the two ways, that of Swann and that of Guermantes, do in fact join. Despite old age and death, narrative can recuperate past time and place. Proust's modernity may in part consist of that recuperation, which stands firmly opposed to the realist texts that preceded it; for Proust, there is no "road not taken."

Before being a social history, before being the story of redemption through art or the recuperation of essence through writing, and in addition to being the story of interpretation, Proust's novel uses interpretation as one of the primary means by which the text continues from sentence to sentence, from page to page. The text is a remembrance of past events, of their interpretation at the moment at which they occurred, and their reinterpretation at the moment at which they are told. Each event, character, motif, and situation has layers of semioticity that far exceed the realms of denotation and connotation. The incident of the *madeleine*, for example, consists of its various layers of interpretation: the initial unawareness, the immediate answer, the repeated musings on the event hundreds or thousands of pages later, as well as the sum of all these. Within the interpretation of any given event in the novel, Proust's text multiplies the explanatory images, deploys numerous metaphors, and inevitably reinscribes the interpretation of another textual point with its own attendant metaphors, figures, and images.

Proust builds his text on the basis of a meager series of banal events and nonevents by elaborating a system of enunciations and discourses whose referents are other enunciations and discourses. Where does this noneventfulness originate? Certainly the novels of Balzac, Stendhal, Flaubert, and Zola had clear plots; characters do something, react to something, or say something relative to a situation and in order to "become." In the nineteenth-century novel, plot is one of the major means of fulfilling a character's destiny and of thereby validating both the subtending ideology of the novel and its narrative structures. In many ways, Proust breaks with that tradition, even as he includes his own nineteenth-century novel, *Un Amour de Swann*, within the larger work. Proust's novel is composed of its internal interpretations, its commentaries, and the authorial intrusions whose combinations are far more important for the structure of the novel than plot twists or "events" themselves. Proust constructs a text where the rather banal aspects of the events serve as a neutral pretext for the virtuosity of interpretation.

The *Recherche* is a break from the integrated structuring of character development and plot, at least as we have just described it. The reality of this novel, the coherence of its characters, and the very organization of the work come out of the discourses of which the work is constructed; in the end, the events are almost beside the point, moot at best. The narrative kernel of the text is not an event, but a nonevent surrounded by a web of discourses. To a great extent, Proust's novel is a reaction against the integrated, unidirectional plots of the nineteenth century; its overarching plot structure may in part derive from that oppositional position. Yet one would not be remiss in saying that Proust found another kind of narrative, almost by serendipity, in the story that rocked France during the 1890's and the early years of this century: the Dreyfus Affair. Of interest to me in the model is not the obvious and well-worn aspect of the story: Dreyfus is an innocent man who is made a scapegoat because of his religion. If you replace religion with sexuality (Charlus) or even with the same religion (Swann), you perhaps have a few threads of plot and structure that stand out. But that for me is not the heart of the relation of the novel to this story.

What one sees in the Dreyfus Affair is an ever-escalating series of discourses based on the nonevent of Dreyfus's treason. In its initial stages, the Dreyfus Affair had an event at its heart, which was an act of treason. But it soon became clear to many, including numerous members of the anti-Dreyfus forces, that this event was a nonevent: Dreyfus himself had committed no such act of treason. At the heart of the Affair is the fact that Dreyfus did nothing and was guilty of nothing. Still, this nonaction led to multiple interpretations, behaviors, actions, alliances, and polemics. So it is not simply that Dreyfus was wrongly accused: whole aspects of the Affair relate to his individuality as a Jew. Had someone else been wrongly accused, one could hypothesize quite a different chain of events from those precipitated by Dreyfus's wrongful accusation, a fact that does not escape the sharp tongue of one of the master interpreters depicted in Proust's novel, the Duchesse de Guermantes.

Proust's interest in the Dreyfus Affair has great social and political import for the novel. From the very first, he recognizes that the nonevent at its heart is more important than the act of treason itself. Proust realizes what a powerful mechanism the Dreyfus Affair is for a reorganization of reflections, signifiers and signifieds, and other "criteria": "These new positions of the kaleidoscope are produced by what a philosopher would call a change in criteria. The Dreyfus Affair brought about such a change . . . and the kaleidoscope again spun its little bits of glass around" (1:508). The Dreyfus Affair serves as a subtext for whole sections of *Le Côté de Guermantes*, where it is always a question of interpretation. And in narrative terms, the Dreyfus Affair already provides a model of figures that surpass the accidental nature of the reality that gives them form. Proust will go so far as to have the Duchesse de Guermantes, who "was anti-Dreyfusard (believing in Dreyfus's innocence all the while)" (2:767), note the importance of the interpretation and recording of that very event:

> "In any case, if this Dreyfus is innocent," interrupted the Duchess, "he is hardly proving it. Such idiotic, overdone letters he writes from his island! I don't know if M. Esterhazy is better than him, but he has a different flair in his writing, another color. That must displease the supporters of M. Dreyfus. What a shame for them that they cannot change innocents." (2:536)

Qualified immediately as one of the Duchess's clever observations, this remark is followed by a structure whose gesture repeats the question of wrongful accusation in another mode; it matters little to the Duke whether a remark is funny or not: "I don't find it funny; or rather, it does not matter to me if it is funny or not" (2:536). Even in a detail about the social ramifications of the Dreyfus Affair, Proust repeats the same basic structure of indeterminacy. In the *Recherche*, the initial kernel of truth or falsity matters far less than the act of interpretation that deems something true or false *pro tem* or *in aeternam*. Neither Dreyfus nor the absolute humor of the Duchess's comment matter in the slightest. What matters is the threads of interpretation that surround an event.

The text that follows will not be a reading of the singularity of Dreyfus's accusation: I have brought up the Affair heuristically as one of the models used for narrative in the *Recherche*. Still, what it tells us is capital: there is no name for what Dreyfus is, for he is only innocent of treason, after the fact, that is, against purported guilt. Just as there is no word to describe Dreyfus without an appeal to this opposition and just as in this Europe there is no name for a Jew except as defined against a Christian, there is also no proper name for homosexuality except as defined against heterosexuality. Proust's project will be a search for these names, separate and apart from oppositions, separate and apart from a dramatic event of discovery, and separate and apart from the dichotomies that reduce minority positions to being the negative other opposed to the majority. Proust will search for the names of the unnamed or the unnameable: sometimes names are found, as the title "Noms de Pays: Le Nom" indicates; sometimes names remain hidden, readable only as an effect of narrative, as the anonymity of Mlle. Vinteuil's friend and the protagonist/narrator himself amply indicate. Does Proust find a name for homosexuality that is not predicated on the normative other of heterosexuality? This is what I hope to show.

The centrality of interpretation *within* the text of the novel immediately affects the reader's understanding of the work and the critic's explanation of it. The reader often hovers between the freedom afforded by complicated imagery and the effects of the internal acts of interpretation that may appear to be a constraint on the protocols of reading. In his well-known study of a passage about reading in *Du Côté de chez Swann*, Paul de Man (57–78) situates the text at a crossroads of transformation and interpretation; he finds the very substance of the text in the flights of meaning. While continuing to accept de Man's gesture, one can criticize his deconstruction because the passage he chooses to examine depends so palpably on the presence of the theme of reading. Since any specificity of "theme" or "object" may be quite accidental for Proust, there is a danger in according too much value to a specific theme as a guide to generalized interpretation. By removing the thematic underpinning on which de Man based his reading, we see that it is possible that the whole novel, and not just the thematically self-reflexive passages, is situated at a crossroads of constant interpretation and transformation.

This solution is not an easy one. The critic's task is complicated by the valuing of interpretation over theme. It is all too easy to make themes out of homosexuality and interpretation; it is difficult to resist the siren call of closure. Moreover, the critic approaching this novel finds his or her task inscribed before beginning, sees his or her view reflected in the text, and discovers a chosen position already interpreted for him or her and undercut by that very process of interpretation. Or, more exactly, the critic may find *his* view already reflected in the text or may find that *her* view is never offered as an interpretation. It is that ever-mobile displacement of interpretation from theme to process, subtended by a continual sexual displacement, a move away from the structures of male heterosexuality, that is at the heart of the novel.

What then can we say about the interpretation of interpretation in the novel? Certain assumptions made about interpretation *in* the work have led both to specific kinds of interpretation *of* the text and to the imposition of models of reading and knowledge. The ways in which critics have interpreted the narrator's own acts of interpretation, I would argue, have been the effective means for bringing the text to thematic and theoretical closure. A given view of interpretation circumscribes the text in a definite way; it determines its themes and, more important, its theoretical perspectives on itself: the means it proposes to explain what is being transformed, what is being interpreted, and what is occurring at any given moment. Since the interpretation of interpretation is a self-reflexive act, a *mise-en-abyme* of the critic's actions, his or her interpretation of interpretation will support the critical position he or she maintains. In fact, I would go further: in every case, Proust's own interpretation of an event within the novel can be seen as the insightful, prescient act that is the precursor to the act of the critic.

II. Miss Interpretation

What can we know from one scene in a novel such as the *Recherche*? More pointedly, is there any intrinsic literary meaning to a scene? How can we know how to interpret it? When we have understood the denotative sense of the language, when we have realized what constitutes the frame of reference for the text, at what point and with what confidence can we say that a passage or scene is critically important? We are all used to making sense of the literary text in a process of rereading: the sense of a passage rarely comes through immediately. We sometimes recognize a passage of strategic literary importance immediately, however, even if no one has told us so, even if we have only just come across the text. One factor spurring this recognition is the presence of what we, as "competent readers," perceive as a "strange" situation: measured implicitly against the other readings we have already done, this text suddenly seems different, new, or strange. Yet, despite the insistence by Russian Formalism on strangeness as an inherently literary value, in and of itself strangeness is no guarantee of significance. The passage in question could merely be a tangent that is not integrated into the work as a whole and could be without any interest other than its strangeness. Or the whole work could be made of such strangenesses. In either case, the difference guarantees nothing for the critical reader.

Another mark of a scene's possible importance is the author's own metacommentary. Less likely to disappoint than the merely aberrant scene, such a passage comes already interpreted for the reader; it is as if the author were saying, "Look, this is important." It is, of course, a frequent phenomenon in Proust's work, yet as we read and reread the novel, we realize that there are problems associated with metacommentary. To say the least, the interpretation is not always correct: many of the earlier parts of the *Recherche* come with their own interpretation, which is often wrong or at least misguided. And the commentary on the events of the first and second volumes is replete with the narrator's false naïveté—which is part and parcel of the interpretation of interpretation in the novel as a whole.

Consider the case of the most famous homosexual character in all of the *Recherche*, the Baron de Charlus. In the early parts of the novel, Marcel does not know that Charlus is homosexual. Yet it stands to reason that the narrator does know this bit of essential information, which he continues to hide from his readers until the character discovers it himself at the beginning of *Sodome et Gomorrhe*. In fact, the wise reader has figured it out in the last part of *A l'ombre des jeunes filles en fleurs* ("Noms de pays: le pays"), in which Charlus's behavior toward Marcel is subtended by a text of homosexual attraction (2:110–24). Regarding this most fundamental point of Charlus's homosexuality, a discovery on which so much depends, the narrator will wait several hundred more pages before confirming the interpretation that the reader has given the events.

In the *Recherche*, the process of misinterpretation is so central that it becomes a part of the narrated events (the *fable*): interpretation is plot and misinterpretation becomes a phantom character in the novel. Consider a remark such as the following about Odette's purported affair with Charlus. Proust puts it in quotation marks but one cannot really definitively attribute it to any one of the characters: "I believe he has lots of problems with his hussy of a wife who, as everyone in Combray knows, lives with a certain Monsieur de Charlus" (1:34). Even one hundred pages later the misinterpretation still stands, though this time it is attributed to Marcel's grandfather: "What a role they make poor Swann play: they make him leave so she can stay alone with her Charlus" (1:140). Nothing, of course, could be further from the truth, but it is not until much later, through a process of rereading, that we realize that this misinterpretation is itself part of the scene. So we can say with some assurance that if misinterpretation can itself appear as an event or a character in the novel, the process of correctly interpreting always depends on return and recursion. When Marcel's own misreadings occur, the narrator does not point to them as wrong, but lets the text develop further, providing cause for the necessary rereading later on.

The misinterpretation of a sequence or event can merely be the signal of a lack of knowledge. Coming at the close of "Combray," the passage about the bell towers of Martinville is emblematic in its deployment of a rhetoric and dialectic of knowledge and ignorance, of interpretation and misinterpretation: "a bit of what had been hidden for me in them appeared to me; I had a thought that had not existed for me the moment before" (1:178). Just as this descriptive page was forgotten and then rediscovered, it emblematically demonstrates the process of forgetting and remembering, misreading and correction, blindness and insight, misinterpretation and interpretation. The image of the bell towers emblematically encapsulates the process of interpretation and rereading. The narrator presents the passage (1:178) and then immediately tells us that he wrote down his interpretation in a "little piece" that he lost and has more recently rediscovered. Just like Combray itself, lost and rediscovered, the mise-en-abyme of the bell towers shows us that rediscovery means rediscovering an event, its echoes, its harmonies, and its layers of interpretation.

There is no better example of this rhetoric of interpretation than the most famous passage in all of the *Recherche*, that of the madeleine. What the madeleine provokes is not memory itself but a will to remember, a will to understand, and a will to interpret. After so many pages devoted to non-knowledge and to misinterpretation, these final paragraphs before the presentation of Combray, the town that springs from the teacup, show to what extent this work has already become a will to knowledge, if only knowledge were possible: "Whence could this powerful joy have come to me? . . . Where did it come from? What did it mean? Where to grasp it? [*Où l'appréhender?*]" (1:44). And yet it will not be an easy event, for the narrator is already changing the format of the structure of enunciation by two verb shifts, from the imperfect to an infinitive and then to a present tense: "I drink a second mouthful in which I find nothing more than in the first, a third, that brings me less than the second" (1:44–45).

The interruption of the present tense would normally be a sign of a shift from *énoncé* to *énonciation*, that is to say, from an event at the level of the plot to a discursive comment that relates to the act of narration. But here it would seem to be nothing more than a feverish desire to find meaning, intensified by the use of the present tense, known as the historical present. As Maurice Grevisse indicates in *Le Bon Usage* (667, para. 715.5), the present can be used to indicate "something that occurred in the distant past, but presented as if it were now happening at the moment at which it is being spoken about; this is the 'historic past,' frequently used to give the story a particular liveliness." Yet one cannot help wondering if that shift is not also perhaps the first sign of a shift from event to discursive interpretation. For not even the immediacy associated with the eruption of the present tense can give meaning to the passage: "And I start wondering again what this unknown state could be . . . I want to make it reappear" (1:45). The desire to interpret is now central and meaningful; the appearance of the present tense is a sign of that desire.

Hence it is not completely accurate to say that this present tense is merely an accepted way of bringing immediacy to a story in order to make it come alive. What comes alive here, if anything, is the act of interpretation itself, certainly not an action. In fact, the use of the present tense at this point is the narratological equivalent of a syllepsis or an amphibology.

While primarily a mark of the immediacy of communicating an experience, this instance of the present tense is also a mark of the need to solidify the enunciative structure for narration to occur. The narrator brings everything into question again as he transforms the rather scattered memories of the first section into the ordered story of the second section; this ordering is a manifestation of his will to write. The very act of questioning, the interruption of discourse, and the presence of metacommentary all constitute the act of interpretation that is a confusion of enunciation and *énoncé*: no one would believe, for example, that the knowledge or the remembering of the little piece of madeleine offered to the narrator by Léonie on Sunday mornings is sufficient for determining the importance of this passage. Rather, the act of interpretation itself, even in its undecidability, opens the text up to a whole series of acts of interpretation, that is, to the rest of the novel; it is that opening that makes the passage important.

We can say, then, that the radical difference of Proust's novel is that interpretation precedes thematics, or even that interpretation replaces thematics. The multiple acts of interpretation in the text forestall the reification of the text's rhetorics into a theme. The acts of interpretation are the text. Tales of jealousy, aesthetics of return and recuperation, readings of society's changes, and even thematics of homosexuality are subsumed under the categories of a novel that frames them all with interpretation itself. We are faced with the interpretation of aesthetics, the aesthetics of interpretation, the function of interpretation according to aesthetics, and the function of aesthetics according to interpretation. The scene of writing or the story about reading is itself subjected to the scene of interpretation, the simultaneous writing and reading of a textuality that never winds up merely in a constitutive mode.

III. The First Time

Since I have been making a case for the complete interweaving of homosexuality and interpretation, because, quite simply, understanding homosexuality in the *Recherche* means the most profound reflection on interpretation possible, I would now argue for looking at the first scene dealing with homosexuality in the novel. By this I mean the scene at Montjouvain between Mlle Vinteuil and her nameless lover, "Mlle Vinteuil's friend [*l'amie de Mlle Vinteuil*]," whose anonymity is important to the structures of encryption and decipherment of the text, as I have shown elsewhere (*Flaubert and Sons* 241–42). Has there ever been another anonymous figure as important to the structure of a classical (readable) narrative as is this nameless lover? The answer is affirmative: the protagonist/narrator of the *Recherche*. So let us turn to this other anonymous individual who, had he had the same first name as the author of the book, would have been named Marcel (3:583). Having fallen asleep on a tumulus, Marcel wakes to espy a flirtatious scene between the two female characters. Just like the emblematic scene of the madeleine that brings the first, disordered memories of Combray to a close, just like the scene of the bell towers of Martinville that brings the first part of *Swann* to a close, the scene at Montjouvain also indicates the end of the passage on the "Méséglise Way."

Three structures seem to come together at this point for the reader who is critically rereading the novel. First, the scene serves as an act of closure that signals a shift to another approach to the text. Second, the scene will be the base for two other scenes of espionage and homosexual discovery later in the novel: the scene between Jupien and Charlus at the beginning of *Sodome et Gomorrhe* and the scene set in the male brothel in *Le Temps retrouvé*. And third, the scene is structurally related to a number of other incidents, both earlier and later in the story.[2]

In the scene between Mlle Vinteuil and her friend, Mlle Vinteuil remarks that she does not know who could have left the picture of her father out (1:160). Her disingenuous remark repeats almost verbatim what her father said of one of his own musical compositions in the presence of Marcel's parents: "I don't know who put that on the piano" (1:112). As Mlle Vinteuil's remark formally repeats her father's, we are reminded that the repetition and interpretation occur with a twist. For, though the scene with M. Vinteuil is witnessed by both Marcel's parents, its barely mentioned repetition is related to Marcel's mother: "Every time my mother made a fresh attempt during the visit . . ." (1:112). When, however, the narrator recalls the earlier event, it is the father called as a witness: "I remembered that those were the words that M. Vinteuil had said to my father about the piece of music" (1:160). Interpretation inverts the figure.

This idea of inversion is carried through the scene. The music on the piano is meant to be seen or read. One would think that the photo is meant to be seen, but it is itself doing the gazing, just as in the remembered version of the earlier scene it is Marcel's father: "this portrait of my father looking at us [ce portrait de mon père qui nous regarde]" (1:160). This will be the scene where the father (Marcel's, or M. Vinteuil) stops looking and

2. The technical terms for that "earlier" and "later" referentiality are "analepsis" and "prolepsis," respectively; they are discussed in depth by Gérard Genette in *Figures III*. Analepsis or retrospection is a reference to a previous event (82–105); prolepsis is the reference to, or the anticipation of, an event later in the story (105–14).

where Marcel begins to look for himself. And when his own active gaze starts, he will make a tentative discovery of a forbidden sexual zone. The discovery will become clear when he realizes that he has all the material for understanding homosexuality in front of him. Repetition is interpretation: the scene at Montjouvain shows the critic how to read the earlier scene, just as the earlier scene shows the difference and interpretation in the later one. And though the critical juxtaposition of these two scenes shows how reading and gazing are themes in the novel, it is far more important to realize that it is ongoing interpretation that structures the events.

The act of interpretation is generalized when we realize that yet another movement or displacement comes of this little game of sexual foreplay: from mother to father (Marcel's), from father to daughter, from woman to woman. As a nameless being and as an interloper, "Mlle Vinteuil's friend" is most decidedly never in her place, if in fact she has a place. Even the town of Combray is aware of the displacement involved:

> Must poor M. Vinteuil be so blinded by tenderness that he does not realize what is being talked about? He, who is scandalized by a word *out of place* [une parole déplacée], allows his daughter to have such a woman live under his roof" (1:145, Proust's emphasis).

The generalization of interpretation depends on a displacement from a singular vision of the narrator to the general hearsay of the town and on the ability of the nameless friend to insert herself anonymously into a situation. Nameless, completely out of place, she is nevertheless comparatively free to interpret. "Mlle Vinteuil's friend" puts the music in "its" place by interpreting the hieroglyphic scrawls on staff paper to produce the composer's posthumous masterpiece, the septet. Far from remaining a theme, the game of interpretation that starts out as narcissism in the case of M. Vinteuil or foreplay in the case of his daughter is re-erected into the modus operandi of narrative itself, becoming the constantly displaced actions of inscription and reading.

One of the reasons for choosing this scene as emblematic of the Proustian process of interpretation is its location at an intersection of structural chains. And even if its place is constantly displaced, these chains are displaced along with it. It stands to reason, then, that any element that is subject to such a theory of interpretation because of its structural relation to other parts of the narrative actualizes a double interlocking chain of signifiers, what structuralism called synchrony and diachrony. One chain operates at a distance by structural homology, repetition, or metaphor: the scene analeptically recalls the scene of M. Vinteuil with Marcel's parents.

It proleptically predicts the other scenes of discovery relating to the revelation of homosexuality (the beginning of *Sodome et Gomorrhe*) and homosexual sadomasochism (Charlus in the brothel). The other chain operates by contiguity within the scene itself as the variations on visibility are explored. Thus the figure of "seeing and being seen" diachronically relates to earlier and later parts of the novel by repetition, with or without slight variation, and by inversion.

The element also relates synchronically to other parts of the same scene in a similar way. The figure of the gazing photo relates to the motif of "seeing and being seen" that is the master figure of the scene. We have reached what might be called a chiasmus at the heart of this figure of interpretation. For a scene of sexual foreplay to be verisimilar, barring a proclivity for exhibitionism, it is necessary for the narrator not to be visibly present. More broadly, the narrative integrity of the scene at Montjouvain, the scene between Charlus and Jupien in the latter's shop, and the scene of Charlus in the brothel all depend absolutely on the narrator *not* being seen. Yet the formal integrity of the scene depends on the idea of being seen: each of those three sexual scenes is a performance of sorts for an audience that is supposedly not there. The characters' every action and word seem to play not only to the invisible narrator but also to an audience of voyeuristic spectators watching homosexuals engage in sex.

The scene at Montjouvain is constantly being remarked for interpretation. Marcel tells us that Mlle Vinteuil is repeating her father's words; this interpretation, as I have said, is itself the substance of the scene. But Mlle Vinteuil interprets her own remarks relative to being seen: "When I say 'see us,' I mean 'see us read'" (1:159). For whom is she interpreting, for whom is she lying? What is this reading? If "seeing us" means "seeing us read," but "really" means "seeing us make love," where is the truth of the scene? Is this reading as much of a lie as one would think? After all, Mlle Vinteuil and her friend are going to make love, and this primal scene of "sadism," to use Proust's own word (1:161; 3:766), or of homosexual lovemaking, is certainly repeated several times in a more or less integral fashion (Saylor 92–94). But it is the reading of this set piece, quite precisely, that gives it its meanings.

The inserted detail of "seeing us read" is an additional clue to the way in which Proust develops his theory of interpretation. As we know, Paul de Man developed his deconstruction of Proust's *volupté de lecture* from a passage in *Du Côté de chez Swann* about reading. What becomes clear from the scene at Montjouvain is that reading itself is an excuse: the last thing a theory of reading, an allegory of reading, or a deconstruction of Proust needs is reading itself as an obligatory part of the *énoncé*. For as de Man shows (77), the allegory of reading makes the absolute meaning of reading undecidable: "The allegory of reading narrates the impossibility of reading. But this impossibility necessarily extends to the word 'reading' which is thus deprived of any referential meaning whatsoever." Why not go to the more radical position, which shows that reading is nonreferential? Thus de Man is right, but he does not go far enough in exploring where that nonreferentiality, much like the misinterpretation I mentioned above, takes us. And as we see, it takes us to the realm of the homosexual, the constantly displaced figure of interpretation for the novel.

The performative nature of this dance of foreplay will be repeated in the courtyard scene enacted at the beginning of *Sodome et Gomorrhe* between Charlus and Jupien and will return in the brothel as Charlus comments on the theatrical performance of his whipper (4:396). I argue that this theatricality is essential to our understanding of the act of interpretation. At every turn, the characters act out a scene for the benefit of the invisible narrator, though they do not know they are being observed. In his own right, the narrator sees that performance and voyeuristically doubles the position of dominance within the scene. The act of interpretation of the narrator is the written equivalent of the sex act. And yet, since the act of interpretation inscribes the event as an event—gives it a beginning, a middle, and an end—it necessarily dominates the act by organizing it. Thus it is not at all daring to say that the figure of sadism in these scenes is the theatrical version, the specular image, even the mise-en-abyme, of the narrator's action in turning a nonevent into textual material. In a perverse way, to narrate is to be a voyeur and a sadist. To narrate oneself is to turn that sadism and voyeurism on oneself and to become, in the process, one's own masochistic, exhibitionistic victim, a blissful homosexual *heautotimoroumenos*, the Baudelairean *bourreau de soi-même*.

Sex, or "reading," is a performance, and until it is interpreted in writing, it has no consistency. Just as the narrator will be disappointed by the performance of Berma (1:437), only to reverse himself when he discovers that it has been written about in the newspapers (1:471), the sex is interesting only when it becomes a narrative act: not reading, but writing. And the key to that transformation is interpretation, which we now realize is another amphibology, pertaining to translation and to theatricality. Thus Proust emphasizes the performative, interpretive nature of sex in the scene at Montjouvain as he shows the reader how the narrative interpretation doubles the performance and how that interpretation, in giving meaning, is sadistic: giving meaning and making ultimate sense, I would argue, are for Proust sadistic acts, since they bring closure to free play.

And even as this theatricality seems to be a necessary element, it is not, for all that, felicitous for the author. In fact, while recognizing the need for a measure of theatricality at this point, Proust will go to great lengths to undercut it. One might hypothesize then that the sense of homosexuality for Proust, or, for that matter, the sense of artistic redemption in *Le Temps retrouvé*, will be the result of the gradual detheatricalization of the event. Here, however, Proust quickly stresses the artifice involved in the theater of sex:

> it is by the footlights of the popular theater rather than by the lamp of a real country house that one can see a girl make her friend spit on the portrait of a father who lived only for her; and there is hardly anything besides sadism that gives a foundation in life to the aesthetic of melodrama. (1:161)

Proust makes a parallel between sadism and theater; reality, which means for him "reality 'aside from sadism'" and the novel can do without that excuse. Just as, I would add, the deconstruction of the text does not need the concrete theme of reading to occur, Proust's narrative does not need the tangible, visible light to come into being. Such an excuse turns real life and narrative into melodrama. As the narrator comments later on in *Le Côté de Guermantes*: "As will be seen, I finally met highnesses and majesties of another sort, queens who play at being queens, and who do not speak according to the customs of their ilk, but like Sardou's queens" (2:718–19). Throughout the novel, the rehearsed dialogues of various social situations, sexual or not, are seen as mere theater, deprecated in favor of the aestheticization of real life in novelistic form. Moreover, if Mlle Vinteuil really were a sadist, she would not perform an act "of such rudimentary and naive symbolism." If she really were what she says she is, or more exactly, what she seemingly shows herself to be (for she says she is reading), she would not read her own actions. Were she really a sadist, her behavior "would be more veiled both to others' eyes and her own."

I would argue then that the realization of a homosexual hermeneutic that does not rely on performance will be the key to understanding the turn away from the theatrical. Hence, when the scene in Montjouvain returns in *La Prisonnière*, the narrator excuses the theatricality as a kind of madness:

> Moreover, Mlle Vinteuil had acted only out of sadism, which didn't excuse her, but later I thought about it with tenderness. I said to myself that she had to realize,

at the moment she and her friend were profaning her father's photograph, that all that was sick behavior and madness and not the true joyous evil she would have liked. The idea that it was only a simulation of evil spoiled her pleasure. (3:766)

Sadism is no longer a transgressive sexual activity, but rather a performance based on role-playing, as distant as possible from the "voluptuousness" of the sexual. Even in what would seem to be the most scabrous part of the novel, Proust maintains the theatricality of sadism. In the scene in the male brothel run by Jupien, Proust continues to insist on the asymmetry of sadism and masochism: the supposedly dissolute, crime-ridden life of the male prostitutes sent to whip Charlus is theatrical, whereas Charlus's sexual pleasure depends on the absence of theatricality: "he calls me a scoundrel [*crapule*] as if he had memorized a lesson" (4:396). This is, to say the least, no longer sexuality but pure melodramatic performance. Just as the narrator has learned to distinguish (homo)sexuality from sadistic performance, Charlus too has changed, wishing for an orgasm and finding himself in a bad raree-show.

Let us return to examining the ramifications of the scene at Montjouvain. When we have integrated the raw material of the *récit* with the interpretation given the material in the discourse of the narrator, when we have reinterpreted that complex of récit and discourse, we are then on the road to understanding a section of the work. Still, we must perform the same act of interpretation on the narrator's discourse that he has just performed on the story. I mean that we need to examine the interpretive solutions to the scene: first, that against the theatricality of a scene, the narrative will be true, and second, that this sadism is itself nothing more than a performance. As I will show, the points are not merely reinterpretations or corrections of misinterpretations but keys to an understanding of the processes of interpretation at work based on the constant displacement that homosexuality affords the text.

The first point is that the performance Mlle Vinteuil gives is theatrical and that what is being given to us is "true." By interpreting the meaning of the scene, by showing to what extent Mlle Vinteuil is giving a performance, the narrator has proposed that narrative will be the locus in which truth is revealed through the processes of interpretation. One of the dangers of life as performance is precisely that infection of the interpretation of a scene: one runs a risk that the performative aesthetics of the theater may take over life itself, as will be the case with the whole Verdurin clan. The members of the Verdurin clan do not live, they perform their parts by rote every night. The narrator gives us a theatrical scene to examine, and at every turn, the performance is geared to making the invisible audience aware that it is an audience and to making the observer understand what is going on. The performance is there for Marcel who has fallen asleep on the hillside; the performance is there for us, as we allow Marcel to see vicariously for us.

We can effectively interpret the scene by simultaneously accepting and refusing its theatricality, just as we have accepted and refused the implications of the present tense in the madeleine episode. The scene is both a performance, the "interpretation" of a role, and the rejection of performativity in favor of a narrative form that is itself proposed as the model of the revelation of truth. The novel is the locus in which we assume we can distinguish between truth and falsity, where we eschew the bad mimesis of theatricality, and where récit without discourse is a banality. In the novel, the narrator proposes, interpretation in the performative sense is subsumed under the category of interpretation in general. Again, we see a familiar mechanism at work: interpretation structures the narrative when the theme of interpretation (like the theme of reading, for example) is discarded in favor of a generalized theory.

It is not so easy to dismiss the performance, however, for the question of sadism is neither negligible nor epiphenomenal. In retrospect—and how can we read this novel without the benefit of retrospection?—we know that Proust will repeat the scene of sadism as theater in the homosexual brothel. But it is already clear that if Mlle Vinteuil really were a sadist, she would not perform such a simple act of "ritual profanations" (1:160). I would venture to say that such an expression is the indication of the theatricality that Proust seems to be simultaneously affirming and denying. This private theater in which we see Mlle Vinteuil "read" is a locus for reading that interprets, where interpretation always includes a dysfunctional component of misinterpretation. Also, when we read, we are as likely to intercalate our own fantasies and our own subjectivities as we are to read what the author has placed before us in his act of representation, which affirms and denies its theatricality:

> I wanted to put down the volume I still thought I had in my hands and blow out my light; I had not ceased, while sleeping, to reflect on what I had just read, but those reflections had taken rather a particular turn: I thought I was what the work was talking about. (1:3)

So Mlle Vinteuil is not really lying; "reading" is just as good a name as any for what she is doing: interpreting her own situation, mixing her "true" nature with a theatricalized version of herself, being, like the narrator, "a church" (for ritual), "a quartet" (a sonata or a septet), "the rivalry" between two individuals (1:3). Reading means the surrender of the self to the text of the other; and neither Marcel, Mlle Vinteuil, nor any of the other characters in the novel ever performs this act absolutely. Without the interpretation, the act does not exist: it is pure theater, as distant from reality as possible. Without the act, however, the interpretation has a life of its own as the novel.

Now that we have looked at some of the ramifications of this passage, I would like to turn briefly to the context in which it is found in the novel. As I have already suggested, the meaning of any given passage never starts and stops at the limits of the passage. The scene at Montjouvain does not begin its own interpretive chain. It is predicated analeptically on the fact that Vinteuil had already performed a homologous scene for Marcel's mother, one totally bereft of sadomasochistic implications. It is predicated on the hearsay of the good citizens of Combray, who are aware of what is going on, that is to say, what they assume to be going on, even if M. Vinteuil turns a blind eye or a deaf ear and even if the narrator does not yet know what is going on. It is predicated as well on the germ of the very first paragraph of the novel: Marcel falls asleep and intermittently observes, relates, and identifies with what he has been reading. So Marcel's reading is an act of interpretation equivalent to Mlle Vinteuil's reading and vice versa. Again, any reading of the scene at Montjouvain depends on how it is articulated with what precedes it, in the alternation of scenes of reading and voluptuousness. Yet to see the scene at Montjouvain as a scene of interpretation is to note that it is the locus in which reading and voluptuousness become mutually indistinguishable as interpretation.

The series of scenes of interpretation could arguably start with the passage on walks taken after hours spent reading. But even then, the narrator has just spent a paragraph interpreting his own interpretations of Françoise's speech patterns and, not surprisingly, has ended in the realm of the theatrical. Not the least of the points in the paragraph is that the errors Françoise makes, the relation of which constitutes a subtext throughout the *Recherche*, relate to language itself:

> If, filled like a poet with a rush of confused thoughts about chagrin or about family memories, Françoise apologized for not knowing how to answer my theories and said: "I don't know how to espress [*sic*] myself [Je ne sais pas m'esprimer]," I triumphed over that admission with a brutal irony worthy of Doctor Percepied; and if she added: "She was still a relativity [de la parenthèse], there's still the respect owed to relativity [à la parenthèse]," I would shrug my shoulders and think "I am so generous to discuss things with an illiterate who makes such howlers." (1:152)

So Françoise is simultaneously illiterate and poetic; her errors are as lettered as possible, especially the misuse of the word "parenthesis" (*parenthèse*) for the word for "relatives" (*parenté*). Even an illiterate joins family members in a parenthetic act of reading as interpretation, to be remarked by the narrator who is as sadistically "brutal" as Percepied, even as he is theorizing, giving his point of view, and interpreting for an illiterate. The same "error" is repeated much later: "In any case it's the same relativity [*parenthèse*]" (2:323), but this time the interpretation of her errors goes far beyond the personal: "Like the French language itself, her speech, especially her place-names, was bestrewn with errors." Françoise's errors often show the spark of creativity, as she invents "Antoinesse" as the feminine of Antoine, based on the model of "chanoine" and "chanoinesse" (2:234). Elevated to the levels of idiosyncratic linguistic purity and of creativity, Françoise's errors appear, through the act of interpretation at a distance, to parallel the creative act of the author himself. In fact, this whole interpretive process is comparable to the scene at Montjouvain: Mlle Vinteuil repeats her father, misnames what she is doing, and only eventually allows the deciphering of her father's septet to occur through the nameless friend's dedicated musicological Egyptology, as she establishes "the definitive reading of those unknown hieroglyphics" (3:766). Here, Françoise's errors, initially disdained by the narrator, wind up being the very herald of what he himself is idiosyncratically doing in his acts of interpretation of the world.

Even when we arbitrarily say that a sequence of interpretations begins at a given point, this beginning depends on a pretext where interpretation constantly joins what the reader may think of as different realms: the world of text and the world of emotion. Just as there is alternation and ultimate confusion between an act and its interpretation in almost any sentence or paragraph, similar alternation occurs from paragraph to paragraph. So the walks in the woods that follow an act of reading are themselves followed by daydreams, an act of masturbation, and the scene at Montjouvain itself (155–57). The Montjouvain scene is inserted into a chain of events in the novel, each of which is an act of interpretation, a mixture of memory and desire, a combination of interpretation and act. The reference to masturbation ends with an analogy between the products of one's imagination and the act of reading a novel:

My desires seemed to be no more than the purely subjective, powerless, illusory creations of my temperament. They no longer had a link to nature or to reality, which thereafter lost all its charm and meaning and was, in my life, no more than a conventional frame, as is, for the fiction of a novel, the train on whose bench the traveler reads it to kill time. (1:157)

The scene at Montjouvain shows us how interpretation works in the novel by setting up a model for interpretation that alternates meaning and desire as the privileged signifieds for an ongoing, ever-spinning narrative. From that scene at Montjouvain, let us turn to a general view of interpretation.

IV. Names of the Interpretation: The Name

From an elemental scene at Montjouvain, we pass to an excerpt that has become Proust's most (in)famous text on homosexuality. Like the scene of the madeleine, that of Martinville, and that at Montjouvain, it too signals a shift in strategy, for it comes at the end of a long meditation on interpretation which we shall examine in the last part of the chapter. But before looking at that meditation, let us recall the well-known beginning of *Sodome et Gomorrhe*. In this part of the novel, Proust writes thirty-odd pages of essay mixed with fiction in which he details "the first appearance of men-women" (3:3). In describing the encounter between Charlus and Jupien, the narrator develops an extensive set of natural metaphors, provides some generalized, even stereotypical, commentary on homosexuals, and describes the sounds of sexual congress he has overheard.

In addition to being Proust's most famous text about homosexuality, it is also widely disliked. Sedgwick (*EpCl* 216) speaks for many when she says: "Suppose we agree—as most readers, I among them, do—in perceiving Proust's chapter on *la race maudite*, in its direct thematization of gay identity, as sentimental and reductive." And Bersani (24) talks of "the banal thematization of homosexuality in the essay that opens the volume." Gray (129) is one of the few critics not to lambaste Proust for the episode of Charlus and Jupien: she says that the image of the bee and flower "breaches its containment as image to invade and overturn the narrative proper." Whereas I am aligning myself with the minority position that finds the section of interest and one of the least thematic parts of the novel, I differ from Gray in one significant way: I see this breach as the standard figure for the novel. In fact, I wonder if we can even talk about the "narrative proper" when we are talking about Proust, so much do the figures of the text seem the most proper (and improper) of its parts. Indeed, attempting to talk about the "narrative proper" would be part of a will to closure in which narrative itself is made a theme of the work. In such a case, one might talk about the thematization of homosexuality in this "reductive" chapter, but one would be contributing to the "heroically resolute banalization" (*EpCl* 216), not of the issue of sexual choice, but of the narrative itself. As I shall suggest below, one would do well to see how *Le Côté de Guermantes*, while proposing a framework and thus a kind of closure, retains the possibility of theme that is always "open to interpretation."

At first glance, however, one may be inclined to agree with the general assessment offered by Sedgwick. Seemingly feeding on stereotypes of homosexuals and predictable behavioral patterns, Proust writes of the history of these individuals, gives a brief sociology of their behavior, and tells specifically of his protagonist's discovery of the nature of the relation between two of these special creatures, Charlus and Jupien. Now, obviously, for a writer like Foucault, the very fact that Proust is engaging in this collective social biography is a sign of the changes that the nineteenth century made in its view of the homosexual as an individual. Proust's arguments seem to be in line with the standard views, for, in inventing the homosexual as a so-called individual, what the end of the nineteenth century really did was invent the homosexual as a type of individual with a type of behavior pattern.

In seeming to rely on the banal, the general, and the stereotypical, Proust appears to be asserting general truths. Yet at the same time, he is providing a ground for the specific truths and interpretations of the novel, and especially for the characters of Charlus, Jupien, and Saint-Loup among others. On the one hand then, Proust's discourse operates at a level wholly consonant with the typology of the homosexual at the end of the century: each individual is a subset of a general "they." On the other hand, Proust is making great efforts to distinguish his major male homosexual characters, not only from one another, but also from the general typology. How are we to understand these pages which seem to be self-justifying in that they reaffirm the stereotypical typology and which seem even to be independent of the fiction in which they are found, since they purport to contain an extra-narrative general truth?

In the discussion that follows, I shall consider several possible approaches to this material, and will look at how certain critics have approached it. My aim here is not to denigrate the insights of these critics but rather to underline the ways in which this section of the novel is troublesome and resistant to interpretation. In this examination of what I perceive as a set of strong misreadings, in the most complimentary Bloomian sense, I make an implicit argument about the novel as a whole: far from being stereotypical, reductive, and hackneyed description, this section of *Sodome et Gomorrhe* is a mise-en-abyme of the whole novel. It resists clear interpretation, just as the whole novel does. And, if I may jump the gun, the reason that homosexuality becomes an overt theme of the novel at this point in the novel is that it is precisely here that Proust seizes the novel as a self-reflexive interpretive structure, whose echoes of interpretation ripple out toward a lack of closure.

Obviously, we could ignore this section as Proust's unfortunate, politically incorrect slip. But I argue that we have to look at it as being of fundamental importance to the novel as a whole. In fact, the reductive banality itself turns out to be a narrative trick. If we do read the passage, we could see it as being Proust's statement of a general truth. This truth can take several forms: it can refer to the referential world and thus be the sign of a typology or it can refer to the world of the novel and be a law of the universe of the novel. And it can also be nothing more than the convenient framing device that serves, not as a general law for the novel, but as the mixture of inductive and deductive remarks about the homosexual characters in the novel. Let us now apply these views to the novel.

It is no wonder that so many critics find these pages so banal, awful, and reductive. Even the sympathetic critic cannot fail to notice that by labeling Charlus as a homosexual, Proust has foisted a set of conventional interpretations of "the homosexual" upon his reader. After 32 pages in which the author drags up every stereotype about homosexual men of the "invert" variety, how can the reader possibly look at Charlus without prejudice? By classifying Charlus in this category, Proust seems to be making the same gesture as does Balzac before him for so many of his characters. In both cases, the author relies on a typology grounded in the popular science of the day. Proust thus seems to be saying that readers can rely on their own stereotypes of the invert, or on late-nineteenth-century psychosexology. Proust also seems to be saying that there is no other way to approach the question of the homosexual aside from this typical, typological, and conventional format. But as he already has shown us, he can sneak up on homosexuality, something he will do again.

Still, one should ask what the problems are with typology itself, for one could easily argue that any novelistic character is somehow a type to a greater or lesser extent. Let us think, then, about the results of having a homosexual character grounded in an extended discursive passage. The effect of this typology is to raise a specific truth about a character to the level of a general truth about a certain segment of human nature. And if this general truth is universal, the unique nature of the novelistic creation is lost: instead of being the singular creation that Proust produced, Charlus would be of a type, part of an undifferentiated set. Thus, rather than providing the rational basis for the unexpected turn of having a rather overt homosexual as a protagonist, the initial effect of the didactic passage may be counterproductive to the literary aspirations of the text: the most enduring effect would be to take individuality away from the character and make him a trivial reflection of himself.

Certainly an author may choose to interpret his text for us in a way that sets it up as representative: I am telling you, he says, about one individual, but what I am saying is true for many. Yet with Proust, the initial reading of *Sodome et Gomorrhe* does not follow that model, nor does it follow a strict Cartesian model. (By "Cartesian model," I mean a text *à thèse*, in which the author gives a general law and deduces a case of behavior from it. Examples of such deduction-driven texts include Goethe's *Elective Affinities* or numerous texts in *Les Rougon-Macquart*; but even then, the narrative art deflects the strict interpretation of the theory.) Proust's relation of didacticism to example is different; he seems to be giving both a representative example and the law, both the theory and a case, both a singularity and the type.

We can certainly choose to see the double logic as a means of internal validation, a crisscrossing game that is often an effective means of textual legerdemain, as I have shown in a study of Stendhal, "A Chronicle of Production." Precisely because of the apparent self-sufficiency of the text, which seems to have created a world completely parallel to the real one, we are not sure whether Proust is commenting on his novel or on the world. It is not even clear to what extent Proust intends his mixture of aesthetics and sociology to refer to a nonfictional world. Two laws seem to be at work: one of internal coherence and one of external representability. The law of internal coherence states that the text should be internally consistent: it should make sense, follow through with its paradigms, and not contradict its own structures. The law of external representability says that the relation between the text and the real world can be known and articulated, this articulation occurring through the mediation of enunciation and the theories of representation provided by the enunciative framework. Now obviously, these laws are not laws in the sense that they stand outside the text, but are laws within the paradigms of fiction: they are the rules for interpretation on which all interpretations depend. In this world the specific case is in the book; the general theory is in the world at large.

In situations in which the general theory seems to precede the case, that is to say, where the author has set up a general law of the universe, the version of the law in the text is cast as a representation of the general law. So the laws of determinism posited as the general rules for a naturalist text are there as the exact representation of these laws as they exist in the world. Proust's text is different in that he seems to be proceeding from a specific case (Charlus, for example) to general theory. But at other times, a general theory appears from which the case is expected to be deduced. On the one hand, then, Charlus is supposed to be a singular case whose comportment inductively points to a general rule about the behavior of homosexuals. At the same time, there are general rules that do not derive from the case at hand but which also do not represent the theory of the world, since they are also rules arrived at inductively.

The ambiguity of the modes of reference can be seen at the end of the section, where Proust writes, "Certainly in every country they are an oriental, cultivated, musical, gossiping colony that has charming qualities and unbearable faults" (3:33). Is Charlus, for example, to be constrained by a general statement that seems to derive from other observations or even future observations promised in "the pages to come" (3:33)? Is our further interpretation of his behavior to be determined by his actions, by Proust's interpretations of his actions, by our interpretations of his actions, or by our interpretations of Proust's interpretations? Or is our interpretation to be guided by conclusions about behavior drawn from Proust's general theory of homosexuality?

By juxtaposing a remark that comments on the world outside his text and a proleptic statement about future action of the novel, Proust presents us with a dilemma about the nature and status of fiction. If we accept the continuity between the sentence about homosexuals being a colony and the sentence about what we shall see in "the pages to come," our act of reading forfeits a measure of the fictional text's independence because the fiction is considered to be secondary to an eternal truth presented as a generality. Hence, even within a realist praxis, the construct of a fictional situation is not merely the reflection of a world. More important, this construct is the parasitic repetition of an eternal sign present in the world *before* the arrival of the fictional text; it is a sign and a world that the fiction can never replace. Yet if we separate the remarks, we still have to clarify the truth-value of the global statement; we still need to understand the function assigned to the present tense.

Along with the questions that relate to the exemplarity of Charlus's behavior and psychology comes an additional concern about the relation of the discourse to the real world: What status does referentiality have? To what extent do the enunciations of the narrator have a truth value, either for the world or for the text of which they form a part? The Proustian narrator is not omniscient; he cannot pretend to the truth, but can offer statements of an admittedly subjective consciousness. And even if it is considered to be only the effect of narration, this consciousness is motivated to maintain both its subjective integrity and that of the text as a coherent object marked with general truth statements. Thus Charlus must act according to a coherently ordered individual psychology, but must also obey the laws that the narrator has proposed for homosexuals in general. At every turn, therefore, there is an additional hermeneutic constraint on how we read Charlus. Along with the tension between the needs of the story and the psychological consistency of the character that is a hallmark of realist fiction, Proust is proposing an additional interpretive mechanism for reading Charlus's homosexuality. At every turn, Charlus risks having his individuality dissolved into a stereotype.

How do we resolve the question of the constraints upon the character? It is not a simple question nor is it a secondary one. For if we are right in having assumed that homosexuality is the base for interpretation in the *Recherche*, it is necessary to understand the articulation of these parts of the novel. The opening pages of *Sodome et Gomorrhe* are not problematic because they are banal, thematic, reductive, or garden-variety homophobic. They are problematic because they complicate the way in which Proust articulates the structures and systems that are founded in and on a homosexual hermeneutic. Perhaps the narrator of the beginning section of *Sodome et Gomorrhe* is somehow different from the narrator of the other parts of the book. S. Y. Kuroda (287–93) proposes eliminating the theory of the omniscient narrator in favor of narration without narrators or in favor of local narrators who would narrate part of the text. While Kuroda's theory certainly offers an insightful approach to reading the text of a so-called omniscient narrator, using it with the *Recherche* creates more problems than solutions. Seeing the beginning of *Sodome et Gomorrhe* as a local narration whose narrator is unrelated to the other narrators of the novel would fracture the novel. Certainly the narrator changes over time, as we have already seen. And certainly there is a manifest difference, though without a rupture, between the character, especially in his young years, and the narrator, who knows more than the younger incarnation of the character but sees fit to hide it on many occasions.

At least superficially, the interpretation of the text depends on the perceived validity and seamlessness of the narrative voice whose truth should be coterminous with the truth derived from the text. This is not to say that the placement or locus of the narrator is an easy one to define. Like the anonymous friend of Mlle Vinteuil, the narrative voice must constantly be dislocated relative to an imaginary third-person omniscient subject whose truth is the truth of the didactic passage. But it must also remain dislocated relative to the object, homosexuality, whose comprehension is itself always deferred along interpretative lines.

Understanding *Sodome et Gomorrhe* and, I would argue, *Le Côté de Guermantes* as well as the *Recherche* as a whole depends on an integration of the discourse of this section but we are still not sure how to do this. Traditional criticism would tell us that the novel is the transposition of its own theoretical statements and thus that the quotation about the "cultivated, oriental colony" refers seamlessly to its environment and has a truth-value for the book as a whole, if not for the world outside the text (Pavel; Riffaterre). Thus, wherever one looks in the world described or alluded to in the *Recherche*, whatever the relations of this world are to the "real" world, there is a "cultivated, oriental colony" of homosexuals. We could thus consider, for example, that the views developed about homosexuality at the beginning of *Sodome et Gomorrhe* apply only to the homosexual characters of this fictional world, a world that in many ways, but not *necessarily* in *this* one, happens to be a verisimilar one. In that case, Proust would be describing a world where the interpretive value of having a "cultivated, oriental colony" is important to the structures of the *Recherche* but not necessarily to the referential world. Certainly, one could argue, the number of characters revealed sooner or later as homosexual is sizable. Furthermore, the revelation of a character's homosexuality might form an analogy to the conversion of the narrator from passive reader to active narrator. Revealing homosexuality, the hidden meaning of things, would be an exemplary case for the process of artistic revelation that structures much of the novel.

Yet even in this light, the problem is not completely explained. Do the remarks pertain both analeptically and proleptically or only for the text that follows? If the remarks are to have retrospective value, how do we align the general truths of the narrator at the moment of the narration of *Sodome et Gomorrhe* with the ignorance of the earlier narrator? The position of the narrator of *Du côté de chez Swann*, for reasons of narrative strategy, seems more closely to mime the character of the young Marcel. We need only mention in passing the comments about Odette and Charlus, the scene at Montjouvain, or the exchanges between Marcel and Charlus in *A l'ombre des jeunes filles en fleurs* to see that the position of the earlier narrator is made problematic by the current didacticism. Even at those points in the narrative, the narrator knows that Odette is not having an affair with Charlus or that Charlus has become smitten with Marcel, yet the narrator says nothing. For the narrator to say what he knows would mean destroying the whole process of gradual interpretation and retrospective understanding of which the text is made. How do we reconcile this new information, which amounts to a hermeneutics of reading, with what was necessarily the narrator's and our own misreading of earlier passages?

But perhaps the didacticism has no theoretical pretensions and is absolutely equivalent to statements about an individual character. The remarks about the "cultivated, oriental colony" refer no further than the "cultivated, oriental colony" in this fiction. Charlus then would be an example of this group and the group would be the category in which Charlus and a few other characters fit. Then the relation of an individual case to a general law or the general law to an individual deduction would be a synecdoche, where the part stands for the whole or the whole stands for the part. Now, in the nineteenth-century novel, where the so-called omniscient third-person narrator is both transcendental and transparent, the process of textual law based on synecdoche or on metonymy is frequent. But because the narrator in such cases is constantly pretending he or she is not there, his or her uses of metonymy and synecdoche are consistently subjected to laws of representation and ideology. The brackets of the closed set—the one containing the homosexual characters, for example—silently disappear and the closure gives way to implicit referentiality. There is at least one stellar example of this process in Proust: "Un Amour de Swann." The more the text is aligned with the rhetoric of nineteenth-century representation, the more consistent the tropology is with such representation's external criteria. Hence we can generalize from individual and set to the real world, because the laws of representation of the text allow that to happen. But this is not the case in the *Recherche* as a whole, where the narrator in no way attempts to mime the position of the transcendental third person.

In this passage, then, Proust might initially seem to be miming the didacticism of Zola or even the pretension to absolute knowledge maintained by Balzac. Yet we must remember one cardinal point: this text, *like any other in the novel*, is subject to the same laws of interpretation we have already discussed. So there is a vacillation between wholes and parts such that the critic does not know in which direction to look: proleptically or analeptically, from part to whole or from whole to part. When I agreed above with Margaret Gray's assessment that the figurality of the passage overturns the narrative, I noted that I disagreed with her use of the term "narrative proper." For me, that expression implied that in Proust there was some hypothetical metaphor-free zone. What I am arguing, on the contrary, is that this section makes interpretation clearly a three-dimensional process. At any given point, the narrator's conclusions lead the text to spin in a third direction, that of metaphoricity.

Risking the apparent heterogeneity of a scientific or mathematical model, I would put this schematically in terms of a three-dimensional system of coordinates. Given a point "A" in the text—for example, in the discussion of homosexuality in *Sodome et Gomorrhe*—there are three components to that point. The x-component of the point's location relates, we shall say, to the degree of exemplarity of the point. The x-component tells us to what extent the point is an example from which conclusions may be drawn and/or to what extent it is a rule from which examples may come. More likely than not, the situation is in fact (am)bivalent: the interpretation of interpretation in Proust's text allows every point to be simultaneously example and theory. The y-component is temporal: Does the point refer back to another as theory or as example, or ahead? Again, more likely than not, it is simultaneously proleptic and analeptic. The z-component would be the degree of verisimilar representability. It indicates to what extent the point approximates representation according to a verisimilar model of enunciation. But it also shows to what extent the point is borne away from representation toward metaphoricity. And as is the case for the x- and y-components, there is no doubt that both are happening at the same time.[3] Rather than fixing the point in its "place," each of these components is a continuous displacement away from a solution.

To resolve the problem of interpreting didactic enunciation in the novel, some critics have displaced the problem of the status of enunciation by relating its "truths" to other representational systems. In the terms of the mathematical system just described, critics collapse the x- and z-components into one and thereby make the system a manageable two-dimensional one. So the truth is not narrative in nature, but may become, for example, semiotic in the eyes of Gilles Deleuze, psychoanalytic in the eyes of Serge Doubrovsky, and philosophical in the eyes of Vincent Descombes. Descombes is most specific in his reflection on the process of narrative translation and it will be useful to recall his approach.

Descombes posits a rupture in the text between discourse and plot: in narratological terms, Proust's enunciative remarks are less profound philo-

3. This is only a contradiction if we restrict our graphing of the three components to real numbers. If, however, we see each component as being a complex number having a real and an imaginary component, such as "4 + 3i," the contradiction disappears. Technically, this would schematically be represented by the intersection of three Argand planes. See Penrose 87–92.

sophically than what can be logically extrapolated from the *énoncé*. And for Descombes, "the novel is philosophically more daring than Proust is as a theoretician" (*Pr* 15). For example, the general laws of love that can be deduced from "Un Amour de Swann" are more profound than the statements about desire, jealousy, or love that Proust gives us in the narrator's voice. Thus, in this view, the fiction about homosexuality is stronger than any discursive enunciation: Proust's disquisitions may be tied to a limiting turn-of-the-century philosophy, but Charlus is not. In coming alive, so to speak, Charlus outstrips the discourse that might tie him down. Moreover, for Descombes, the work "is a *novel* that gives the narrative transposition of the theoretical propositions of an essay" (*Pr* 14). Thus, the beginning pages of *Sodome et Gomorrhe* can be seen as an anecdotal study of ethics or behavior whose fullest explanation occurs in the narrative that follows. For Descombes, the examples will go far beyond the original essay. These pages then illustrate a philosophical position whose truth is located at a historical moment in philosophical praxis and has no real pretension to being a universal law of behavior.

Despite Descombes's optimistic remark about the status of philosophical theory, I would maintain that no theory in Proust's text can ever be initially exposed as pure theory, untouched by exempla: there is always mutual deformation between what passes for theory and the rest of the narrative. By hypothesizing the possibility of extracting pure statements of philosophy from the text, either through deductive or inductive reasoning, one is simultaneously positing the existence of some such statements that resist such a process of reading. What is the future of those statements? They are either repressed by the act of reading to a level at which they no longer seem to function as anything but figures or they are reduced to being part of a neatly circumscribed theme.

To think that the philosophical or narrative theory is present within the text and recuperable as such is to repeat the Proustian project of recuperation that subtends the whole work. It is thus the most fictional of gestures. From the vantage point of the critic, it is a repetition of a form of Kantian idealism that also underlies the text. But there is a tension between demonstrating a Kantian ideal with transcendental value as a law and showing both a singularity, such as Charlus, and the structure of the novel. Still, if only to demonstrate that this tension exists, critics need a means of approaching the text that relies on being able neatly to frame the author's didactic and theoretical statements—a framing, as Derrida has shown in "Parergon" for Kant himself, that is ultimately impossible to complete. What has happened, then, is that the idealism in Proust's text is doubled by a recuperative act in literary criticism that takes the theoretical positions of Proust's text and normalizes them into a thematics. Proust's theories of aesthetics or sexuality are channeled into a constituted thematics, perceived as a whole, subject to closure, and able, therefore, to provide form to what is subjected to it.

To sum up then: the *Recherche* is recalcitrant and it resists interpretation in myriad ways. There is no better example of this resistance than the didactic passage at the beginning of *Sodome et Gomorrhe*. Taken alone, the passage causes the reader to question the validity of standard interpretive models of enunciation and *énoncé* and of representation. Taken in relation to the rest of the novel, the passage brings to light problems of hermeneutics: How does a text mean, or how indicate what it signifies? Standard critical approaches have either discounted the chapter or ignored the problems it repeatedly implies. In one way or another, the received criticism of Proust has assumed homosexuality was a theme *tout court* of the novel, despite the problems that this section poses. And not the least of those problems is the reductive essentialism conjured up by the specter of thematic closure.

Yet no critic would deny that homosexuality seems to become a "theme" at this precise point in the novel. So I would offer the following hypothesis: the move toward thematic closure is accompanied by a simultaneous resistance to closure and to thematization precisely because the entire hermeneutic model of the novel is at stake. If homosexuality becomes a full-fledged theme subject to closure, the author has nowhere to go. And yet he needs that superficial thematics to propel the text. Just as Proust makes a theoretical pitch that bears some of the hallmarks of essentialism and of thematic closure—the referential and textual faces of the same argument—he imbues his text with a recalcitrance and a resistance to closure, to theme, and to essence. It is to that recalcitrance I now turn by looking at how the contemporary critical scene has negotiated that resistance.

With its copious notes, sketches, and variants, the recent Pléiade edition of the *Recherche* helps show readers and critics the recalcitrance of the Proustian text. In Antoine Compagnon's introduction to *Sodome et Gomorrhe*, we read that "the Sodomite theme and the Gomorrhan theme crisscross" (3:1186). In the notes to the first sketch for this material, he marks "the theme of sexual inversion" (3:1797).[4] Again, we wonder why it is

4. Compagnon has also published a collection of essays on Proust, *Proust entre deux siècles*, an examination of some literary-historical points in the *Recherche*. Compagnon's study of Proust is the most recent in a series of critical studies that seek to understand the novel through reference to institutional and literary history. For him, the novel is at least partly the erasure of the visible signs of systems external to the text itself, the text's prehistory in

here that homosexuality becomes an overt theme of the novel. But we also wonder whether heterosexuality has been the theme heretofore. The odd nature of that second remark seems to indicate either that the "theme" of homosexuality does not exist in Proust except as a fuzzy catch-all critical term for what is most resistant or that the only thing that can be thematized is difference from a norm. In the first case, we seem to fly in the face of reason, for common sense tells us that the theme of homosexuality does exist in the novel. The second choice therefore is more plausible; however, by constantly dissociating difference from dominance, Proust will himself begin to undo the very thematics about which he is supposedly writing.

We have already seen that a model like that of the Dreyfus Affair can serve as an interpretive analogue for the *Recherche*. We recall that what is salient about the Dreyfus Affair as paradigm is that, at the heart of the Affair, there is no act of treason by Dreyfus. I would propose, then, that if homosexuality is as powerful a mechanism as I have suggested for the novel, the superficial chain of genesis is not where one should look for its power and meaning. Like the nothing at the heart of the Dreyfus Affair, the homosexual act or story is itself the merest excuse, on the superficial level, for the homosexual text.

Critics may have been attracted to the genesis of homosexuality in the Proustian text because a historical genesis is a less radical solution than the double one I am proposing: the strength of homosexuality is in its ability to serve as a means of interpretation and as a generator of metaphors. Still, looking at the arguments about a historic background for homosexuality in the novel can be instructive. According to Compagnon, the traces of this theme can be seen in *Les Plaisirs et les jours*, the Eulenbourg Affair of 1908, the correspondence, and the like. No one would deny that these all deal with the question of homosexuality, but no one could predict that these little papers would unfold to form a tree, a house, or a master-theme of homosexuality in the novel. In no way do these works necessarily predict the *Recherche*. Proust's novel creates its predecessors, but are these or other

---

previous writings, letters, historical considerations, and the like. The task of the interpreter is to make that invisible writing visible again. His or her task is to bring to light what Compagnon calls the "same" material in the correspondence and the novel (140). By relying on this version of textual prehistory and the development of an ordered thematics, he does not allow himself to explore the possible contradictions between the idea of sameness inherited from thematics and the problematic concept of rupture that comes from history. By accepting this sameness, Compagnon makes his reading a thematics of Proustian writing, which places him in the company of Paul de Man, whose writing was a thematics of Proustian reading. For Compagnon, interpretation becomes the search for the incarnations of identity, with or without variation.

predecessors the only answer to the generation of a thematics? Borges's comment on each writer creating his precursors strikes a cautionary note: "The first Kafka . . . is less a precursor of the Kafka of the shadowy myths and atrocious institutions than is Browning or Lord Dunsany" (108). Despite all the clarifications of textual genetics, the most compelling argument is that the thematics of homosexuality of the *Recherche* is a product of the *Recherche* itself.

Much of the thematics of homosexuality has also been covered by J. E. Rivers in *Proust and the Art of Love*. He states (ix) that his "study began as an attempt to understand the thirty-two pages that constitute the first part of Proust's *Sodome et Gomorrhe*." The author devotes a large part of his monograph to a thematics of homosexuality grounded in literary history, psychosexual studies, and sociology, a thematics for which Sedgwick has criticized him (*EpCl* 212–13). If the reader follows Rivers or Compagnon, he is bound to take the first thirty-two pages as a guide to the novel as a whole. The reader will have to justify the enunciations of the fiction through recourse to outside models such as history, biography, or sociology, where discourse has an assigned truth-value. In so doing, the critic once again diminishes fiction, which becomes a secondary and derivative discourse parasitic on the social truths of the world.

Each of the critics chooses his or her thematics by organizing the monstrosity of the text with some mechanism of closure. Gray (105–6) speaks quite correctly of "the critical tradition's tendency to close the space of mastery and possession." Thus, for example, de Man's deconstructive Proust is related to a thematics of reading, Deleuze's semiotician is related to a thematics of signs, and Rivers's Proust is related to a thematics of homosexuality. But for me, Proust's novel is a theory of reading even when reading is not the theme, a theory of signs when there are no "signs" to read, a theory of homosexuality even when it does not seem to be a question of homosexuality. And most generally, all of these themes and theories rely on the underlying homosexual hermeneutics of the work, its most basic interpretive mode.

Against these versions of the text that rely on external social truths or internal philosophical ones, I would maintain that as an overt theme relying (like other themes) on the subtending homosexual hermeneutics, homosexuality is constituted by a meeting of two strands, chains, or itineraries in the novel. Just as with the scene at Montjouvain, there is a synchronic chain linked from page to page and a diachronic one stretching across thousands of pages. The synchronic chain is of enormous proportions: the whole volume of *Le Côté de Guermantes*, which develops a general theory of interpretation and reading. Through his reading of social structures, systems of desire, and semiotics of difference, Proust develops a general view of interpretation that stands as a theorization of the very act: What does it mean to interpret? Diachronically, there is a heterogeneous set of texts made up of the various passages and scenes relating to homosexuality that have preceded *Sodome et Gomorrhe*. These include, but are not limited to, the scene at Montjouvain, the interactions between Charlus and the narrator in *A l'ombre des jeunes filles en fleurs*, the hints at lesbianism in the first two volumes, and the supposed relations between Odette and Charlus. When coupled with the explanations of the generation(s) of homosexuality in the first pages of *Sodome et Gomorrhe*, the general theory of interpretation submits the text to an act of closure by making the exegesis understandable.

The linking of these two parts of the novel, the social semiotics and the generation of homosexuality, takes the didacticism of *Sodome et Gomorrhe* and turns it into a thematics by indicating the way in which the material is to be used. This is not to say that no theme of homosexuality would have been possible without these pages, but rather, that the direction of the theme, its import, and especially the effect it has on readers all find their direction from the thrust of the reductive essay. As a theme homosexuality is thus framed by a general theory of interpretation; the open-ended anthropological and botanic exegesis on the generation of this "race" becomes a closed theme, the solid base on which the thematics is grounded. The border between fiction and apodictic truth is ensured as the truth within the novel becomes the mimetic version of the truth outside the text.

It would be easy to stop there, were it not for the troubling fact that interpretation, as we have seen, is open-ended for any given part of the novel. Proust's development of a generalized hermeneutics is itself subject to interpretation and thus is its own ironic deformation. This irony necessarily has an effect on the closure we have just projected for the Proustian theory and thematics of homosexuality: the confirmation of a theory of homosexuality, that is to say, its thematization, by a theory of reading, a hermeneutics, or an interpretive model puts both theories into question.

When we speak of the theory of interpretation of *Le Côté de Guermantes*, it is in full realization that this is not the first theory of interpretation proposed by the novel, nor is it even the first formal Proustian hermeneutics. The reading of reading given in *Du côté de chez Swann* is well known, not merely in the passage about the "*volupté de lecture*" discussed by de Man in *Allegories of Reading*, but in the more general form of an idealism of transmittable meaning, be it the Cartesianism of the first few pages of the novel, where elementary knowledge arises from doubt, or the more obvious Kantianism of the ideal exchange of form and contents perceived by the young Marcel as the objective correlative of a text: "The novelist's discovery was the idea of replacing those parts impenetrable to the soul with an equal amount of immaterial parts, that is to say, that our souls can assimilate" (1:84). This combination is perceivable in the text of the other; but as a potential author himself, Marcel sees a gap that must be filled if he is to write: "this absence of genius, this black hole being dug in my writing, was it not also only an illusion without consistency?" (1:171).

In the early part of novel, the primary function of theory is to allow a set of contents to enter and be situated within the framework of the text. Though seemingly straightforward, this early function seems to bridge a gap at the origin of the literary text. It is a gap that Proust proposes to fill in various manners, not all of which are expeditious, but which are generated according to an economy of reading. The clearest example is the nineteenth-century novel within a novel, not *Sodome et Gomorrhe*, but "Un Amour de Swann," with its wealth of details available only to someone with the omnipresent and impossible vision of the Balzacian narrator. "Un Amour de Swann" does not solve the problem: it offers a normalized base on which to construct a *roman d'apprentissage* by providing the general foundation instead of a gap and a modeling system, yet it does so at a price. At one remove, after the textual recursion of *Sodome et Gomorrhe*, the whole Albertine section of the novel could be read as a twentieth-century gloss on, tribute to, and translation of a nineteenth-century novel—not one by Balzac, Stendhal, Flaubert, or Zola, but precisely on "Un Amour de Swann." With the example of "Un Amour de Swann" and the meta-example of the Albertine texts, we see that Proust uses the forms of literary history, the imposed view of how a text means, in order to help structure his text.

The hermeneutics in *Le Côté de Guermantes* is the mechanism allowing for the interpretation of homosexuality in *Sodome et Gomorrhe*. Rather than being an embarrassing graft onto the fictional text, the first 30 pages of *Sodome et Gomorrhe* can be considered the general law of interpretation derived inductively from the examples of interpretation in *Le Côté de Guermantes*. With the focus shifted, those pages no longer seem a pretension to an apodictic truth, but rather the natural conclusion to the disparate exempla of the earlier volume. The theory of homosexuality is a specific example of interpretation and not a separate truth from which examples are deduced. Hence a theory of origins for the "theme" of homosexuality is put into question because it is seen to arise as a result of making a general law out of previous examples, a law that is then applied to this or that situation—in this case, to homosexuality.

V. *Names of the Interpretation: The Interpretation*

Bearing in mind the reductivism of any equation, I would still posit that the meaning of the *Recherche* resides in its interpretations of interpretation. The master act of interpretation of interpretation in the novel is homosexuality itself, ultimately less a thing or a theory than an interpretant, telescope, telegraph, microscope, and black box all in one. With this in mind, we return once more to the scene of the initial encounter between Charlus and Jupien. In the space of 32 pages Proust sets up one of the striking plot devices of the book, for much in the last four volumes will depend on this accidental meeting between two characters. Obviously, this is not an accident of which Proust is unaware. But since so much of the remainder of the book relates in one way or another to this meeting, I am trying to discern the novelistic (narrative, theoretical, interpretive) dimensions of having these two characters meet precisely at this point in the novel. The chance event of their meeting segues into a sexual act accompanied by the narrator's having espied, or more precisely overheard, the event. Thus the sexual activity between Jupien and Charlus is already redoubled by its own interpretation:

> For given what I heard at first in Jupien's shop, which was only inarticulate sounds, I suppose [je suppose] that few words were spoken. It is true that those sounds were so violent that, if they had not always been repeated an octave higher in a parallel wail, I might have thought that one person was strangling another right next to me and that after, the murderer and his resuscitated victim were taking a bath in order to remove the traces of the crime. From that I concluded that there is one thing as noisy as suffering, and that is pleasure. (3:11)

The effect of the present tense of "je suppose," instead of the expected preterite or imperfect, is dramatic. It is as if the tentative present tense of wonder associated with the shift to discursive interpretation in the episode of the madeleine had reappeared in a strengthened form of supposition in this passage. Where once the narrator wondered, he now seems tentatively to have more knowledge, more deftness in interpreting, and ultimately, a greater recognition of the centrality of interpretation to the construction of the text. Proust reinforces the importance of the interpretive system by stressing the eternal or atemporal nature of the enunciation. The narrator remains silent about what he sees, if in fact he sees at all: he perceives the event "through the transom which I did not open." In the meantime, the narrator repeats what he has heard and interprets the act as one example of the great problematic of homosexuality for which these pages are, in some sort, an excuse.

The general metaphor for homosexuality is nature, something as natural as the fertilization of flowers by bees. According to this apology, homosexuality is natural in man because there are so many cases of it in nature. In following this line, Proust is making an argument similar to that found in the second dialogue of *Corydon* (38–83), with which he was familiar. The narrator is a reader of nature or a naturalist who sees the various behaviors in the wild and brings them back as evidence both of the appropriateness of the behavior and of the precision of the metaphor. But what a difference there is between Gide's procedure and that of Proust! Whereas Gide makes a litany of ordered examples, the Proustian narrator, much like the bumblebee he will soon mention, flits from figure to figure so quickly (a speed of narrative rare in Proust) that it prevents the construction of a litany, an order, or a raison d'être other than metaphor and interpretation themselves. The narrator compares himself to a botanist (3:3) and wonders if the insect will come to fertilize the flower (3:4). He is knowledgeable in botanical matters, since he knows about the tropism of stamens in general (3:4), about the growth patterns of morning glories (3:23), and about the fertilization of trimorphic heterostyle flowers in particular (3:30). He knows things a naturalist would know about trained monkeys (3:21), the domestication of animals (3:26), the hermaphroditic nature of snails (3:31), and, of course, the behavior of bumblebees (3:8).

Whereas in *Corydon* Gide brings the natural argument to the fore as a rational apologia in the pastoral mode, Proust lets his text take off. Instead of a reality that from time to time is the excuse for a flight of metaphoric fancy, it is the metaphor, or more precisely, the interpretation of metaphor, that seems to bring about human reality:

> At the same moment that M. de Charlus had gone through the door while sounding [*sifflant*] like a big bumblebee, another one, a real one this time, entered the courtyard. Who knows if it was not the one for which the orchid had waited for so long and if it was bringing the rare pollen without which the orchid would remain a virgin? (3:8)

In other words, the narrator sees a real bumblebee, whose presence occasions a metaphoric one, in this case, Charlus himself. Charlus's rogue bumblebee has Jupien as his flower, with all "the coquettishness that an orchid could have had for a bumblebee" (3:6).

At this point the critic is likely to ask about the appropriateness of the metaphor. One of its functions is to naturalize homosexuality and to show that there is a seamless continuity between the world of human beings and that of nature. Yet the ramifications of the metaphor hardly suffice; in fact, they undercut the situation: the qualities of virginity and coquettishness hardly describe the two characters in this scene. So the qualities attributed to the characters in the situation do little to dispel the reader's feeling that the metaphor is developed for its own sake as text instead of as an explanation for homosexuality. The usual Proustian technique of using an overarching metaphor is followed through to its end; the metaphor relates to other figures in the text as it develops its own internal intertextuality.[5]

While the figure of the bee and the flower is carried through the passage as a metaphoric explanation for homosexuality, there is a veritable explosion of comparisons, as if somehow, after having been bottled up so long, the figure of homosexuality had to burst both from the apologetic mode and from the pages of the book. But there is too much noise in the explosion, there are too many comparisons for the sake of comparison. Many have nothing to do with this natural metaphor of bees and flowers. The heterogeneity of the submetaphors, or what I earlier called the z-component, undercuts the efficacy of the overarching figure and makes the supposed didacticism of the whole section rather less banal in its outrageousness.

In the playing out of the figure, there is a comparison between self-fertilization and inbreeding in marriage (3:5), followed by a comparison between self-fertilization and the use of an antitoxin, the function of the thyroid gland, and the value of sleep. Charlus, who a few lines later is compared to a bumblebee, is as pale as marble (3:5). Jupien, compared to a plant, behaves as if he were following some arcane laws (3:6). Charlus, the bumblebee, asks questions that are like Beethoven's phrases (3:7) and compares himself to the caliph of *The Arabian Nights*, to a teacher, and to a doctor. On the other hand, the narrator has behaved as if he had been absentminded and unknowingly faced with a pregnant woman (3:15) or ignorant of the horselike nature of a centaur (3:16). A particular homosexual is like Oscar Wilde who himself is like Samson (3:17); he can also be like a schoolteacher or a notary (3:20). Another may be like Griselidis, Andromeda, or a sterile jellyfish (3:27–28). In general, homosexuals are like Jews (3:17–18), but they also behave like doctors looking for cases of appendicitis everywhere (3:18). Homosexuals are like schismatic political groups, music aficionados, or people reacting against progress (3:21), when they are not like people with certain inborn skills or innate tendencies toward a medical condition: "having, unbeknownst to them, inherited a disposition for drawing, music, or blindness" (3:20) and "those who

5. One well-known example of this extended metaphoricity is the water imagery in what Riffaterre (96–98) calls the "Night at the Opera" passage (2:339–40), where text is produced from the syllepsis in the double meaning of the word "*baignoire*" as opera stall and bathtub. This passage is also discussed by Lang (164) and Gray (124–26).

seem predisposed to it like the addict for morphine" (3:22). Still others are like Zionists, Saint-Simonians, people against the draft, vegetarians, or anarchists (3:22). Again, certain homosexuals are like people with a case of hives (3:27) when others are like self-interested listeners "who, at the Collège de France . . . go to take a class, but only to get warm" (3:28). Still others are like Lot's wife, and thus they are like a female resident of Sodom. And heterosexual women, by the way, faced with effeminate men may be like "those who, in Shakespeare's comedies, are disappointed by a disguised girl who is taken for an adolescent boy" (3:23). Banal, reductive, sentimental? Hardly.

The comparisons are a route to other comparisons, tautologically supporting one another when they can and failing to do so when they cannot. Eventually, the circle closes and the text is brought back to the original metaphor which, we have seen, is not at all foundational:

> Jellyfish! Orchid! When I was following only my instinct, the jellyfish disgusted me at Balbec; but if I knew how to look at it, as had Michelet, from the point of view of natural history and aesthetics, I saw a delicious cluster of azure blooms. With the transparent velvet of their petals, are they not like the mauve orchids of the sea? Like so many creatures of the animal and vegetable kingdoms, like the plant that produces vanilla. (3:28)

Returning to the basic figure is a means of starting anew, as the text jumps from color to color (azure to mauve) and from specific to general, to "so many creatures." What then will have been the value of this exercise? The explanation of homosexuality at this point is superfluous if we follow the imagery used to describe it and try to come up with a coherent explanation of or analogy to its situation. Piling metaphor upon metaphor, Proust essentially opens up the interpretation in a myriad of ways and effectively blocks interpretive closure: all these half-definitions of homosexuality wind up undefining it. The explanation of homosexuality serves another purpose, however: in this section of the novel, the imagery is the means by which discourse starts referring to itself as such. The chapter is not an excuse or apology for homosexuality; rather, homosexuality is an excuse for discourse.

The narrator knows how to read a jellyfish, an orchid, and a homosexual. The narrator needs visible, that is, readable, signs to launch his writing. He does not have to transcribe; he can create the scene out of belief in his own power of interpretation. Whereas at Montjouvain he needed to see the scene and repeat it as a theatrical act of representation in his writing, all he needs now is a spot in which to read without moving his lips and to listen and record without a sound. Or, more accurately, what he needs is the sign that what he is about to hear is going to happen. Having internalized an interpretive system for the world at large, the narrator needs nothing more than the equivalent of the ringing of the telephone to announce that a call is coming. With that, he can play what he hears on his "internal stereopticon." In fact, his interpretive talent is such that he can understand groans and silences, as in the case of Jupien and Charlus.

The initial world of *Du côté de chez Swann* is already divided into the visible and the audible. The visible exists for what needs to be read. Off in a slightly proleptic future, the sense of what is seen inevitably comes a bit after the fact. Visibility and readability are marked with a *Nachträglichkeit* that confers meaning after the fact through a process of rereading. Not so for the audible: always understood, the audible is the realm of the familial or the familiar. Everyone, including the narrator, knows what the little bell means (1:14); Swann's voice is recognizable before he is visible; the narrator hears the steps of his parents (1:33) and manages to overhear an entire conversation (1:33–34). Hearing his aunt in the next room talking to herself, the narrator always understands, even to the point of being able to infer the words under the words: "I must remember that I did not sleep" (1:50). But when his mother is finally in front of him and his father arrives on the scene, Marcel misreads the situation: he errs in thinking that he will be punished, since his father gives his mother permission to stay.

If we pursue this understanding of the narrator's acts of interpretation, we realize that homosexuality has become familiar to him. There is no need for watching a scene that he can already play out in the theater of his mind. Like the author alone in his cork-lined room, the narrator has no need to see the homosexual world in order to describe it. Through an internalization of the interpretive mechanism, the activity of the voyeur becomes that of the listener, who transcribes into writing what he hears. There is no longer a need to read, only a need to write. Writing cannot occur all at once; having traded immediacy for understanding and visible presence for comprehensible absence, the narrator has to make adequations in his explanation of what he already understands.

I argue that there is narratological evidence for this implicit understanding of homosexuality as a means to interpretation, evidence found in the anachronies in the section. As Prince (5) defines it, anachrony is a "discordance between the order in which events (are said to) occur and the order in which they are recounted." As Genette has so admirably pointed out, much of the narrative is structured by an alternation between two kinds of anachronies: prospective comments on future events (prolepsis) and retrospective comments on previous events (analepsis). The prolepses and analepses are discursive moments that order the récit in a way other than the "original" chain of events, the chronological story ordered on an absolute time line. And as Genette (115) indicates, the importance of these two kinds of anachronies is linked to the "retrospectively synthetic nature of the Proustian story, which, at every moment, is entirely present to itself in the narrator's mind."

The novel as a whole is rife with anachronies, but in this section, the use of anachrony centers on a specific kind of prolepsis, the "*annonce*," translated as a "repetitive prolepsis" or an "advanced notice." Whereas a prolepsis in general announces a future event, an advanced notice announces the event and indicates that the event will be recounted later on. Prince defines the advanced notice as a "narrative unit referring in advance to situations and events that will occur and be recounted at a later point" (4). Genette describes the "canonic formula" of an advanced notice as generally "a 'we shall see' or 'as will be seen later'" (111).

Three of these advanced notices can be found in the last two pages of the chapter: Charlus sets up Jupien in "conditions that we shall see later" (3:32), which we take to be the male brothel that is the third version of the scene of sexual espionage; "those exceptional beings who are pitied are numerous, as will be seen in this work, for a reason that will not be revealed until the end" (3:32); and homosexuals "will be seen in a certain way in the pages that follow" (3:33). But neither the second nor the third of these is a pure advanced notice as Genette and Prince define the term, for both these critics emphasize the fact that "advanced notice" refers to récit. This is not the case, however, with the second and third examples given, because both examples refer proleptically to discourse: "in this work" and "the pages that follow." Rather than alluding to the event that "we shall see," the narrator is alluding to the writing or interpretation of the event. Looking further, we find that the two previous instances of advanced notice in this section do not refer to récit at all but *only* to discourse. There are no events that we shall see, but solely writing: "my reflections had taken a turn that I shall describe later" (3:5); the narrator writes of a theory "that will later be seen to be modified" (3:17). And the last example of anachrony in the chapter, a "recall" of events "already told" (Prince 80) is the parallel to the repetitive prolepsis. It too refers to the discursive act: "the young man whom we have just tried to paint" (3:23). Even here then, it is not "as we have seen" but "as we have told."

Thus out of six instances of repetitive anachrony—five advanced notices and one recall—five of the instances refer either to the acts of narration and discursive analysis alone or to narration linked to the récit. There has been a shift from the expected formulas of "as we have seen" and "as we shall see" to "as we have written" and "as we shall write." Of the six examples of repetitive anachrony, only one is an example of the pure advanced notice as it is defined by narratologists as a reference to the récit. Yet even this instance of récit is not an arbitrary event, but the reinscribed homosexual matrix of the novel: Montjouvain, *Sodome et Gomorrhe*, the male brothel. Thus the unique example of standard repetitive anachrony is focused on the representation of the very act of interpretation in which discourse and récit intertwine. Even behind this seemingly pure case of advanced notice, then, lurk questions of narration, discourse, and interpretation. I find the insistence of repetitive anachrony all the more striking since I have not been able to discern such an imbalance between pure advanced notice and discursive advanced notice earlier in the novel. Here, however, the discursive advanced notice is more or less exclusive. What is going on here?

Far from being an aberrant embarrassment, the beginning of *Sodome et Gomorrhe* should be viewed as the point at which the novel redoubles itself as its own metadiscourse. Perhaps this return, redoubling, inversion, or invagination is troubling, troubled, awkward, or scarred: such virgin births are seldom easy. A double invisibility marks the scene: first, there is the narrator's invisibility to Charlus and Jupien. He can see them but they cannot see him. That aspect is structurally a repetition of his voyeuristic position at Montjouvain. His invisibility is redoubled by the invisibility of the sexual act. They still cannot see him, but now he cannot see them. Yet he knows everything that is going on. And whereas once he had gotten details about "a love that Swann had had before my birth" (1:184), now he needs no details, no outside facts, and no discourse of the other. That other discourse is now completely internalized. Sex between Charlus and Jupien happens within the narrator, within some internalized interpretive system; it is not an event in the outside world to be transcribed after the fact. So this double invisibility is the mark of the internalization of interpretation. Through the introduction of the discursive advanced notice, the novelist sets language up as its own object. Primal scenes of a mother's kiss or a jealous lover fade in favor of scenes that refer to production in narrative. And in fact, the little *aventure* that occurs between Charlus and Jupien is far less important than the excuse for interpretation it provides. The singular qualities of the referent have as little absolute sense as does the guilt of Dreyfus.

Heretofore in the novel there have not been so many signifiers referring to other signifiers. To neutralize their hallucinatory juxtaposition, the narrator makes a metadiscursive remark about the number of comparisons: "the multiplicity of these comparisons is itself all the more natural" (3:8). The metadiscursive remark is itself counterbalanced by an apology: "without the least scientific pretense at relating certain laws of botany and what is called, often quite in error, homosexuality" (3:9). In fact, the specific kind of prolepses that refer to a moment of discourse find their intradiegetic echo in a series of metadiscursive remarks that go so far as to enter into the very speech of Charlus to Jupien: "I see you are deaf to metaphors" (3:14). The narrator is left wondering if his comparisons are even appropriate: "Perhaps the example of Jews, from a different colony, is not even strong enough" (3:25).

Homosexuality is a difference; it is the interpretant as difference: things are not what they seem, only a good interpreter armed with a theory of the invisible can determine what homosexuality is, if in fact it "is" at all. For Proust, homosexuality exists as a difference from itself, in its modifications, its displacements, and its variants. No apology can explain this difference. Rather, the difference is figured as the trope of its gap: homosexuality is the text's own metaphor for interpretation. In that it produces figures, it is a machine generating text across its own difference from itself. In the *Recherche*, heterosexuality produces a stultifying sameness of discourse: heterosexuality is thematic. In the "real world," of course, heterosexuality is as different from itself as is Proust's version of homosexuality. Or one could say that in its insistence on being doxological, heterosexuality is as closeted as homosexuality. In *Proust et les signes*, Deleuze (17) goes so far as to say that "intersexual loves are less deep than homosexuality and find their truth in homosexuality." Opposed to the closures of doxologically represented heterosexuality, homosexuality, for Proust, produces a constant deferral of meaning along a chain of signifiers: homosexuality is theoretical.

VI. Homosexuality as Interpretation

In the remainder of this chapter, I hope to cast a new light on interpretation by focusing on interpretive strategies in *Le Côté de Guermantes*. A whole series of theories of interpretation precedes the formal constitution of a homosexual hermeneutic in the beginning pages of *Sodome et Gomorrhe*. This includes the methodic Cartesianism of the first pages of the whole enterprise that helps in the initial *débrouillage*, the solipsistic and masturbatory fantasies about writing that inform the text as an allegory of reading, and the syllepses that in establishing a map of figurality deform the map at the same time (I tried to show some of this in *Flaubert and Sons*, 165–79). The aesthetic viewpoint combines architectonic construction with the phenomenological impressionism that serves, on the surface, as the operative mode of descriptive writing. Yet the architectonic construction of the text occurs through a minute series of analyses and correspondences that rely on the presence of a transcendental ideal to effect them. For example, in the famous passages in the first volume about hawthorns, understanding the text depends on an a priori comprehension of the transcendental value of metaphoricity in Proust. Similarly, the phenomenology of the surface play of impressions in the text is always undercut by an anagogic imperative that forces us to seek the text's ultimate meaning.

Now, as I have said, the beginning of *Sodome et Gomorrhe* is the point at which the narrator and the reader recognize the internalization of interpretation that is emblematically indicated by the absent scene of homosexual congress and by the presence of a dizzying series of tropes. I have also maintained that this occurs precisely at the conjunction of the diachronic repetition of the homosexual scene of Montjouvain and the sequential semiotics of *Le Côté de Guermantes*. It is to that sequence that I now turn. The very presentation of Guermantes gives a framework rather than a base. It provides a format, what is called a *dispositif* in French, beginning with which one could begin to represent and decipher: "This Guermantes was like the frame of a novel, an imaginary landscape that I had difficulty representing to myself" (2:31).

With this dispositif, the impossible act of representation has been replaced by a subjectively defined and arbitrarily determined act of naming that in turn formulates the rules of representation within the system. The incantatory action of the naming, motivated by desire as early as the famous third part of *Du côté de chez Swann*, "Noms du Pays: le nom," shows itself to be the means by which a dispositif takes its place. It is in the nature of the frame itself to be excessive and problematic in its borderline status, for the frame is the format or border within the novel and the novel or the novelistic serves as a frame for what is contained. Though the two cannot be separated, the frame delimits the realm of representation in a constructive way that allows the rules of the game to come into play. The framing delimits a space as infinite as a "*paysage imaginaire*," whose rules are given by the act of framing.

The operative rule is one of deciphering. No longer—at least in this work—will Proust attempt to found the novelistic system on a universal categorical law of representation. The act of deciphering is an act of judgment, deforming in its own right, precisely because as an act of judgment it does not have "its own right" but is necessarily predicated on the presumed right. But this deformation is limited, as it cannot exceed the general law of production given by the imposed frame. At the same time, since there is a limit to error, the absence of a sign is now no longer perceived as a gaping abyss, but rather as what is not yet readable. Proust therefore has displaced absence by a universal claim to potential readability: text is readable now or it will be in the future in a rereading or a revision. Thus Proust has troped an earlier nineteenth-century model whereby reality and language are seen to be coterminous and continuous. For Proust, it is not language and reality that are continuous, but language and interpretation, the extension of space having been translated into the extension of time.

Proust begins to generate his theory of interpretation from the known. As an illustration one might take Françoise, who, during the drama of the maternal kiss in *Du côté de chez Swann*, is the bearer of a full letter and an empty response that says "there is no answer" (1:31). But now, she is framed by what Proust determines to be the novelistic, not the act of representation, but the acts of translation, transformation, and deciphering: "All day long Françoise would not have failed to present a face covered with little red cuneiform marks that deployed externally, though rather undecipherably, the long list of her grievances" (2:317). Thus Françoise has become a set of poorly decipherable symbols, with the cuneiform writing being the novelist's *trouvaille*, the written equivalent of Françoise's function as the repository of the French language. But here the signs themselves are the object of attention, not the presence or absence of a thing. This insistence highlights the functions of writing in the novelistic realm, where written marks are the very substance of the text. Interpretation becomes the primary function of the text as well as its object. When, however, in a later passage it is a question of direct, silent interpretation instead of the redoubled act, Françoise is no more than a stage performer:

> Thus, when I inadvertently left on the table, among other letters, a certain letter that she should not have seen . . . the compromising document first struck my eyes as it had not been able *not* to strike Françoise's, placed as it was by her right on top, almost alone, as evidence that was a language, had its eloquence, and which, like a yell, made me tremble from the doorway. She excelled in orchestrating these scenes destined to instruct the spectator so well. (2:655)

Thus, by *Le Côté de Guermantes*, the mere act of reference or the gesture of meaning has taken its place inside the realm of the theatrical, as now the redoubled act of interpretation comes to the fore.

The subtle shift operated by the frame is the move from a theory of representation to a theory of interpretation—and with interpretation the question, representation is assumed. "Un Amour de Swann" replaces the gap of the forgotten past with a third-person, nineteenth-century novel onto which the Bildungsroman is grafted. Similarly, the theory of interpretation of *Le Côté de Guermantes* replaces the theory of interpretation of the first two volumes and will serve as the basis for the massive set of interpretations of *Sodome et Gomorrhe* and the whole Albertine sequence as well. In "Combray," for example, we are presented with transformed writing in the description of the tombstones of the church on which the magnificent Gothic capital letter seems to have spread beyond its limits and the "elliptical Latin inscription, introducing an additional whim [*caprice*] in the order of these shortened characters, putting two letters together of a word, where the others had been inordinately distended" (1:58). The absent, present, shrunken, and distended letters on the effaced stones become transformed in Gilberte's message announcing her marriage (4:220) in *Albertine disparue*, which is misread as being from the dead Albertine (4:234–35). In Combray, the tombstones are above the noble dead of the city; the disfigured letters refer to a forgotten past that will now be revived in an act that makes Combray present once again. After *Le Côté de Guermantes* and *Sodome et Gomorrhe*, there will be no revival of the dead, just letters referring to other letters, readings correcting misreadings, and interpretations rewriting another text palimpsestically:

> The rather artificial originality of Gilberte's handwriting mainly consisted, when she wrote a line, of having figure [*figurer*] in the line above the bars of the "t's" which seemed to underline words or the dots on the "i's" which seemed to interrupt the sentences of the line above. Moreover, inserted in the line below were the curls and loops of words that were superposed on the next line. It was completely natural that the employee of the telegraph office had read the loops of the "s's" or the "y's" of the line above like an "ine" finishing the word of Gilberte. The dot on the "i" of Gilberte had climbed above to look like an ellipsis. As for her "G," it seemed like a Gothic "A." (4:235)

The Gothic letter in Combray that names a dead body to be resurrected out of the magical cup of tea now represents only another Gothic letter.

In *Le Côté de Guermantes*, desire is reborn in the aesthetic object in the act of deciphering the written word, in the very movement of deciphering. This object is neither the thing in itself nor the sign taken as thing, as is the case, for example, of the letter the narrator waits for from his mother in *Du côté de chez Swann*. Rather, the infinite variation afforded by interpretation that is determined but never limited by the novelistic framework of interpretation replaces elementary signs as the means for bringing about desire: "These traits were moreover enough to charm, since, with only the conventional value of writing, they allowed a well-known name to be read" (2:342). It is as if Proust were effecting a reversal of his own text. The world in which Swann, consumed by his desire, looks for telltale signs of Odette's infidelity, caprices, or affairs no longer exists in *Le Côté de Guermantes* or *Sodome et Gomorrhe*. The framework of the novelistic, given as the name surging out of a mixture of memory and desire, fosters the system of interpretations that reaches its conclusion in a reinvention and reaffirmation of the act of naming.

Even if the Duchesse de Guermantes and Charles Swann seem to have the same speech patterns and the same interpretive skills, the duchess turns her tongue on the signs of others, whereas Swann is concerned with the object of desire. The wrong window of Swann's frenzied pursuit of Odette (1:268–71)—where, interestingly enough, Swann finds two old men who seem to be sharing a bedroom—and the letter to Forcheville (1:277–78) have given way to the wrong signs. But even in the face of death, these wrong signs amount to nothing more than the wrong color of a pair of shoes (2:883–84). In the first half of the novel there are real bodies of desire; in the second half, the wrong sign refers to another sign: the shoes should match the dress, according to a semiotics of fashion. Desire has given way to aesthetics, which will, by *Le Temps retrouvé*, become the object of a renewed, inverted desire expressed in every word of the text, as the narrator, "smitten with a work [*amoureux d'une oeuvre*]," will try to produce another (4:621).

Through the development of a view on interpretation in *Le Côté de Guermantes*, the act of interpreting that reaffirms naming is capable of producing the aesthetic object as a product of interpretations. Again, it is not the object of the earlier books nor even the incompletely captured object distorted by a phenomenology of vision, as was the case for the belfries of Martinville. Here, the possibility of creating the iconic sign as an aesthetic object comes in the act of naming: "certain artists who, instead of the letters of their name, put at the bottom of their canvas a form that is beautiful by itself, a butterfly, a lizard, a flower" (2:342). So the sign, here iconic but eventually written, comes to stand in a place determined by a frame. The sign no longer indicates the object or stands in the object's place. The sign is allotted its own frame, the novelistic itself, born both of the translation into art of the world and of the replacement of one sign, the name, with another: the butterfly, lizard, or flower. The aesthetic object is a double substitution, a double replacement of name for thing and picture for name. This double replacement or distortion is a sleight-of-hand recovery of the act of representation and interpretation by which Proust can sign his work—not with his name, but with the work itself. Proust's signature to the novel, nothing as simple as a flower, even hawthorns, a cattleya, or an iris, is the novel itself: his signature is the whole novel.

Product of a double substitution, transformation, or anamorphosis, the signature is nothing if not internalized, brought home, frame and all. The great interpretive project of *Le Côté de Guermantes* and, even more so, of *Sodome et Gomorrhe*, will not work unless the signature is brought home with its frame. The laws of interpretation determined by the frame now fit in the *for intérieur* where the correction of error occurs:

> And even the evenings that some change in the atmosphere or in my own health brought to mind some forgotten scroll on which there were impressions of long ago, instead of profiting from the forces of renewal that had just been reborn in me, instead of using them to decipher within myself thoughts that usually escaped me, instead of finally getting to work, I preferred to speak aloud, to think in an agitated and distant fashion which was only useless discourse and gestures, a whole adventure novel that was sterile and truthless. (2:367)

The written text is not the distant lost paper of the belfries of Martinville but some primary text written within the novelistic realm. The space of interpretation is the space of reinscription now internalized; it is in that inner space that interpretation will occur. With the novelistic frame internalized as well, its limiting nature disappears; the novelistic bounds out explosively to escape entirely from truth, a separation viewed here as sterile. This separation and sterility will gradually be brought under domination in *Sodome et Gomorrhe* and in the Albertine sequence. Again, it will not be with a simple antidote or bridge to negate the gaps, but rather with a trope that includes the negativity. So the lack of truth in the "adventure novel" will be compensated for by the forced living of a "*roman d'aventures*" as truth in *La Prisonnière*. Closer to us, closer to the text of *Le Côté de Guermantes*, is the compensation for sterility that is the theory of homosexuality of *Sodome et Gomorrhe* and, in fact, the use of the same as the fertilizing mechanism for all of the next book of the *Recherche*.

Thus the theory of homosexuality of *Sodome et Gomorrhe*, with its attendant figures of fertilization, is a way of making the sterile fecund. But the figure is automatically fecund, because, as the reader remembers, that figure too is subject to the process of proleptic and analeptic reference. Specifically, the figure of the fertilization of flowers recalls most immediately the discussion of fertilization of flowers between the Princesse de

Parme and the Duchesse de Guermantes (2:805–6), as well as the metaphor or euphemism of the cattleya used by Swann and Odette for their lovemaking, and the discussion of the name of the cathedral of Florence in "Noms du pays: le nom." Even the phrase brought up so often in contemporary readings of Proust, the pejorative remark about a "race of fairies [*tantes*]," itself gives the lie to the sterility implied by many. For where does a race come from if all are sterile? Product of the interpretation of interpretation, just as if it were a trope of tropes, the race produces flowers, butterflies, pages, and books.

Pigeonholing *Sodome et Gomorrhe* as a book whose "theme" is homosexuality does not give enough credit to the critical process, in which, moreover, Proust himself is clearly putting faith: the reading and the interpretation through that reading which make the sterile fecund. Charlus and Jupien's mutual reading of each other comes under that category, as does the narrator's fully developed ability to read the exterior and interior signs present for the good interpreter. For the internalization of the text is like the renaming of the name, the act of inversion par excellence for Proust. From the barely decipherable marks on the face of Françoise we pass to the eternally etched notes on the face of the narrator's grandmother: "until that moment, every time that my grandmother had spoken with me, I had always followed what she said on the open score of her face" (2:433). With an adequation between the two kinds of writing, external and internal, the difference as such is quashed and the narrator is almost ready to read the world of inversion, where every sign comments on others, alternately visible and invisible.

With a newfound ability to read and interpret the narrator is even capable of seeing the signs or marks that are barely present if they are present at all: "A young servant, with a hardy look and a charming face (but trimmed so closely to stay perfect that his nose was a bit red and his skin lightly inflamed, as if they had kept something of the recent, sculptural incision)" (2:497). One can now understand the narrative function of "Un Amour de Swann" more clearly. If this text makes sense thematically where it stands, it does not do so at a narratological level, since its narrator is far more insightful than the narrator of Combray or *A l'ombre des jeunes filles en fleurs*. The invisible narrator telling the nineteenth-century novel of "Un Amour de Swann" is the one who can replay conversations on an "internal stereopticon" (2:837), the one who knows that Swann himself is as dead as any nineteenth-century text. *Le Côté de Guermantes* is the means of working through the process of interpretation in order to arrive at a precise system of replay, reinscription, and reinterpretation. Through this process, the narrator moves far beyond the situation in which this section of the novel starts, where "our imagination is like a malfunctioning barrel organ that always plays something other than the indicated melody" (2:342).

What then of the theoretical thematics of *Sodome et Gomorrhe*? Proust establishes a text whose ontology depends entirely on insightful powers of reading. Thus it is only the effective reader, who has theorized his or her own position throughout *Le Côté de Guermantes* and who is thereby able to read the barely known signs of Jupien's and Charlus's flutterings and posturings, who can erect the singular event into a general law. In light of the transformation springing from the process of internalization and inversion, it is the narrator's own position that is seen equally to be homosexual. Not merely the half-hidden, half-visible ghost of the author, and certainly not an ironic and impossible contrast with the protagonist of whom he is the continuation, the narrator internalizes the criteria of reading in a focused but productive fertilization and construction of his own text.

Barthes: Writing Desire or Desiring Writing

I. Pleasures

The number of diverse subjects that Roland Barthes addressed is staggering. From Michelet to Racine to Brecht to Proust, from Japan to Panzani pasta to rhetoric to photography, from Erté to Arcimboldo to realism to the art of singing Schumann, from Loyola to Fourier to Sade to Roland Barthes, the sheer volume is impressive; the variety is even more so. What astonishes the reader is that there seems to be no thread except for the pleasure of writing itself and the pleasure at being read. Barthes frequently notes that he writes only "to fill an order." His writing, in being an answer, could thus be said to be a writing that lacks aggression, that does not seek initially to be showy. As Susan Sontag (170) remarks, "All his writings are polemical. But the deepest impulse of his temperament was not combative. It was celebratory." It is rather a writing modestly proffered to fill a gap. On a biographic level, as Louis-Jean Calvet notes, Barthes greatly regretted that his tuberculosis had kept him from pursuing the path of the Ecole Normale Supérieure and the Doctorat d'Etat. Perhaps then, Barthes's pride in always writing "to fill an order" is partly a manifestation of an insecurity, a hesitation to express his own desire to write without having the proper authorization to do so.

I would go further than this autobiographical explanation, but not by the reductive ploy of recreating Oedipal mythology, having the writing replace the absent phallic father or be a love-gift for the mother. It seems to me that Barthes's writing is not predicated on a physical sickness, on an absence of authorization, or on an endless repetition of Oedipal love. Even if any of those were the case, they would not provide much enlightenment; when those pat answers have been given, there is nothing more to say. As will be seen below, the Oedipal model returns not as an answer but as part of an endless discourse. One could make a very schematic contrast here between psychoanalysis as a set of structures such as the Oedipus complex, and psychoanalysis as process, as an interminable analysis, which, even in repeating Oedipal structures, far exceeds their reductive nature. Like Deleuze, Barthes rejects the "mommy-daddy-me" version of the Oedipal model. Barthes will come back to a *loquèle* of discourse that resembles nothing more than stringing out an interminable, unending discourse of analysis.

I would hypothesize that Barthes's writing is predicated most basically on a difference, the difference of homosexuality. Recently, D. A. Miller published a retrospective view of Barthes's writing/homosexuality and discusses the hiddenness or, for that matter, the "open secret" of homosexuality in Barthes's earlier texts. Though I agree by and large with Miller's assessment, I would like to push the matter further toward a reading that relates the changes between Barthes's structuralist writing and his writing of the seventies to a reconsideration of the sexuality of the writing subject. Unavowed, fictionalized, metaphorized, and even deified, homosexuality is made a motor by Barthes, one that is sometimes silent and sometimes roaring, and which always helps the continued flow of his writing. Quite frankly, Barthes may choose discretion or privacy *as a person*, but I believe that *as a writer*, Barthes seizes the opportunity of being a nonauthorized subject. Sometimes invisibly, sometimes palpably, Barthes accepts the challenge of authorial and critical free fall, as he writes without a model to determine who he must be. Sontag (171) notes his "amorous relation" to writing. I would say then that Barthes's writing is the celebration of a homosexual love affair with writing. Barthes's writing is the transfigured expression of homosexual love for the text of the other. The writing that has preceded him is the object of desire. Once invited by that other, or its vicars, to desire, he can seize the opportunity, but he cannot make the first move: he must be asked to desire; he must be seduced by the other whom he will seduce in turn.

A quarter of a century after its publication, *S/Z* seems, now more than ever, to have been a revolutionary work. It is the text of a cultural revolution, a work where the rhetoric seems to be of permanent revolution, where the very upset of structuralism, which was engendered in great part by Barthes's own work, is left behind. Barthes had become an institution, a darling of the media, an *éminence grise*, and a legend in his own time. Perhaps he felt it necessary to underline his break with what was rapidly becoming institutionalized and thus normalized structuralist rhetoric, grounded in its own centers of power. In no other work does Barthes seem to take such pleasure in daring to transgress, even when the transgression is of his own past. The text on Sade, an author used by others such as Klossowski, Bataille, and Blanchot as a rallying cry for transgression, is chaste in comparison.

An early reading of Barthes's works of this period, like Culler's *Structuralist Poetics* (226–30), still sees *S/Z* as a continuation of the structuralist model. Later readers, such as Bensmaïa in his excellent study of the rhetoric of writing entitled *The Barthes Effect*, see *S/Z*, along with *Le Plaisir du texte* and *Roland Barthes*, as a break with the paradigms of the past. Certainly, coming out of a seminar held in 1968 and 1969, part of the rhetoric of *S/Z* relates to the historically revolutionary moment of May 1968. Today, however, no one would doubt that the work is revolutionary within the context of Barthes's writing, separate and apart from its historical moment: it is demonstrably Barthes's first poststructuralist work. In it, he challenges the fixed structures inherent in the models of structuralism, models that he himself had in no small way promulgated.

With *S/Z*, Roland Barthes starts a new phase of his career that is a focused exploration of the subject; Wiseman (134) notes Barthes's "experimental rewriting of concepts surrounding the notion of the human subject" in the seventies. This exploration continues through works like *Le Plaisir du Texte* and the fragmentary autobiography entitled *Roland Barthes*. Polemically, *S/Z* is the first turn away from, or step beyond, structuralism into what was subsequently called "poststructuralism" in the United States. On the surface in *S/Z*, Barthes seems to remain more or less faithful to his semiotic and structural systems. But the reader soon realizes that Barthes is undercutting the explanatory capabilities of the structural. He gives five codes by which to explain the world, but he also gives a number of fragments where the law is not one of paired structural oppositions. In many fragments, the law, if we can even call it that, is of ambiguity, fading, or the greatest anathema of structuralism, the unbridled subject. As Andrew Brown (6) puts it in his thoughtful study of the figures of writing in Barthes, one of the best works to appear on Barthes in a long time, Barthes starts with a binary opposition, then "drifts away" from that opposition. *S/Z* is the text in which the law of the subject, a law of drift and difference, begins to take over as the main law of language.

S/Z also evinces a turning away from what had been implicit in Barthes's previous understanding of the subject, to wit, its constitution and division according to structural lines. Extensively influenced by Marxist theory both directly and indirectly in his study of and interest in Bertolt Brecht, Barthes earlier constructed a subject of opposition immersed in language but alienated from it. In a text like *Mythologies*, the subject is perceived as being divided between denotation and connotation. Simultaneously, the validity of the subject is denied by the dominant language in power through the very act of language that seeks to make "norms and facts" coincide. Long after *S/Z*, when his writing has turned to a more complicated vision of the subject, the public Barthes still maintains this polemical position in *Leçon*, a speech given as his introductory lecture at the Collège de France. He says that language "is neither reactionary nor progressive; it is quite simply: Fascist. For Fascism is not the prevention of speech, it is the obligation to speak" (*L* 14).

During the same time, there is a shift away from the constructs of the psychoanalytic subject. Increasingly sensitive to the complexity of a model for language that must go beyond the oppositions of his early post-Marxist, post-Brechtian model, the Barthes of the sixties still remains sympathetic to psychoanalysis, and specifically to a Lacanian reading of the divisions of the subject. As we shall see below, while Barthes does not adopt the complete Lacanian concept of the subject, he does use the Lacanian category of the symbolic as a means of overturning the structures of identity that seem to be one of the outcomes of structuralism. Barthes was certainly not a faithful adept of Lacan, but like Jacques Derrida (*Positions* 112–19) up to the same moment (about 1968), Barthes maintains a "neutrality" vis-à-vis Lacan. At first glance, *S/Z* seems to continue a line of argument influenced by Lacan, especially given the subject matter of castration at the heart of the Balzac story treated in the work. In fact, Barthes's seemingly procedural but in fact very theatrical gesture of dividing the Balzac tale into *lexies* repeats the text's castration 561 times. Yet the notion of drift that Brown so strongly promotes shows us clearly that castration is/is not a theme (in Balzac, in Barthes), and the text drifts away from that closure, decision, or cut. Barthes's study itself drifts away from the mimetic repetition of the theatricalized act to head toward a surplus of signifier that makes the very pretext of castration a theatrical prop, the very division into *lexies* an excuse for text.

More or less at the same time, Barthes and Derrida begin their individual "dis-implications" (as Derrida puts it) from Lacan by questioning the Lacanian categories of the "imaginary," the locus of the images of the whole, and the "symbolic," the locus of the signs of the subject. For Barthes, the dis-implication is complex; ever generous, Barthes weaves the Lacanian symbolic into his own work only to weave it out again: "what is marked here with the name of the *symbolic* does not come from psychoanalytical knowledge" (*S/Z* 170). Perhaps this is a Freudian denial, but in any case, it is a canny way to read Lacan and ultimately to unread him. *S/Z* is the first work Barthes publishes in which we see the line of difference and division displaced from the sign itself or the semiotic in general to the territory of the subject.

The subject is the figure or person who produces writing and who is constituted by that writing. The person writing has various avatars and the subject changes according to the writing: the subject is both the person organizing fragments and the figure of fragmentation itself. In addition, the central moment and figure of the subject, the figure within the figure, replaces the structurality of structuralism (Derrida, *Ecriture* 409–28) or the mise-en-abyme as the figure of the literary. Barthes's figure becomes the gap, the gape, and the line between: the absolute of writing, and the line between pleasure and *jouissance*. Like invisible ink suddenly appearing on the page, the complex lines of joining and division appear when there is no clear opposition, be it intrinsic to the text or extrinsically imposed by a system such as the structuralist method. In the realm of the literary, as well as in the realm of the subject as a figure of writing, this line marks the border between textuality and sexuality. The focus of the current chapter will be on following the various ramifications and modulations of this line as they appear in the works of the later Barthes.[1]

A cursory reading of *S/Z* would indicate that the model used by the text belongs to fairly pure semiology if not to structuralism. One might liken the project to Barthes's own *Système de la mode*, which proposes a codification of the language of fashion, or to Genette's *Figures III*. In *S/Z*, the system of five codes, discussed at length by Kaja Silverman (*Subject* 250–82), seems at first to cover all the possible ramifications of meaning and signification, at the level of content and of narrative form. The hermeneutic

1. De la Croix sees *Le Plaisir du texte*, *Roland Barthes*, and *Fragments d'un discours amoureux* as a trilogy with their joint concepts of pleasure, jouissance, love, and the body of love, all of which are joined in a systematic discourse of fragments. As I shall try to show below, there are differences among these texts that relate to the uncomfortable relation among the concepts of pleasure, jouissance, love, and the body. Jouve stresses the erotic in his study; he points out (97) that it is not until Barthes's last writings that one finds the most intense effect of literature in full force, that effect being its erotic effect. The movement of signifiers is the locus in which textual erotics are played out. In an excellent article, "Du fragment au détail," Bensmaïa discusses the poetics of the fragment in these later texts of Barthes.

code deals with questions about plot; the proairetic code functions as the reader's organization of the material into actions and events. The semantic and the cultural codes deal with meaning: one at the level of denotation, the other at the level of connotation. The fifth code is the symbolic code, a field of reversal and ambiguity where there is a "shimmer of meaning" [*miroitement du sens*]" (*S/Z* 26).

S/Z is not Barthes's first reading of Balzac's "Sarrasine." An earlier text called "Masculin, féminin, neutre" is part of a Festschrift for Claude Lévi-Strauss, and in it Barthes pays due homage to the father of structuralism. In this article, Barthes distinguishes *four* kinds of suspense: "Who?," "What?," "What will the result of the drama be?," and "How will the text get from beginning to end?" ("MFN" 895). The four types of suspense, two of being and two of doing, do not correspond to the codes of *S/Z*, but the symbolic, which is not a "code" but just "the symbolic," is already related in a complex that involves the neuter/neutral and the antithetical. As opposed to later work in which he will theorize the neuter/neutral, in "Masculin, féminin, neutre" Barthes deems the "*neutre*" an impossible construct:

> The neuter is truly impossible in our language; were it grammatically possible, it would be no less dangerous discursively, for it would either reveal the castrato too early (neither man nor woman: we have seen that in our mythology the neuter is perceived as a desexualization and not as a "disanimation"), or it would mark the will of not choosing between the two sexes, which would already be saying too much. ("MFN" 906)

Barthes seems to have two props here, both false in the long run. On the one hand there is the grammatical prop. Barthes seems willingly to confuse grammatical and sexual gender: no one would assert that a *Fräulein*, for example, is neuter just because the noun is neuter. The historical pretext is also a problem in this earlier study of "Sarrasine," where Barthes is still quite attached to the idea of a historically representable reality. Part of his argument relates to historical facts about castrati but unfortunately the kernel of the historical argument is wrong: Barthes says incorrectly that the "last two castrati died in 1846 and 1861" ("MFN" 899), that is, after Balzac but before Barthes. Domenico Mustafà died in 1912, however, and there were recordings made of at least one castrato, Alessandro Moreschi, who died in 1922 (Pleasants 51). Implicitly, with this wrong information, Barthes is safe from castration. One might safely say that the debatable props of the essay are necessary because Barthes has not yet found out how to shake the structures of structuralism. But in the later *S/Z*, the effects of the shimmer of meaning of the symbolic code will undo the presumed solidity of a historical ground for representation. He is perhaps no longer safe from castration, but is certainly able to play with meaning and signs more creatively before the mythical knife falls or fails to fall.

Before proceeding any further with an examination of Barthes's version of the symbolic, I should briefly like to remind the reader of the structuralist and Lacanian versions of the symbolic, for him or her to realize in what ways Barthes is writing against those versions of the symbolic. The very name that Barthes gives to his "symbolic" code is itself a heavily coded act, as it brings together both the structuralist and Lacanian versions of the "symbolic" while overturning them in the process. As Jean Laplanche and J.-B. Pontalis (475) point out in their *Vocabulaire de la psychanalyse*, "the symbolic" is a term used by Saussure and later by Lévi-Strauss, the latter seeing intersubjective reality as being organized by a symbolic order. The structuralist version of the symbolic is thus part of a structure of similitudes that organizes parts of the system to resemble wholes. Structuralism has demetaphorized the symbolic by producing a concept of a symbol devoid of symbolism, but it has exchanged the metaphors of a more standard symbolism for figures of metonymy and synecdoche, not coincidentally the figures of narrative itself. So the structuralist version of the symbolic is able to proceed from whole to part by proposing that the act of representation is a resolvable figure of rhetoric. Again according to Laplanche and Pontalis, the Lacanian symbolic, like that of the structuralists, is deprived of symbolism. As Laplanche and Pontalis (475) remark: "There is a clear difference between the [*la*] Freudian symbolic and the [*le*] Lacanian symbolic: Freud stresses unifying . . . the symbol to what it represents, while, for Lacan, it is the structure of the symbolic system that is primary; the link with the symbolized . . . is second and impregnated with the imaginary." For Lacan the symbolic is the locus of the signifier, as well as being the locus structured *like* a signifier. On the other hand, the Lacanian imaginary is the locus of the image of the whole. Thus the structuralists' concept of the symbolic is not related to the Lacanian symbolic, where the subject is constantly fleeting, but to the realm of the *imaginary*, concerned with the images of the whole.

Despite the five codes and the lexematic divisions, despite the residual apparatus of structuralism in *S/Z*, Barthes warns the reader not to "structure the symbolic field" (*S/Z* 26). He is careful to distinguish the reversibility and multivalence of the symbolic from the reversibility inherent in the structures of structuralism. So how is the symbolic field unstructured, or how does it unstructure the structures of a semiological reading? It is no coincidence that Barthes strategically places the symbolic field as the third of the five fields elaborated in his initial discussion. It is posited as the middle point between the inside of the text, the hermeneutic and semantic codes, and the outside, the proairetic and cultural codes. Whereas the latter are organized or marshaled by the reader to the extent that he or she can be a good reader, the former participate more clearly in formal textual systems. Hence, far from being a renewal of structure, the symbolic is between inside and outside; the symbolic is found on the borderline where subject and object meet. This borderline provides no easy link. The meaning is destabilized and pulverized in multiple mirror images: "a dust, a shimmer of meaning [*un miroitement du sens*]" (*S/Z* 26). At the very heart of the system there is no heart, there is destabilization, a motor gone awry, a spin that unstructures the very center of the structure that is no more. It would not be an exaggeration to say that the rest of Barthes's career will be devoted to an exploration of this symbolic code that is not a code, for it is in this reversibility, in the multiplicity of entryways, and in the resulting reconfiguration of inside and outside that the problem will reside: "the main task still remains: to show that this field is reached by several equal entries, which makes depth and secret problematic" (*S/Z* 26).

Barthes rejects the image of the whole that structuralism produced as a totalizing figure; with it, he rejects the structuralist symbolic with its attendant figure of metonymy. The advantage that the Lacanian symbolic has over the structuralist version is that the former does not submit to closure, though it maintains supremacy over the two other divisions of the Lacanian psyche, the imaginary and the real, the locus of what is real for the subject. The Lacanian symbolic is multiple and not whole. It allows for the play of language, the constant fading from pure presence of the subject, and most important, the contact between textuality and desire. Barthes adopts the Lacanian symbolic as a replacement for structuralism's totalizing figure of the symbolic. This action is simultaneous with the rejection of a concept of closure.

Retrospectively, I see this adoption as a heuristic move, for by the time Barthes publishes *Le Plaisir du texte* some three years after the publication of *S/Z*, the Lacanianism will have disappeared in favor of a sympathy toward some of Gilles Deleuze's and Félix Guattari's insights in *L'Anti-Oedipe* about desiring machines. In a text like *Fragments d'un discours amoureux*, Barthes's version of desire relates more to the fragmentation of the subject than to a Foucault-Deleuze–inspired position about the "*effet de sujet*." So where structuralism shies away from the subject and Deleuze and Guattari espouse a position of desubjectivized desire, Barthes arrives at his position of the fragmented desiring subject through a recognition of the limits on the constitution of a whole and through a *miroitement* that shakes the very core of the desiring being and upsets the meaning of writing. He uses the Lacanian idea of the absent object of desire and the Lacanian symbolic in general as ways of liberating himself and his writing both from the totalizing weight of the structuralist symbolic and from the imaginary of orthodox Lacanianism.

By placing this "symbolic" code at the middle of his five codes and by redefining the symbolic in Lacanian terms, Barthes upsets any closure the system of codes might provide. *S/Z* plays on this multivalence to the point of eschewing the insights afforded by the four other codes in favor of their undoing by the *miroitement* of the symbolic. *S/Z* is not the first text in which one sees this destabilization. Whereas in the Festschrift article Barthes still seems to be a structuralist, on the other side of the Atlantic Barthes has already sent up a poststructuralist trial balloon in the work entitled "Ecrire, verbe intransitif?" This work has the ambiguous and singularly appropriate status of coming chronologically before *and* after *S/Z*. Actually the text "before" *S/Z* is the English version, entitled "To Write: An Intransitive Verb?" This paper was presented at Johns Hopkins University at the famous structuralist conference held in 1966, a conference that was already arguably poststructuralist in many ways: it was the conference of Jacques Derrida's "Structure, Sign and Play in the Discourses of the Human Sciences" and the conference at which Lacan made the pronouncement that the unconscious was like Baltimore in the morning. The text "after" *S/Z* is the French version, published posthumously in *Le Bruissement de la langue*.

In "To Write: An Intransitive Verb?" Barthes suggests that the verb "to write" (*écrire*) should be considered, at least in the modern sense of writing, to be in the middle voice, opposed to both the active and passive voices. The middle voice refers to an action reflected back on the subject. It is different from an action performed on an outside object, signaled by an active verb. But it is also different from an action performed on the subject by another agent, signaled by the passive voice. Hayden White has discussed the concept of the middle voice in Barthes in his article "Writing in the Middle Voice." White relates Barthes to Foucault by reminding the reader that Foucault had already discussed the intransitivity of writing in *Les Mots et les choses*. White hypothesizes that Barthes's article is in some respects an answer to Foucault, for whereas Foucault saw language "demoted" from a medium to a thing, Barthes envisioned a "metatransitive relationship between an agent, an act, and an effect"—in short, the middle voice (180–81). Even understood polemically, Barthes's concept of the middle voice relates to a return of the problematic of the subject.

Though one might initially be tempted to make an analogy between the unmoved center of structuralist endeavor and the middleness of writing, they are quite different. The unmoved center of the structures of structuralism is a mark of the presence of structure unto itself (the structurality of structure), one of the major foci of the critique of the structuralist enterprise that Derrida develops in "Structure, Sign and Play," given at the same Baltimore symposium. The middle voice occurs, however, in the movement of displacement and replacement as the action changes the subject performing the action. By putting the subject back into the action, by placing this action at the very reversible, symbolic middle of the function of the subject, Barthes reinvents the subject in and through language. The subject is no longer Marxist, structuralist, or psychoanalytic; it is a subject of enunciation whose action is that very enunciation: "To write today is to put oneself at the center of the process of words, it is to effect writing in affecting oneself, it is to make action and affection coincide, it is to leave the writer inside writing . . . as the agent of the action" (*BL* 28–29).

Writing occurs by reflexively turning back on the subject, and in so doing, it participates in the definition of the subject as the subject of writing. The fact that the subject is writing "a text" more and more seems to be evidence of the internal accusative nature of such an expression, more like "dancing a dance" or "singing a song" than it is like a real direct object (*Pr* 97). The difference between affect and effect takes place in this newly defined realm of the symbolic, where the differences will eventually be blended to form a sinuous curve that is no longer oppositional but differential, and whose trace will sketch the middle voice of writing.

I shall return to the concept of the middle voice later in this chapter, but for now, let us turn to *S/Z* and read that work with the assumption that "To Write: An Intransitive Verb?" is a predecessor of *S/Z*. Just as *S/Z* initially seems not at all revolutionary in its procedural mechanisms, nothing in the work's poetic dimensions prepares the reader for the revolution in the work. *S/Z* starts out from an ascetic locus of enunciation: "It is said that through ascesis certain Buddhists are able to see a whole landscape in a bean" (*S/Z* 9). This ascetic locus holds out the possibility of pure vision; through ascetic endeavor, one might arrive at plenitude. Things have changed vastly since the positing of the utopia that some structuralist analysts saw in the infinite possibilities of the story. The utopia of the opening line of *S/Z* is posited nostalgically, for the subject is already engaged, and no amount of Buddhist or structuralist asceticism can completely negate the function of the subject or the necessary presence of the desire of the subject and the attendant erotics of that desire.

From an ascetic, dispassionate point of view that sees the whole as a mise-en-abyme, a reflection of the whole world, analysis moves toward a plurality of voices. There is no longer a whole posited that has the purity of an egoless world. Whether it admits as much or not, each critical text has to make a place for some of these voices; in so doing, it is able to maintain the illusion of readability. *S/Z* undercuts the possibility of reducing the infinite play of differences to a manageable set of plural voices. Despite the fact that Barthes posits and maintains the five codes as the rules of the game for a polytopic reading, the discursive parts of *S/Z* tell a different story from the one he is purportedly reading. In *S/Z*, we move quickly from the asceticism that favors fullness to a game of differences that is both ludic and hedonistic in its pursuit of the fleeting voices that make up its own writing. *S/Z* is a text critical to our understanding of all of Barthes's work because it is the first of his writings to enunciate its own critical position as a text situated between control and explosion, between structuralist objectivity and incidental and fragmentary subjectivity. This latter position, as I have indicated, will fully come to light in works like *Fragments d'un discours amoureux*, where it is the subject, or better, the traces of a subject in discourse, that is, the decentered center of the text.

S/Z posits an opposition between the "writable" and the "readable." Barthes begs the question of whether this is an all-inclusive categorization by setting up the readable as the negative, reactive variant of the writable. Barthes first posits the writable as "what can be written (re-written) today" (*S/Z* 10). Barthes starts with "today" because what is at stake "is making the reader no longer a consumer, but a producer, of text." This "today" is an interesting shifter: participating in writing in a nowhere, it sets up writing as the precondition to reading and not the reverse. In his autobiography (*RB 169*) Barthes relates the shifter to a utopian discourse of desire, situated at the antipodes of the asceticism with which he begins *S/Z*. Here, however, the question of utopian discourse has not yet been broached: the general discourse of desire will ensue after a thorough working through of the problems posed by the encoding of the text.

Writability includes iteration: "rewriting" is part of the definition, though parenthetically, as if the parentheses were indicating that the concept might be problematic. This iteration necessarily implies that an act of reading is included in writability: to know that something is "writable today" we must have read it at some moment anterior to the absolute up-to-the-minute act of rewriting. To "write today" we must be willing to cross out the today-ness of the writing by realizing that there is a previous moment, perhaps one in which reading also has a middle voice to correspond to its own internal accusative. Thus there are gaps in the so-called opposition between readability and writability, and writability includes readability. Finally, there is the definition of readability as a negation: it is the "negative, reactive value" of the writable text: the readable is "what can be read but no longer written" (*S/Z* 10). For something no longer to be writable, there must be a criterion in writing that indicates this impossibility. Yet the oppositional definition, the definition by negation, does not allow a place for this absence of iterability. If what is readable is merely what is no longer writable, readability has the same constraints as writability. Writability is what is rewritable and thus readable; readability is what is readable but not rewritable. Hence, aside from any historical questions of reception, the opposition between writability and readability is deceptive, for it is neither simple nor all-inclusive. It does, however, provide a place for the subject writing and reading in the feedback of the nonwritability of the readable and that of the rewritability of the writable.

The subject "today" sits on the border between writability and readability, no longer able to observe dispassionately but not yet able to enter into the fray to create his or her own fragments. In *S/Z* the position of the subject is as a subject of writing: the one writing today or the one rewriting today. The position of the subject—the subject of the critic, this critic—is that of someone who is not yet able to allow himself to be read as the subject of reading but someone who is beginning to engage himself as a writer able to deal with specific acts of sexual power. Barthes is moving toward the enunciation of the subjectively sexual and has gone far beyond the dispassionate sexual dynamic that depends on formal interdiction in *Sur Racine*: "Hippolytus hates the flesh as a literal evil: Eros is contagious, one must cut oneself off from him" (*SR* 117). In *S/Z*, the cut is internal: it is read in the very mark that divides the title, in the castrato, and in the text itself: "what is called 'real' (in the theory of realist texts) is never anything but a code of representation (of signification): it is never a code of execution: *the novelistic real is not operable*" (*S/Z* 87). The play on words is not negligible: if the words "operable" and "execution" refer to whether something is workable or not, they also refer to legal and medical discourses.[2] Racine's Hippolytus was executable and so he was destroyed by

2. Medical discourse also comes into play in *Roland Barthes* with the concept of "diathesis." It would perhaps be a useful exercise to trace the function of the medical in Barthes's work: how a very real case of tuberculosis has echoes in the writer's repertoire of the imagi-

wild horses. The realist text cannot undergo an operation, for the mark of having been operated on is, to use a cliché, "always already" there. Thus even within the realm of the readable there is some difference between what is readable and not remarkable, a work such as Racine's *Phèdre*, and what is readable and still can be remarked, a realist story such as Balzac's "Sarrasine."

After *S/Z*, the position of the subject undergoes a slippage, or drift, as Brown calls it. Barthes moves from considering the function of the subject of writing in *S/Z* to allowing the subject to become a subject of reading, a receiver of pleasure, the very locus at which pleasure and orgasm occur in *Le Plaisir du texte*. In *S/Z*, the technique of reversal is at stake; Barthes is writing today about rewritability as he writes about a text, "Sarrasine," whose rewriting is impossible. Yet even if it were possible, the rewriting would consign the rewriter to a dangerous territory of the neuter, of the castrated, and of dangerous supplementarity. After *S/Z*, Barthes will be able to get beyond the reversibilities of certain kinds of logical oppositions or binarisms. There is a line of difference between *S/Z* and *Le Plaisir du texte*, just as there is a difference between a story of castration subject to a certain kind of heterosexually oriented power structure that includes homosexuality as a perverse variant and a story directly about homosexuality. Whereas in *S/Z* the subject of the text is disparate, in *Le Plaisir du texte* the subject emerges as a complex surface ready for bliss.

In a general sense, there is a change in logic between the structuralist works before *S/Z* and an unabashedly poststructuralist work like *Le Plaisir du texte*. In his structuralist phase, Barthes relies on a sort of Aristotelian categorization and a Cartesian logic of division; the vestigial traces of that double logic remain in the armature of lexemes and codes in *S/Z*. But this once unshakable logic begins to come apart in the *miroitement* of the prose between the disquisitions on codes and the ordered semiological analyses of the sequential fragments. There is no more important example of this change than the renewed concept of the sign. For the early Barthes, the opposition between signifier and signified is totalizing. In *Eléments de sémiologie*, published in 1964, he writes: "The nature of the signifier largely suggests the same remarks as those about the signified: it is a pure *relatum*, its definition cannot be separated from that of the signified" (*AS* 45). Along the same lines, the system of denotation and connotation is not first seen

nary, how "pneumothorax" constantly reinvents itself in the very breathing of his text. François-Bernard Michel has undertaken part of this project with a study of the idea of breathing in the work of certain writers, including Barthes, who have respiratory illnesses or syndromes.

as problematic: connotation is seen as being in a metalinguistic relation to the denotative meaning of a word, expression, or syntagm (*AS* 76–79).

In *S/Z* and, a fortiori, in *Le Plaisir du texte*, the notions of signified, metalanguage, and denotation have themselves become suspect. The signified seems to have become an endlessly recessive chain of signifiers. The opposition between denotation and connotation gives way to a Derridean play of differences in which no "pure" denotation can be observed. In *S/Z*, connotation "assures a (limited) dissemination of meanings, spread out like gold dust on the apparent surface of the text" (*S/Z* 15). If the denotative statement says that connotation is limited, the entry into the poetic with the simile ("like gold dust") assures us that connotation is not limited. The dissemination spreads like gold dust across the surface. The once overvalued transcendental signified of pure meaning or translatability, erected into a transcendental signifier that bestows meaning on a system, is decentered, multiplied, and atomized. Any transvaluation of a position is undercut by the impossibility of having denotative value congeal at that position. The tone is apocalyptic, or at least evangelic, as Barthes damns the denotative meaning that has always stood at the head of the line. Finally, all is connotation: "denotation is not the first meaning but feigns being so; under this illusion, it is finally only the *last* connotation" (*S/Z* 16). Once again the opposition fades with the discovery that one of the terms of an opposition is actually included in the other: denotation no longer has a separate status but is part of the connotative world. Eventually the whole semiological adventure will give way to a staggered deployment of signifier and work (*BL* 91). Amid that deployment will be the place of the desiring subject.

It would be useful to examine briefly here three versions of opposition that are inherent critiques of the structuralist model of neat, bivalent oppositions, for Barthes's version contrasts with those of Derrida and Foucault. I say they are inherent critiques, for both Foucault and Derrida were already exploring the question before structuralism found institutional acceptance. Each, however, continues his critique in an explicit fashion, Foucault in *Les Mots et les choses* and Derrida in *De la grammatologie* and in "Structure, Sign and Play." In Foucault's opposition, the world is divided, but one term sets up a grid of discursive praxes and power to repress the other: sanity represses madness, the legal and licit juridically or sexually repress the illegal and the illicit. In the Derridean notion of opposition, one term is seen to take precedence and acts thereupon to repress the first through its inscription in metaphysics: thus writing is repressed by speech; absence by presence; femaleness by maleness; homosexuality by heterosexuality; and so forth. Derrida's early critique of Foucault's study of madness offers a useful contrast between these two positions. Derrida sees the metaphysics of opposition as being more complicated than Foucault's vision. For Foucault, the members of the opposition can be separated or controlled; for Derrida (*Ecriture* 51–97), the opposition only "makes sense" in the act of repression of the second term. Thus "sanity," for example, has no meaning except *as* a member of the pair of "sanity and madness" and *in* the act of repressing the other member of that pair, madness.

Barthes erects an opposition only to dismember it by folding one part of the opposition in on the other; one might well ask if they remain opposed or if one is included in the other. Does, for example, the opposition between connotation and denotation that collapses into connotation fully cover the field? Are writability and readability true opposites? It is as if Barthes has decided to choose the incompleteness of fragmentation both as a generic form and as a value: there is virtue, Barthes seems to be saying, in the incomplete. The difference between Barthes and Foucault, the sexual dynamic of which has been studied by Naomi Schor in "Dreaming Dissymmetry," is easy to categorize in a general sense, for Foucault's synchronic approach to the whole of a historical moment is as far away as possible from Barthes's flirting with the incomplete. The difference between Barthes and Derrida is more entangled, and the clues come in the play of words used by Derrida on the one hand and Barthes on the other. Derrida's terms, such as "trace," "supplement," "hymen," and "pharmakos," live on the borderline between two registers; the words both separate and join the registers. In Barthes's later works, indebted to Derrida without being "Derridean," the terms play on the collapse of difference between registers: "jouissance," "punctum," and so forth. Whereas Barthes's work from this period tries to approach the excluded third, Derrida's work during the same time seems to focus more on the repressed other. When Derrida writes of the woman in a text like *Eperons*, Barthes is writing of neither the man nor the woman. Barthes writes instead of the neuter (*neuter*), of the homosexual, of the uncategorizable excess that goes beyond the oppositions of a bivalent system. Of course, the contrast is not absolute: we have Derrida's text on Kant and excess in "Parergon" as well as the very Barthesian word "dissemination."

Let us return then to examining Barthes's writing after *S/Z*: we find new oppositions that are not really oppositions. Not the least of these new oppositions is between pleasure and jouissance, which seem initially to cover or be covered by the realms of readability and writability respectively. Yet jouissance becomes completely ineffable: to say it is to name it in an act of reading, not in an act of instantly complicitous rewriting in the utopia without difference that Barthes seems to desire. The jouissance is ultimately the mark of each *instance* in the Lacanian sense (493–528), each *incident*, and each moment of the flow of desire or text. Thus jouissance is a figure that marks the subject of the text as being problematic to constitute as a whole. As Deleuze puts it in a remark to which the Barthes of this era would wholly subscribe:

> There is no subject of desire, any more than there is an object. There is no subject of enunciation. Only the flows are the objectivity of desire itself. Desire is the system of meaningless [*a-signifiants*] signs with which flows of the unconscious are produced in a social field. (Deleuze and Parnet 96–97)

The model of jouissance is the same as that of the gold dust spread over an apparent surface. The problem is that this desubjectivized jouissance still coexists with the subject. In fact, the reinvention of the subject has brought about the simultaneous possibility of desubjectivation. In other words, it becomes necessary to reintroduce the subject in order to question its validity, not as the "disappeared" other of the structuralist model, but as the perpetually self-inventing, and therefore fictional, figure that allows for the desubjectivation of flows.

The model of deployment that Barthes develops is structured around a line that separates without totalizing. In the texts that follow *S/Z*, Barthes continues to elaborate on the sense of the middle ground. It is as if in earlier texts, more structuralist or semiotic, it is the very bar within the sign that gave the sign its totality: the bar that separates signifier and signified ensures that it is dividing up a whole world. With the new, poststructuralist model in place, totality is no longer the *terminus ab quo* or the *terminus ad quem* of textuality. The line merely separates or joins; it is neither a guarantee of totality nor a means of ensuring an active voice wholly distinct from the passive or middle operations the voice undergoes in its very enunciations. The line becomes a flaw that divides the subject into inside and outside or into desire and discourse. The process of enunciation changes from one in which the subject seeks its wholeness into one where the wholeness is never there, neither posited at the beginning as an undifferentiated origin nor the goal aimed for in a nonrecuperative development toward an entelechy.

Writing is then no longer fundamentally a product of ideology or even of pleasure. Writing is the articulation of the flaw in the subject, the jagged edge at which inside and outside meet. Synonymous with the jouissance of the subject, writing introduces its own marginality to the center. Speaking of the fuzzy distinction between the two effects of writing, pleasure and jouissance, while remarking the very middle-voicedness of writing itself,

Barthes says "distinction will not be the source of certain classifications, the paradigm will creak, meaning will be precarious, revocable, reversible, discourse will be incomplete" (*PT* 10). The effect is revolutionary, for not only has the figure of totality disappeared, but the heuristic value of such a totality is gone as well. No longer is there a scientific paradigm at work in which the model of an experiment in a closed universe can be seen as the more or less accurate, microcosmic figure of the whole in the open universe. Again, this new view of discourse is the epistemological version of the death of metonymy and synecdoche as the master-figures or tropes of the truth.

For Barthes, writing has become the true version of the talking cure, but it is the talking cure of an interminable analysis where there is no cure or closure. It is moreover an analysis in which there are no structures of transference and countertransference. Finally, it is an acceptance of the Oedipalization of the world, a recognition allowing that the subject is, to use Derrida's adverbs, always and already castrated. Ultimately this means that for the Barthes of *Le Plaisir du texte*, the notion of castration has no transcendental meaning: each instance of this talking cure or each incident of the writing is the rewriting that implies the fact of having read. Thus each instance of writing implies that there was a point before writing, a utopian whole always inscribed as an impossible absence "today." Saying that means, for Barthes, we have learned nothing, for we have once again fallen into the nostalgia of bivalent opposition between now and then, between castrated and uncastrated.

This is ultimately where Barthes realizes that Lacan has been a heuristic tool; Lacanianism is a convenient stepping stone rather than an article of faith. While I do not mean to reduce the complex nature of Lacan's thought to a commonplace, one can safely say that whereas Freud used his terminology heuristically, Lacan sees the structures of his own discourse as part of the very psyche of the analysand. At times it would seem as if the "truth" of the analysand's psyche resided not in the psyche itself but in Lacan's description of the Lacanian psyche in general. Barthes is insistent on the singularity of his discourse and his desire. Even if he knows that everyone is "always already" castrated, even if everyone desires, everyone desires differently. No totalizing structure—neither the paradigms of structuralism nor the psychoanalysis of Lacan—can negate or subsume this singularity.

If writing has become the postmodern version of the talking cure, speech for Barthes has become no more than a poor substitute for, or even a supplement to, writing. While no complete erasure or crossing out of writing exists—while the text is always readable even when it is partially crossed out—speech cannot have even the illusion of erasure. Speech is impoverished in its very excess; it is an unchanneled flow distinct from the articulations that writing gives to the flaws, wounds, and fault lines of the subject. As Barthes says in the autobiography: "an internal flow of words [*loquèle*] grabs me, a bombardment of sentences. . . . It is the opposition of writing, stingy in its very disbursement" (*RB* 124). This *loquèle* is certainly something more than the flow of language or logorrhea. In the chapter of *Fragments d'un discours amoureux* on the loquèle, Barthes notes that he borrows the term from Loyola to designate "the flow of words through which the subject tirelessly argues in his mind about the effects of a wound or the consequences of some behavior: the exaggerated form of the lover's 'palaver' ['*discourir*' *amoureux*]" (*FDA* 191).

The loquèle covers the space of discourse in which writing would otherwise be found: it masks the flaw or wound instead of articulating it. Speech substitutes for writing and drowns it (out) with a constant flow of words. Is it therefore in the nature of the loquèle or of speech in general to overflow in generosity and in the nature of writing to be stingy or parsimonious? Certainly in that speech cannot be erased, in that one cannot literally take back one's words or literally go back on one's word, speech fades away and dies out. When we give our word, when we plight our troth, it is literally irrevocable and can only be removed if that speech is considered to be writing. So the border between speech and writing is defined by the fact that writing contains its own potential negation whereas speech can only deny a posteriori. If speech comes after a wound, does writing come before?

Why is there a wound at all, mark of the medical discourse already mentioned, but index of a martyrology as well? What is Barthes "talking" about? If we return to "Ecrire: verbe intransitif?" we find a clue about this wound. It is precisely in the word that is only half there. This is how Barthes approaches a definition of the middle voice, the locus in which writing takes place:

> Another linguistic notion will perhaps give us the key: that of diathesis, or, as the grammar books say, of "voice" (active, passive, middle). Diathesis designates the way in which the subject of the verb is affected by the process. (*BL* 28)

Behind the linguistic definition of "diathesis" lurks another definition: diathesis is the propensity of an individual for getting a certain kind of illness.[3] This other definition is even signaled in passing in the fragment

3. For a discussion of diathesis in linguistics, the reader is referred to Benveniste's article, "Actif et moyen dans le verbe" (170–75). Ulmer (86–87) discusses both Barthes's concept of diathesis and Derrida's relation of *différance* to the middle voice. Derrida (*Marges* 9) himself has

on amphibology in *Roland Barthes*, where voice is defined as both "bodily organ and grammatical diathesis" (*RB* 77). The middle voice, then, that of the verb "to write" and, need we recall, of the standard example, "to sacrifice," is a double diathesis: a middle voice, sitting in the middle of the reversible symbolic field where one can always choose "not to write," and a disposition toward the illness of writing that is both its own fulfillment and its own cure.

Writing precedes the *blessure*; writing is where one can sacrifice oneself or the other without spilling a drop of blood, without there being a wound. Benveniste's examples could not be more propitious for Barthes. One comes from Sanskrit: *yajati*, meaning "he sacrifices for another (as a priest)" and *yajate*, meaning "he sacrifices for himself (as a celebrant)." Benveniste's second example is from Greek and it is the example that Barthes *does not* give: *poiei*, meaning "I produce [an action] in another, I give a signal" and *poieitai*, "I produce and participate." Finished with signaling the production of another, ready to produce for himself, Barthes can still only signal, in an active voice, the poetics of the middle voice to come in books such as *Le Plaisir du texte* and *Roland Barthes*. With this poetics announced, the wound is safely forestalled: as long as I am writing, I am avoiding the wound inflicted upon me by another or by myself. As long as I stay within written language, there will be no sacrifice by a priest or by a celebrant: "As far as rites are concerned, is it so disagreeable to be a priest? . . . It would not work for language: the language-priest? Impossible" (*RB* 152).

II. Joys

In *Le Plaisir du texte*, Barthes begins to explore the adventures of this middle voice, with its particular fuzzy logic that can accept the possibility of always contradicting itself. Barthes announces the plan early on; merely a gesture is needed to get rid of the "old ghost" of "logical contradiction" that haunts the text. Barthes proposes a fiction of an individual without "barriers, classes, and exclusions" and "who would mutely withstand all accusations of illogic and unfaithfulness; who would remain intransigent

---

commented on the middle voice as follows: "And we shall see why what is designated by '*différance*' is neither simply active nor passive, announcing or recalling something more like the middle voice. . . . Yet the middle voice, a certain nontransitivity, is perhaps what philosophy, constituted in this repression, began to distribute between the active and passive voices." As Foster (83) reminds the reader in her little-known survey of lesbianism in literature (*Sex Variant Women in Literature*), the word "diathesis" had some currency in sexology earlier in the century, and the word appears in the work of Havelock Ellis. In his study "Sexual Inversion," Ellis (vol. 2, pt. 2:141) notes: "There is no doubt that at this time—that is, between the fifteenth and seventeenth years—a homosexual diathesis had become established."

when faced with Socratic irony . . . and legal terror" (*PT* 9). This fictional individual, an ideal anti-Socrates, is the ironic double of Socrates himself. It is a middle-voiced midwife who assists in his or her own birth: Barthes's figure for the reader-critic, Barthes himself. It is a Socrates of haiku and not of dialogue, of erotic games and free play in the realm of the senses and signs, not a set of adjudged meanings. This individual acts with impunity in his or her reading; his or her incidents of pleasure never add up to a completed act. Such a reader reads in the imperfect of repetition and in the present of incompletion; he or she refuses the *passé simple* of perfect verbs and completed actions and even disdains the *passé composé* of relation. It would not be an exaggeration to state that in *Le Plaisir du texte*, Barthes is quite literally sketching out tenses, voices, and moods for a grammar unique and germane to reading itself.

The first version of this individual is not the "other" reader that Barthes announces on the following page, but Barthes himself, the critic writing this very book in a middle voice. This voice is situated between the readable writing that one always took as criticism and the reading that seemed to form a parallel to that writing. Just as the pairing of signifier and signified is dislocated in *S/Z* by the introduction of the symbolic code, in *Le Plaisir du texte* the pairing of writing and reading is disrupted. No longer do writing and reading relate like the two faces of a coin or like two activities simultaneously joined and separated by a universal bar that is the sign of the universal ego and its language. *Le Plaisir du texte* sketches out the new position of the critic who uses the same middle voice as do modern writers producing writable texts.

The first of these new critics is Barthes himself, who in some sense is coming out of the closet by avowing that the critic has a sexuality. While I have been critical of the use of the expression "coming out of the closet" relative to a French mode of thought and writing, I am using the expression here *sous rature*: the closet out of which Barthes is coming is the closet of structuralism. And while it is of extreme importance that Barthes is homosexual, that particular orientation takes a back seat here to the realization that the critic has a sexuality of any kind. In other words, it is clear to Barthes, as it should be to his readers, that various critical insights come to him from an examination of his homosexuality and from the articulation he gives it: at first it is silent, then enunciated in a stage whisper, but it is always in the middle voice. Right here, though, at the beginning of *Le Plaisir du texte*, is the announcement of sexuality and that is what counts.

This seems as good a point as any to address what I perceive as a general critical shortcoming when it comes to studies of Barthes: the fact that for most readers, Barthes seems to remain basically sexless, as if the famous jouissance could happen without sex organs and sexual orientation. Martin Melkonian promises a body in the title of the book *Le Corps couché de Roland Barthes*, but does not examine the matter. For that matter, despite the tantalizing title, *The Ecstasies of Roland Barthes*, Mary Wiseman offers us a sexless Roland Barthes as well. Saying that what he really wants to examine is "Barthes and the body" (56), Steven Ungar invents for Barthes a sexless body, or the body of the "good homosexual," as Tony Duvert would say, a body deprived of its phallus. Ungar sees the autobiography as being "less an autobiography or confessional essay than a critical fiction" (63). Candace Lang (178) quite rightly criticizes what she terms Ungar's "misconstruction" of the body in his reading of the autobiography, which Ungar seems to see (as Lang phrases it) as an "observable, analyzable organic unity." But it seems that that organic unity depends on a lack of sexuality, an absence of difference, and a misprision of the incomplete nature of the representation of desire in Barthes's work.

In *Le Plaisir du texte*, Barthes is making an important announcement for him and for us. He is asserting that this new kind of critic has a sexuality. To deny that component is to be willfully unaware of the functions and limitations of one's own criticism. It is to deny oneself pleasure; it is to deny one's readers pleasure as well. Again, it is not a question of homosexuality in particular, at least not here and not now, for it might conceivably be more difficult for a heterosexual critic to announce his or her own personal, singular sexuality distinct from the doxa. In a sense then, the homosexual critic has an easier time (for once) in establishing a nondoxological or unorthodox position. Barthes is reaching for the most general statements possible here: in every act of reading, every critical incident, there is a being of desire who cannot be put into parentheses. *Le Plaisir du texte* announces that critics have jouissance, that they "come" too, that they can "come" out of the closet, that their long days of asceticism are over. Barthes includes his once idealized reader in the realm of these new critics: this reader, who thus "comes" as well, will also be able to withstand all accusations of infidelity and promiscuity heaped upon him or her.

But a sexualized reader has other, previously unforeseen problems. The sexualized reader, the one who, like Barthes, has banished the spirit of logical contradiction, can no longer read idealistically as once he or she could. Barthes says in fact that such a reader is figured in dialectical opposition to the work: he or she is the antihero of the text in which his or her pleasure is found (*PT* 10). Given that forced identification, what would normally have been perceived as the *sine qua non* of the readerly text, the process of identification between reader and textual creation, is overturned. A reader cannot, Barthes seems to be saying, identify with Julien Sorel or Eugène de Rastignac, because that reader is also in a charged, nonneutral position. A reader can only see these characters dialectically. This inversion of the readerly model is problematic, because it was always a standard assumption that a reader could "identify" with a character in the "readable" text. According to that assumption, a reader sees the object in the text and seizes it as his or her own in a process of identification. The reader has been figured or can be figured in a process of identification with the subjects of action of the novel or as part of a complete, idealized communicational system. The object, in this case a textual creation, must be internalized and assimilated by the reader through a process of identification. It is only then subject to judgment. The true enlightenment of the reader may come from a Brechtian distantiation, but the pleasure comes from a comfortable seduction, a slipping into the text where opposition has no place.

Barthes seems to be saying that such an idealistic model is no longer possible, because the reader is always in the position of an antihero, whether it is a question of a readable text or a writable one. What then of this antihero? If we understand this "anti-" as a literal inversion, we begin to see Barthes's point. Precisely, the process of identification proceeds through inversion and not according to similarity. Even the heterosexual reader must subject himself or herself to a process of inversion where he or she quite literally becomes the desirer and lover of the text. The desire of the reader re-covers the desire invested by the author in the production of the text. As for the homosexual reader, his or her standard operating procedure always involves inversion of one sort or another for a readerly text: to identify with Julien Sorel, the homosexual reader has to make Mme de Rênal a mister or Mathilde de la Mole her own noble beheaded male ancestor.

Thus the process of reading is redoubled with a sexual cruising [*drague*] by the reader of the text that the author has created. Barthes would have the reader involved in a game of seduction where he or she tries to pick up the text. What is pleasing is neither contents nor structure, but "the scratches imposed on the beautiful envelope: I run, jump, raise my head, and dive in anew" (*PT* 22). The seduction, a two-way street between author and reader and between reader and text, is really an open-ended series of partial sallies, inversions, and identifications. Barthes insists on the partial nature of reading; thus it is no surprise that the figure of this partiality—the wound that represents something less than whole along with the lingering nostalgia for the whole—is related to reading. As we have already noted, this wound reappears in *Fragments d'un discours amoureux* (191) as well as in the definition of the key word, *punctum*, in *La Chambre claire*: "a shot, a little hole, a little spot, a little cut, and a roll of the dice as well. The *punctum* of a photo is the chance event that in and of itself stings me [*me point*], but also wounds me and grabs me" (*CC* 49).

Occurring in the middle voice, the process of writing effects a performative action at a distance: the middle voice produces a delayed action that reverts onto the writing in a redoubled diathesis. The writer writes in the middle voice, and this writing eventually is merged with the reader's remarking action of wounding (*éraflures*). Whereas according to the classical model, the reader's only action was to be absorbed in the text, the reader's actions now are described in a vocabulary of sex and/or athletics. Steadfastly remaining in the middle voice, writing is the locus at which this wounding, the famous sacrifice of linguistics, eventually occurs as an effect of textuality and not as a precedent to the text.

Through this delay over time, Barthes can rhetoricize the absence that writing implies in its very middleness: writing cannot cruise for him. Desire is neither a prelude to writing nor a result of writing; only writing will come of writing. This self-perpetuation of the middle voice is clearest in one of his last texts, "Soirées de Paris," posthumously published in *Incidents*. In fact, it is the line with which the book closes, a suitable last line for a novel: "Then I sent him away, saying that I had to work, and knowing that it was over, and that beyond him, something was finished: the love of *a* boy" (*I* 116). For all the writing he has done, Barthes cannot fulfill his desire. Though the rhetoric and activities of writing may simulate the processes of desire, the middleness of writing returns the action onto the writer. So, despite the likening of writing to cruising or, for that matter, reading to cruising, writing ultimately falls prey to the illusion of representability that Barthes is trying so desperately to escape. Writing stands as the representation of cruising, just as the illusory textuality of previous readerly texts stood for or represented a world. But the relation is the same: writing represents desire two-dimensionally, cannot re-present desire at all, and ironically mocks the acts of desire, cruising, and accomplishment. Once the illusory rhetoric of representation has been pared away, the basic ontology of writing for Barthes is nothing less than pornography. For the writer or for the reader, writing is the simulation in two dimensions both of desire in a general sense and of his own desire in particular.

Still, at least in a theoretical or illusory way, writing is a version of cruising, where the anonymity of the participants guarantees not only a certain success but avoids the pitfalls of the personal. Without names, there is no real active or passive, at least grammatically. When the love of "a boy" is lost, "I" am losing the game; beyond "my" loss is the loss of the addressee, and beyond that, the third person. But with an anonymous text, the personal pronouns begin to lose their effectiveness. The text's position is complicated by the fuzzy border between writing and sexuality and by their relation to the consumer, the receiver, the object. If the text calls to me and seduces me by having cruised me successfully, it is at the price of my own identity. Thus, while admiring Réda Bensmaïa's book *The Barthes Effect* in many ways, I am not fully comfortable with what Bensmaïa says about cruising: "The Barthesian text 'cruises'; it loves its readers (one by one): without equality, (but also) without in-difference" (69). Bensmaïa's discussion relates to a text by Barthes on friendship, a fragment entitled "La relation privilégiée" (*RB* 69); friendship is a state in which we presumably know the other, in which a "*nous*" can be formed, in which loss of identity is recuperable in the bond. But this particularity of friendship cannot be generalized for the relation between writer and reader. In fact, the paradigm here is of anonymity and of *sosies*, doubles, or simulacra, where the real reader is supposed to identify with the posited rhetorical construct. And that can only come with a nonrecuperable loss of identity. For Barthes, then, one has let oneself be seduced by a text that precedes the individual and his or her existence as a subject of reading or sexuality. At the same time, the cruising remains anonymous for the writer, who, cruising for a reader, does not know for whom he is searching or whom his text is attempting to seduce:

> As for the reader, I must look for him ("cruise" for him) *without knowing where he is*. A space of bliss is thus created. It is not the "person" of the other who is necessary to me, but the space: the possibility of a dialectics of desire, of an *unpredictability* of bliss: that the games not end, that there be a game. (*PT* 11)

The space of jouissance is thus the space of the middle voice, the space where questions of active and passive disappear in favor of a "dialectic diathesis": a playing-through of various positions, a space of potentials, a ludic space for action, a spot where speech (*lexis*) and action finally coexist. Jouissance is a means of recuperating speech and action by writing. But, as we have seen, this space of jouissance is also a space of false representation, the space in which the fulfillment of desire cannot occur in an active sense, but can only refer back upon the subject. In terms of writing and reading, this dialectic of desire ultimately opposes a space of representation and thus of false consciousness to a space of middle-voiced but self-referential play.

In a piece called "Digressions," a fragment entitled "Sexualité" is strategically placed between pieces titled "Langue" and "Signifiant" (*BL* 89). As it was written as a response to a questionnaire by Guy Scarpetta, the paratactic arrangement may simply be fortuitous. But we should seize on the chance event, as we recognize that for Barthes sexuality does serve as a channel between the global entity of language and the single instance of the signifier. Sexuality functions between the presumed wholeness of the discourse of the nonwounded other and every single fragmentary instance of language for the wounded self. Thus the constitution of the other through sexuality, posited itself as a whole, ties the text to discourse. Certainly the relation of the signifier to the signified is far more complicated than the opposition originally posited by structural linguistics and semiology. Barthes says that it was an error to think that the signifier was the simple correlate of the signified (90); he now knows that the signifier and the signified are opponents. Finding the true correlate of the signifier in "work" (91) does not help elucidate the substance of this opposition. The opposition between signifier and signified ultimately involves the struggle of the signifier to produce its meaning, but, through the mediation of sexuality, the instance of the signifier is linked to the phantasmically complete discourse in the realm of the imaginary.

Sexuality is the vehicle for reintroducing a figure of *pars pro toto* into poetics. In rejecting the structuralist version of the symbolic, Barthes denies the viability of synecdoche as a master trope, since synecdoche depends on the possibility of an axiomatic vision of a whole subtending the figure. By introducing sexuality as a mediating device between the individual instance of discourse and the global entity of language, Barthes is metaphorically reintroducing the missing figure. The sexual body is the vehicle for moving from part to whole: synecdoche exists but only through the mediation offered by metaphor. The whole is reconceived as the object of metaphor and the vehicle to that end is the imaginary representation of the sexual desire of the self and the body of the other. This troping of a trope is tantamount to the ironization of all three positions: the instance of discourse, the vehicle carrying instance to totality, and the totality of language itself. The production of discourse and the announcement of the self are now out in the open. But they are never fully themselves and are always under the troping of an irony that posits incompletion, blanks, or *différance* at the end of the line.

Thus when we read about sexuality at this point, we realize that Barthes is necessarily referring to an ironization of sexuality, in fact, a double irony because we are dealing only with the imaginary representation of sexuality. For Barthes, however, the effect is capital since this double movement allows him to restore to sexuality what disappeared with the failure of representation. Earlier we indicated that the problem with introducing sexuality into the text was that it depended on its own representation and was therefore necessarily a failure. Barthes now allows sexuality to come back to itself: the representation of the representation or the troping of the trope brings sexuality back. But it comes back freed of the fictions of representation and, more important, freed of the structures imposed on it by the ideologies and metaphysics of the world from which it came.

Barthes thus liberates sexuality both from the process of representation and from the constraints imposed by representation. Despite the Western mode of treating sexuality under the sign of the doxa, the general opinion that allows or forbids the juridico-discursive power and moral suasion, true sexuality is far more polymorphous. In reducing sexuality to a simple bivalent system, in keeping it "prisoner of a binary opposition, a paradigm, a meaning" (89), the doxa maintains sexuality as the third term of the opposition between signifier and signified: sexuality defines the famous bar between the two as a bar of transgression. Moreover, even a deconstruction of the binarism would itself come under the sway of the doxa. It is the task of the signifier to reorient this sexuality in the realm of the textual and to signify desire by opening up the position of the subject to a chain of signifiers in the realm of the imaginary as well as in the realm of the symbolic. The sexuality of the signifying praxis provides the intersection between the phantasmic completion of the imaginary and the fragmentary nature of the symbolic.

By accepting a secondary status defined by the discourse of dominance, that is to say, the doxa of heterosexuality, homosexuality reproduces the binary imprisonment that Barthes sees as the bane of sexuality and its discourses. The transgression of certain rules of "good" sexuality "remains implacably subject to the rule of exact meaning: homosexuality, a transgressive praxis, thus immediately reproduces in itself . . . the purest imaginable paradigm of active/passive, possessor/possessed, screwer/screwed, fucker/fuckee" (*BL* 89). Homosexuality becomes a privileged paradigm because it is subject to a double imposition of binary logic: subject to the doxa of dominant heterosexuality, it is also endlessly resubjected to a division into a grammar of actions where there is no middle ground. The interpellated doxa of activity and passivity conspires at every level to stop jouissance: "A slight teacher from Marrakesh: I'll do whatever you [*vous*] want, he said, filled with effusion, goodness and complicity in his eyes. And that means: *I will screw you*, and only that" (*I* 54–55). And it is not without a degree of sadness that Barthes sees this reduced to a mechanics of penetration, for he knows that writing, as opposed to this interpretation of the doxa, promises far many more possibilities than the simple oppositional one to which most homosexuality has been reduced.

Barthes envisions the possibility of sexuality untainted by the internalization of its own representations. The possible freeing of the desiring subject from imprisonment in the representations given by the other and internalized at the level of the imaginary allows Barthes to try to liberate writing in a similar fashion. We have seen that the reintroduction of sexuality into writing first leads to a questioning of the act of representation of sexuality, then to a false consciousness because of that representation. Barthes moves toward a freedom from that consciousness, and it is at this point that he can jump back toward the same liberation at the level of writing and reading. What is to be avoided is fixing roles in the active and passive, be it in matters of sex or in the middle actions or voices of writing and reading. Numerous are the texts in which Barthes opposes the strict classification of actions in this bivalent system. He promotes instead the middle voice of sexuality and textuality, an erotization of the entire field: "Erotization is a production of the erotic: light, diffuse, mercurial; it circulates without landing; a multiple, mobile flirtation links the subject to what takes place, feigns holding one, then lets go for something else" (*RB* 66–67). Again it is a question of retroping the tropes that lead to the freedom of the erotic within its own realm; one is free to be gay on the rue de Rennes with its gigolos, or on the rue Ste Anne, the location of the gay bars of the era, but is that an authentic freedom? By reversing the movement, by providing one's own irony, one can turn the act of writing into a flirtation completely freed from the constraints of the doxa.

By maintaining a rhetoric that tropes the tropes of division, by a middle-voiced refiguration of rhetoric as irony, both bathmology, a science of "levels of language" (*RB* 71), and amphibology are means of avoiding the dialectic of active and passive and of remaining in the diathetic middle. Will is not enough to avoid the dialectic: the doxa is a constant threat looming large on the textual horizon. It is not enough constantly to ironize one's own position, nor is it sufficient to introduce figures with limited use such as amphibology and the irony of bathmological observations. The surest process of refusing the congealing of behavior, be it erotic or authorial, into a fixed activity or passivity is through the process of fragmentation of text and being: erotic existence is a series of incidents without serial value; texts become a paratactically (dis)organized set of fragments.[4]

At the same time, texts constructed of fragments show obvious authorial self-awareness to a greater degree than do more cohesive units that conceal their laws of construction and organization. Perhaps an earlier Barthes would have said that he was providing a fragmentology in the form of a metadiscourse on fragments. This unconcealing of the law of the text is its fragmentology, yet this fragmentology is simultaneously and bathmologically a fictional unification of the pieces of text. The apparently unified text may have a hidden law that destroys unity; openly submitted to the law of the fragmentary, the fragmentary text may be given a false unity by that very law. To avoid the specious fiction, Barthes inevitably accompanies the fragments with a bathmological rhetoric, as fragmented as the initial fragments and ultimately indistinguishable as a separate metadiscourse.

At certain points of autoreflexivity, the discourse on the fragment, itself in fragmentary form, replaces the fragmentary discourse on the object. To what extent is this metadiscourse itself fragmentary because of the author's

4. Bannet (63–93) maintains that part of the raison d'être of the fragment in Barthes's writing relates to the process of note-taking inculcated into French schoolchildren: "Like all French schoolchildren, Barthes had been taught to take notes on the books he was reading as he was reading them by the '*fiche*' or index method—that is to say, he had been taught to note down everything about a given character or theme on a separate piece of paper and to put the name of the character or theme clearly at the top of each piece of paper" (72). The banality of the act explains nothing of what an earlier generation would have called the "genius" of Barthes; everyone else in his school learned the same technique, yet there was only one Roland Barthes. Bannet seems at times to mix the differences between Barthes and the text of the other: in one case, Balzac, and more generally, the famous doxa. For example, in reference to *S/Z*, Bannet omits a few words and changes the meaning of the text. She seems to be saying that Barthes sees danger in transgression when Barthes is saying that Balzac sees that: "'It is lethal,' Barthes points out, 'to remove the separating line.'" But the French has the following: "il est mortel, *dit le texte* [says Balzac's text], de lever le trait séparateur." (*S/Z* 221, my emphasis). She has left out "says the text" and this *brouillage* between the position of Balzac as interpreted by Barthes and that of Barthes allows her to posit a simultaneous and thus oppositional will to transgression in Barthes. It is not clear to me, however, how Barthes "buys in" to the lethal nature of transgression. Rather, to quote Bannet herself, Barthes makes the transgression of the doxa the very standard of his being-in-the-world: "Barthes turned homosexuality, perceived as the condition of being neither male nor female, into a third term, a neuter, which subverts all the reproductive paradigmatic forms of extant society. And he made homosexuality's own practices—*la drague*, the cruising in quest of a series of acutely pleasurable but transitory sexual encounters, the close, accepting friendships with non-sexual partners and the perversion of exhibitionism with its thrill and fear of discovery—he made these his standard of pleasure, love and social disalienation and his counter-weight to extant social practices" (86). As I have shown, the language of the closet—"*acutely* pleasurable," "thrill and fear," "social disalienation," "counter-weight"—is, quite simply, irrelevant. Barthes's interest (double genitive) is in going beyond phenomena of transgression to examine imprisonment in a doxa that sets up transgression as a value.

predilection for that form? To what extent is it due to the logic or rules of fragmentary discourse? If we opt for the first choice, we continue to subject questions of form and genre to a set of psychological constraints. Style then becomes the manifestation of the author's personality and we resurrect the absolute subject as something that precedes its discourses. Barthes himself seems to lean in the direction of a logic of the fragment that does not depend for its authorization on a psychology of an author who favors the fragmentary approach: "The fragment is not only cut off from its neighbors but also parataxis reigns within each fragment" (*RB* 97). Obviously, the choice is paradoxical: if we opt for the nonpsychological interpretation because Barthes touts it, then we are in essence opting for the psychological interpretation. So we should opt for the second choice because the first is not viable, and then allow Barthes tacitly to agree. For Barthes, then, the very nature of the fragmentary approach informs the parameters of the discourse. The fragment has its own rules precisely because it is a fragment.

To follow this logic is not to posit a psychologism but a whole discourse that is the imaginary, ideal construct from which the fragment has been taken. Barthes thus seems to be simultaneously suggesting that along with the fragments as such there is a whole of which the fragments are only pieces. Whether Barthes actually "believed" or not in this plenitude of discourse is moot. In any case, it is posited both as a construct with its own rhetoric (as opposed to a rhetorical construct) and as a textuality, a map, or even a symptomology of the imaginary:

> I have the illusion of believing that in shattering my discourse, I cease imaginarily discoursing on myself, I draw out the risk of transcendence; but since the fragment (the haiku, the maxim, the thought, the bit of a diary) is *finally* a rhetorical genre and since rhetoric is that level of language that is best suited for interpretation, while thinking I disperse myself, I do nothing but wisely return to the bed of the imaginary. (*RB* 99)

The act of denial or its transcription in its own self-avowal as denial is replaced by a rhetoric that refers back to two wholes posited as preceding the fragmentary text: the whole of discourse and the whole of the self, or its replacement as a symptomology of the imaginary, once again medical in nature. Barthes posits the possibility of liberation only to fall prey to the illusions that this possibility seems to offer. While the possibilities of the fragmentary still exceed those offered by other strategies that seek liberation from the doxa, Barthes does not delude himself into thinking that there can ever be a pure liberation from the doxa's insistent representations. Firmly aware that such impure representations will always return, Barthes seems to get comfort from and take pleasure in the simultaneously medical and erotic "bed of the imaginary." The expression adds another amphibology to Barthes's list: the bed is the locus of erotic pleasure and of sickness and pain, as well as, one might add, the middle-voicedness of sleep.

This rhetoric about the fragmentary is the means by which recourse to these two posited wholes of discourse and body is undone. Maurice Blanchot's remarks (229) about the fragment in Nietzsche's writing could be convincingly applied to Barthes's work as well: "The word in which the need of the fragmentary is revealed, a word that is not sufficient, but not by insufficiency an unfinished word (because it is foreign to the category of accomplishment), does not contradict the whole."[5] Rather than being a fragment of a preexisting discourse or a symptom of a preexisting imaginary whole, be it psyche or body, the fragment is self-sufficiently itself, neither preceding from nor heading toward a whole.

The fragment is an act of representation whose particular rhetoric represents not a set of contents but the fragmentary nature of any discourse. Just like the announcements in *Sodome et Gomorrhe* that refer to discourse and not to contents, the fragment represents a form instead of representing contents. It is not part of some imaginary whole discourse but a sign of the incompletion of any discourse: all discourses are fragmentary and they merely show their jagged edges to a greater or lesser extent. Just as the fragment returns us to the fragmentary nature of all discourse, it simultaneously returns us to the fragmentary nature of the imaginary. The fragment relates split to split and seam to seam. The fragments of the imaginary are connected, albeit tenuously and rhetorically, to their distorted representation in an equally fragmentary discourse.

Parataxis is both the internal rhetoric of the fragment and the external rhetoric of the organization of fragments knowledgeably juxtaposed by the author. The reader is called to read this juxtaposition before or after he or she reads the fragments themselves. So if the whole process of cruising the reader is an anonymous one in which the reader is created as he or she does the reading, the parataxis itself creates a geography of reading. Now, I do not believe that Barthes imagines a female reader, though obviously

5. As Deleuze and Guattari remark (50): "Maurice Blanchot successfully formulated the problem in a rigorous manner on the level of a literary machine: How can fragments be produced and thought that have relations of difference as such between them, that have their own difference as their own relation, without referring to an original totality, be it a lost one, or to an eventual totality to come?"

he could imagine women reading his work. The rhetorical construct of the reader in works like *Le Plaisir du texte* and *Roland Barthes*, however, seems to be a homoerotic male reader. Both the straight male reader and every female reader are placed in the position of having to perform the same act of self-effacement that has implicitly and traditionally been asked of the gay reader faced with a heterosexual love story. Literally, it is as if the reader were being told at what intersection the cruising might take place, at what textual street corner he might be picked up by another man.

Barthes invites the reader to apply the laws of fragmentology in order to see an opposition between a linear discourse with a closed hermeneutic circle and a fragmentary discourse built as much on the gaps between the fragments as it is on the pieces themselves. The straightforward discourse, with its pretension to completion, inevitably heads toward the doxa, and in this case, toward the doxa of heterosexuality based on mastery, *parade*, and oppositional role-playing.[6] But with its voluptuous association of states and situations beyond simple opposition, the fragmentary discourse is the discourse of homosexuality: an ongoing series of incidents and a liberating sexuality that is simultaneously jouissance and a sign of death, since it is not reproductive. And finally, this fragmentary discourse is the locus in which the *neutre* will come about.

Barthes juxtaposes a fragment on the *neutre* (which means both "neuter" and "neutral") with a fragment on active and passive. The *neutre* includes white writing, flow, and bliss—anything, in fact, that renders "*parade*, mastery, and intimidation" ridiculous (*RB* 136). The *neutre* is of primary importance, for it defines a space in which writing may potentially take place. In his brilliant book on utopias, Louis Marin (30) analyzes the definitions accorded to the *neutre* in various discursive praxes. Marin's definition is one that would have pleased Barthes, even though the Barthes who is consciously writing these fragments as fragments tends to stay as far away from definition as possible. Marin writes:

6. The word "parade" in French covers three areas: a military parade, in the sense of a review; show or ostentation; and parrying, be it physical (in fencing) or verbal, in the sense of repartee. Since there is no English word that covers these various meanings, I am keeping the French word here. And we should not forget that Barthes claims that he willfully keeps the various meaning of amphibologies or enantiosemes of a word: "Each time he encounters one of these double words, R.B., on the contrary, keeps both meanings of the word, as if one of them were winking at the other and that as if the meaning of the word were in this wink, which makes *one word*, in *one sentence* mean two different things *at the same time* and that one semantically enjoys each through the other" (*RB* 76). I am maintaining italics for *parade* and for *neutre* to underline that, in the first case, I am using the French word, and in the second, that it is not simply a typographical error.

> The *neutre* could henceforth be defined in relation to a dynamic totality whose parts are *in opposition*, *in a position of marked difference*, a relation that would still have the unique characteristic of putting itself outside this totality, *in a position of difference relative to the internal difference of the whole*.

While not identical to the diathesis of the middle voice of writing, the *neutre* is the locus in which that writing can occur without being collapsed into a doxa or protracted into a marginality. As Blanchot (449) notes, the *neutre* is related to what Barthes would call bathmology: "The *neutre* would thus relate to what, in the language of writing, emphasizes certain words . . . by putting them between inverted commas or parentheses." Blanchot indicates that the *neutre* relates to the very literal aspect of text as writing. For him, the *neutre* is autoreflexive in its insistence on its literality. Blanchot's remark has a darker side too: the very process of bracketing, the suspension of decision that still involves the imposition of brackets, parentheses, or "inverted commas," is simultaneously, as is the case with the Husserlian *epoche*, a continuation of an idealism, and thus of a belief in a transcendental valuation of the very process and possibility of bracketing. For Barthes, the *neutre* takes a preeminent position that is a sign of what an earlier avatar of Barthes would have called "writerliness." Sign of the writable, the *neutre* is the escape from opposition, the devalorization or annihilation of the imposition of the doxa, and the liberation of the text from received opinion and laws of *genre*: the laws of both genre and gender.

One must wonder then if this *neutre* is an ideal position, a product or strategy of the author's idealism. Or does it produce the author's idealism as the ground on which a "happy sexuality" and a "happy writability" can both simultaneously occur? We must first consider how Barthes makes the *neutre* an operative concept, since it begins as a product of readability, as the signed mark of castration. As long as we consider the *neutre* for itself, however, and understand that this "self" does not exist except in its own diathesis, the *neutre* remains an operative concept untouched by idealism. First of all, the *neutre* is the product of a reversal and not an average of active and passive, of male and female; the *neutre* is the bathmological rereading or rewriting of the concept of center that underlies such oppositions:

> The *Neutre* is thus not the third term—the zero degree—of an opposition that is both semantic and conflictual; at another turn of the infinite chain of language, it is the second term of a new paradigm, whose violence (combat, victory, theater, arrogance) is the full term.[7] (*RB* 136)

7. Gallop also relates the problem of the *neutre* to the ambiguous zone in which sexuality and textuality seem to mingle. Discussing the *neutre* in *Le Plaisir du texte* and in *Leçon*, she

As Bensmaïa says in his book: "Since it [the Neutral] is not the third term (category Zero) of an unimaginatively semantic or purely conflictual opposition . . . the Neutral gives rise to a 'generalized collapse' of the economies of the Text" (48–49). We realize that this collapse includes both the economy of language and the economy of genres. Even if there is violence lurking at the position of plenitude, and thus even if the utopian position is marked, on the far side, by its own ending, the free play of the *neutre* has made that violence ridiculous (*RB* 136).

This passage on the *neutre* is immediately followed by one entitled "Actif/passif," which starts out with the opposition between virile and nonvirile. From all the possible subcategories of active and passive, Barthes chooses one that relates to sexuality and erects it monumentally as the dominant dyad for the doxa itself: "This celebrated couple, reigning over all the Doxa, resumes all the games of alternation (every well-formed meaning is a *parade*, a coupling and an execution" (*RB* 136). Now this *parade* is what has just been made ridiculous by the *neutre*, not by the contents of the preceding fragment, but by the intersection of the two fragments: the presence of the first neutralizes the content of the second. The author uses the rhetoric of parataxis to jump to a utopia of joyful neutrality: "However, as soon as the alternative is refused (as soon as the paradigm is scrambled), utopia begins: meaning and sex become the object of a free play, at whose heart the (polysemic) forms and (sensual) practices, freed from binary prison, will be in an infinite expansion" (*RB* 137).

Once again, Sedgwick finds herself in the realm of the "peculiar," as she warns us that Barthes's utopianism may in fact be premature. Disagreeing with Barthes, she says that

> a deconstructive understanding of these binarisms makes it possible to identify them as sites that are *peculiarly* densely charged with lasting potentials for powerful manipulation—through precisely the mechanisms of self-contradictory definition or, more succinctly, the double bind. (*EpCl* 10)

Marin (15–25), however, more germanely points out that the two roads to utopia are the *neutre* and the plural. Barthes agrees wholeheartedly with

---

says, "This utopic italicized *neutre* may be a sensitive zone of Barthes's homotextuality. It certainly is part of a wish to escape the constraints of bipolar gender differentiation. And so perhaps he shares in feminism's liberatory project" (113). As this last sentence shows, Gallop's concern is with feminism in this very interesting piece. She goes on to say: "The pleasure of Proust. A guilty pleasure. On the question of feminism: *neutre*. The pleasure of Barthes, but what about feminism? What is Barthes's position on women? He never takes a position on women. (Out of homosexuality perhaps? Neutrality? Exclusion?) A possible exception: the word 'woman' occurs *once* in *The Pleasure of the Text*."

this assessment. By escaping from a bivalent logic that is also a double bind, a logic that endlessly forces subjects into constraining dyads and that repeatedly submits them to repressive doxologies, the subject in its manifestations of sexuality and textuality can be liberated to enter into a baroque utopia of endless ramifications. Certain parataxes seem privileged in that they lead toward an erotics of the intersection of texts. Those erotic intersections, we might say, are the loci of successful cruisings: they call the previously anonymous reader and they map out a road to utopia. Refusing a "heterosexual" binarism of active and passive, or its epitome in the opposition of virile and non-virile that shows the heterosexual doxology to be a phallocentric ideology, Barthes develops a nonoppositional tropics of desire, whereby the positing of neutrality leads to a utopia and a "happy sexuality."

Barthes gives an emblematic name to this utopia and it is "shifter." This word is central to formalist and structuralist linguistics, and much is made of it in the development of structuralist literary theory in the sixties. As defined by Roman Jakobson in a famous essay entitled "Shifters, Verbal Categories, and the Russian Verb," a shifter is a word whose meaning cannot be defined outside of a reference to the specific message in which it is contained. Examples of shifters are words like "today" or "I," whose "meaning" can only be clear from within the context in which they are found. This category of shifters names utopia for Barthes, a realm of fragments and of Deleuzian *machines désirantes*:

> Can one image the freedom and even the loving fluidity of a group that speaks only with first names and shifters, each saying nothing but "*I, tomorrow, over there*," without referring to anything legal, and in which the *flow of difference* . . . would be the language's most precious value? (*RB* 169)

The discourse of utopia, the discourse of fragmentation, and ultimately the discourse of sexuality, that is to say, homosexuality, intersect in a textuality that refuses to move toward violence and that proceeds by making its own nonreproductivity the means by which it produces.

The *neutre* receives special attention in the discussion about the French philosopher Charles Fourier. Barthes makes a list of words that Fourier uses for the reserved part, the part of the "happy few," and that list includes "*neutre*," along with others like "passage, mixed, and ambiguous." Translating Fourier, Barthes says "we could call it *supplement*" (*SFL* 111). The space of the neuter is the space of supplementarity; by naming the neuter the supplement, Barthes enters into a sphere of Derridean deconstruction, for the *neutre* "is a purely qualitative and structural notion; it disrupts meaning, norms, and normality" (*SFL* 113). The supplementarity of this neuter is troubling to the text and to the reader, as is the return of the word "structural." Barthes seems to be saying two things; that ambiguity is worth exploring.

On the one hand, the neuter as supplement occupies the position of the signifier as writing—writing that, in its Lacanian insistence, opens up to the symbolic (*SFL* 11). Patrizia Lombardo points out that *The Pleasure of the Text* has a Lacanian context, which can be seen in Barthes's vocabulary. But there is a difference for her: "Barthes posits a fundamental opposition between desire and the law, pleasure and the institution, while Lacan cannot conceive of one without the other" (59). I would go further: as we have seen, when Barthes is using Lacanian language after *S/Z*, there is a simultaneous undermining of that language. So in *Sade, Fourier, Loyola*, the supplement is ultimately the supplement to nothing, for Barthes has already attempted to void the symbolic. In its insistence and its instances, the supplement is itself all there is in writing. At the same time, there is the lingering notion of a pure structure. Barthes is also saying that there is a language without a supplement—a "utopia of poetry"—and a kind of "Adamic language, stubborn in not meaning" (*SFL* 138). Barthes continues to hold out for a position without a supplement and to think that the supplement adds itself to language that might otherwise be without a supplement. Such thinking maintains the closure of the original language, posited as a whole and as "Adamic" in nature.

In *Roland Barthes* he says that "Adamic language" is a figure of the neuter (*RB* 136). The neuter is the realm in which closure is possible, but this closure seems to belong to the imaginary. And *Fragments d'un discours amoureux* places Adamic language and the neuter within the realm of the imaginary: "the language of the Imaginary would be nothing else but the utopia of language, a completely original, Edenic language, the language of Adam" (*FDA* 115). For Barthes it is not, as Lacan would have it, that the unconscious is structured like a language, but rather that the realm of the imaginary structures language as a closed system of nonsupplementarity. As Barthes begins to criticize the role of the imaginary in his own writing (a process noted by Jean-Jacques Thomas) and increasingly explores the fragmented subject inserted into the symbolic, this utopian dream fades.

As Barthes begins to see supplementarity in an open system, as he begins to see it as language itself, he abandons this utopian position. I disagree with Domna Stanton, who sees this utopian vision and Adamic language as continuing in Barthes. Her position depends, however, on a binary concept of displacement from the father to the mother, yet accepting a bivalent structure for the imaginary and the symbolic clearly means for Barthes a reintroduction of the doxa, which he certainly does not wish. As Barbara Johnson (4) points out in her commentary on *S/Z*: "In other words, a text's difference is not its uniqueness, its special identity. It is the text's way of differing from itself." If we go with Barthes beyond the opposition to rethinking the endless nontautological dissemination of difference, or if, with him, we make any binary opposition uncomfortable, we must see the fading of the utopian vision and the weakening of the standard systems of symbolic interpretation. The neuter becomes the supplement, and then, in its flight away from the doxa, it becomes the Adamic language of the poststructuralist critic.

The paradoxical conclusion that we have reached is an explanation for the gradual abandoning of the imaginary of the text in favor of the symbolic in the later works. We learn from *Fragments d'un discours amoureux* that this discourse, predicated wholly on the imaginary, takes place within the realm of the neuter: there is ultimately nothing erotic at all about a discourse whose only figure of the subject is a whole and whose cause is a lack. The discourse of love is prompted by a lack, or an absence of the loved one, but it is simultaneously predicated on the image of the whole subject in quest of that missing piece. Following Lacan, Barthes notes in the same book, "desire is missing what one has and giving what one does not have—a question of supplement, not of complement" (*FDA* 268). There is a contradiction in the imaginary, but the contradiction is resolved in favor of the neuter. The discourse of love stands out as a fulfillment of a project, much in the same way that *Système de la mode* was, but the text on love stands opposed to the autobiographical projects and essentially to the writable in general.

For Barthes, literature remains imprisoned in the realm of the imaginary, and the literary space of writers such as Sade and Racine shows us to what extent this plenitude organizes literature. The closed Sadean space resembles the Racinean space that Barthes discussed in *Sur Racine* (*SFL* 22). But *S/Z* opens up the space of the text in a way that the earlier works did not. To believe in the closure of a space is to remain within the frameworks of wholeness defined by the Lacanian imaginary: "one might almost say that *imagination* is the Sadean word for *language*" (*SFL* 36). The critical act liberates the literary text from its prison. Breaking out of that closure, with *S/Z* and also with *L'Empire des signes*, is a means of access to the symbolic order. With an opening up of the microcosm of the text comes an opening up to the infinite.

Two intersecting currents or fields remain that cannot be resolved in terms of any amphibology. Neither a penchant for fragments nor a discourse of supplementarity can reconcile the systems of closure and non-closure. On the one hand, there is the imaginary of literature: filled with images of the whole, marked by discourses whose neutralization always remains possible, the language of the imaginary is figured as the realm of the understandable in literature. Part of the work of the critic certainly involves exploring this imaginary, the figures it uses to determine its own images, the rhetoric involved in positing wholeness, and the ideology that sustains such posited wholes. The job of the critic is to mark the "*imaginary loci of language*," which include "the word as single unit, magic monad, speech as an instrument or expression of thought; writing as transliteration of speech; the sentence as a logical, closed measure" (*PT* 54). On the other hand, there is the realm of the symbolic: the territory of the subject cruising through the text, the realm of fading, and the locus in which rhetorical eruptions show that the supplement is a supplement to nothing. The texts of the later Barthes are crisscrossed with this paradox: cruising versus love, subject versus the neutralized literary object, openness versus closure.

III. Blisses

In the remainder of this chapter, I will explore some additional ramifications of the double current of imaginary and symbolic. Whatever interest *La Chambre claire* might have, it should not be taken as Barthes's singular, absolute, final testament except by default. I find a more plausible final figure to be the gradual will-to-fiction expressed in the autobiography, in *Fragments d'un discours amoureux*, as well as in some of the Proustian passages in *La Chambre claire*. The oft-mentioned desire to write a novel is the resolution Barthes posits to the problem of the wavering line between the sexual and the textual, between the traps of the imaginary and the losses of the symbolic, and between the will-to-representation and the ultimate failure of representation. For a number of years Barthes meditated writing a novel that would undoubtedly have been post-Proustian, but an integral text does not seem to exist.

It could be argued that the last part of *La Chambre claire* is an initial approach to this fiction. The second section of this book is not without its obvious literary intertexts. Proustian in its nostalgic rememoration and in its direct quote of Proust, the section also reminds the reader of *L'Etranger*, as it begins with the death of the mother: "Yet, one November evening, not long after my mother's death, I was filing some photos. I did not hope to 'find' her again, I expected nothing of 'those photos of someone, faced with which one remembers the person less well than when one simply thinks of him' (Proust)" (*CC* 99). Along with that novelistic passage, two others in Barthes's poststructuralist period seem to me to be candidates for inclusion in this approach to fiction: one is the set of posthumous sketches published in "Incidents" and the other is a series of jotted, fragmentary memories in the section of *Roland Barthes* entitled "Pause : anamnèse." What Barthes says about anamnesis recalls the movements of the Proustian text that is ever his model, but it can be applied as well to his own "fictions": "I call *anamnesis* the action—a mixture of bliss and effort—that leads the subject to rediscover, without enlarging it or making it vibrate, a slender memory." As, in *Vigiles* (*Vig* 67), Renaud Camus calls *Incidents* a "collection of anamneses about Morocco," we are not at all surprised to find another narrative thread here in the section on Amidou from that posthumous text (*I* 44–45).

For Barthes, the novel is the genre in which the borders between the imaginary and the symbolic and between Proustian fiction and critical commentary are both the most problematic and the most potentially interesting. Moreover, the novel is the locus par excellence of anamnesis, where deformation begins to operate on the received doxology. Propelled solely by its own singularity, the novel is the genre that refuses the generic; it is the form where loose, baggy monsters coexist with tight texts *à thèse*. The novel presents a whole world, a complete imaginary of signs whose categorization is never entirely finished by the critic but whose figure of the whole looms as the double terminus (*ab quo* and *ad quem*) for the text.

The reading of any nineteenth-century novel is a partial one, predicated on a whole that exists prior to the individual reading and a whole to be reconstituted after the sum of the individual readings. The novel-to-be allows for the possibilities of openness and a transcription of the subject that will parallel its own fading without forcing it into closure, for the closure of the discourse of the subject implies its death. So the novel that is hoped for but never written, utopian in its discursivity, is the figure of the text that Barthes would write or would have written had he been able to close the discourse of the subject. The only way to avoid neutralization is to play Cordelia, who has "nothing" to say: one must not enter into the fray. By regarding a novel as a potential and not as a reality, Barthes could maintain a nondisjunction between the imaginary and the symbolic.

It is interesting to speculate on the title Barthes might have chosen for his text. At one point in *Roland Barthes*, he provides a list of his unwritten books that includes one entitled *Le Discours de l'homosexualité* (*RB* 153). But that title is instantly modified, multiplied into its own fragmentations: "or the discourse of homosexuality or, yet again, the discourse of homosexualities." Barthes is never far from the sexual subject, or from the subject of sex, at this point. Passing through variations on singulars and plurals, Barthes names nothing of this unwritten book except its own incompletion. This text does not exist; Barthes knows that it could not. Though he would perhaps have been capable of writing a novel, that novel would not have resolved the paradox of the subject. Still, what remains interesting in his later writing, from *S/Z* onward, is the way Barthes uses the symbolic, that is to say, the openness of discourse and the eruptions of pleasure, to undermine the images of the whole in the literary imaginary. Parallel to this sabotage is the construction of a discourse of the symbolic, the discourse of cruising that is an open-ended series of incidents for which there can be no closure in discourse.

Each incident of the symbolic, which Barthes does not fail to call a perversion, is simultaneously and erroneously perceived by the subject as being the last one in the imaginary, the one that will provide closure. Each incident, however, is repeatedly the one that will not have provided closure. Figuring the symbolic is an addiction, a perversion, and an openendedness of incidents that stretch out as the discourse of the subject. This perversion pierces the images of the imaginary and produces so many holes as to render the imaginary itself, more obviously than ever, an ideological construct. The perversion in the symbolic names itself with an initial and is concomitantly deified as a goddess. Herewith follows Barthes's most notorious commentary on this goddess, one of whose names (in parentheses) is homosexuality:

> The power of bliss of a perversion (in this case that of the two "H"s: homosexuality and hashish) is always underestimated. The Law, the Doxa, and Science refuse to understand that perversion, quite simply, *makes one happy*; more precisely, it produces something *more*: I am more sensitive, more perceptive, more loquacious, more entertained, etc.—it is in this *more* that difference is found. (*RB* 68)

The unique text "on homosexuality" that Barthes published during his lifetime bears some consideration. It has certainly given at least one writer cause to vent his spleen. Dominique Fernandez (132) sees Barthes's rather neutral confession as nothing better than cowardice, for, according to him, Barthes should really have talked about his homosexuality a lot less coyly than he does in this passage. And it is true that Barthes's "coming out" with that one word "homosexuality" is rather subtle, for even the qualities ascribed to the excess or surplus of perversion seem to relate more to the effects of hashish than they do to a certain sexual proclivity. It is easy to criticize Barthes for not "coming out" more decidedly; it is almost as easy to write an apology for Barthes's failure to "come out." If I hesitate to do either it is neither as a defense nor as a critique of Barthes's position, but rather because for Barthes homosexuality is intensely personal; it is, with no pun intended, what makes up the private parts of his writing. "Coming out" is just not in the picture. A complete "coming out," according to all the rules of good behavior, would undoubtedly relate more to the figure of the self-portrait as corpse admirably discussed by Michel Beaujour (325–34) than it would to the running of a motor for producing textuality. If it is to be useful textually, Barthes's homosexuality must remain part of a game of veils.

For Barthes, sex is the hidden interpretant, the operator of personal liberation in writing, the sign that has no name, but which must proceed masked, the goddess, named with an initial, who is always veiled.[8] Certainly Barthes could have come out, been militant, and advocated gay rights in his writing. But just as certainly, the question of homosexuality operates at a wholly different level in this writing. It is as if he has found a liberating secret formula, a theory of observation and understanding that can function only if he does not fully let on what the secret is; it is his figure in the carpet. Homosexuality will continue to work as an interpretant for Barthes as long as it remains an unavowed transcendental signifier or a secret code book. From *S/Z* on, Barthes's writing is a continuous process of making that transcendental signifier work for him as a means, method, or theory of writing. It is not a question of coming out or of not coming out, but a means of production. To take a militant stand is to move homosexuality from the realm of the productive into that of the reproductive, to take it away from the neuter and force it into an opposition with doxological heterosexuality.

Even as the fading of the subject continues, perversion produces a surplus of signifiers, which is a way to more deeply undercut the hold of the imaginary on the subject prisoned within its walls. The perversion

8. In his study of Descartes, entitled "Larvatus Pro Deo," Nancy develops the sense of the two readings of the Latin expression "*larvatus prodeo*": "I proceed masked" and "masked before God [*pro Deo*]." Nancy's comments (33) on Descartes's text (from the *Préambules*) could certainly hold for Barthes as well: "Behind the mask is no one; there is no figure for thought. . . . There is someone beneath the mask, since masked 'he' goes forward. There is someone confused with no one, since 'he' resembles nothing, someone who is confused with no one [*personne*], that is, in Latin, with the role or mask with which 'he' hides his shame. But this modesty is the condition of knowledge of the subject." Ungar (81) duly notes that Barthes refers to this Cartesian text in *Fragments d'un discours amoureux* and *Le Degré zéro de l'écriture*.

of the subject turns the subject back on the imaginary and thus provides him or her with a means of transgressing its rules. The body of the text is slowly withdrawn from its presumed plenitudes as it is subject first to multiple transgressions and then ultimately to a fragmentation that leaves it resembling nothing more than the figure of the subject himself or herself. Far from being the object of study, the text is now a second subject, crisscrossed with the discourses and fadings of the first. If there can be no plenitude in the symbolic, the subject will, even in his or her explanations, reduce the imaginary wholes of textuality to suspect figures unconsciously produced by the operations of the doxa.

The classical text has a figure in the imaginary that mimes this perverse operation of the subject: the action of storytelling, itself the transgression of the signs of completion that the text fashions for itself. In the text of a writer like Balzac, storytelling participates in the symbolic destruction of the images of the whole. Telling a story means exhuming a body and perversely remarking it for the observer to read as the story is told. The body exhumed within the text, itself a supplement, "is the locus of transgression brought out by the story" (*S/Z* 35). Storytelling is the perverse relation of conquests, where erotic incidents are made permanent in discursive necrophiliac voyeurism. Barthes's supreme irony is to inscribe the quintessence of doxological heterosexuality within a homosexual paradigm. To wit: if a man is telling his story—and Barthes does not seem to consider a female narrator—in one way or another, he is telling how he "won the girl" or "came, saw, and conquered." The storytelling asks that the victory be repeated in the hearing and acknowledgment of the story by the listeners, who, even if female, participate in the re-presentation of the act. Thus a listener repeats the action of a storyteller and re-presents the story to himself or herself, not according to the desire of another but according to the discourse of another. Reading the text and thereby repeating the storytelling is an act that violates the body, but does so subject to a homosexual repetition of the action. The body of the woman (or in the case of "Sarrasine," the castrato), or even the conquered city of Paris at the end of *Le Père Goriot*, described as an odalisque or a beehive, simultaneous metaphor and metonymy of its queen bee, becomes the fetishized object that is repeated through an assimilation of the discourse of another male. Such is the message of "Sarrasine" transmitted by *S/Z*, as it too is written according to the discourse of another.

Barthes sees the possibility of retaining a heterosexual imaginary impenetrable by the perverse remarkings of the pleasures of homosexual reading. In the undeniably heterosexual text of Georges Bataille, whose strength may come from the inclusion of transgression within its own imaginary, Barthes sees a certain imperviousness to the actions of the critic: "Still too much heroism in our languages; in the best of them—I'm thinking of Bataille's—there is an erethism of certain expressions and finally, a sort of *insidious heroism*" (*PT* 50). The difference between Bataille's text and a more readable one is that the former clearly states its own transgressions and thereby erects a stronger wall against the perversions of the critic. But without any transgression announced, a text vacillates between a heterosexual readability that is in itself a transgression and a homosexual complicity that is a perversion. This heterosexual readability means that the act of writing is bound up with a successful completion in the imaginary of the impossible resolution of an Oedipal crisis in the symbolic. Though the subject loses in the symbolic and is reduced to continual fading and incompletion, he or she can win in the imaginary, since "the writer is someone who plays with his mother's body" (*PT* 60). The homosexual complicity comes in telling the tale, in desiring according to the law of the symbolic that is the law of the father, and in repeating in text what could not happen.

We should understand Barthes literally here: playing with the body of the mother means understanding that the text is a toy that represents to the writer both the idealized possibility of fulfillment and a successful solution to an Oedipal crisis. But the toy, marked by the writer as such, becomes a fetish both for him and for the reader: "The text is a fetish; to reduce it to one meaning by an abusively univocal reading is to cut its tress, it is to perform the gesture of castration" (*S/Z* 36). The name of the fetish is thus the phallus itself. This is not the phallus as defined by Lacan, because it is valued by the investment of the desire of the subject as much as it is given a transcendental unity by the appeal to an imaginary and to transcendental "langue." Still, the fetish takes on a certain quality of the phallus, the magic power invested in it by desire. It is a fetish that exists as such, just as the "goddess 'H'" exists as such only when there is a threat of removal. And it is obviously not the role of the reader to castrate; the reader does not imitate the gesture of the father who limits meaning and determines direction. The task of the critic is to refuse this overt act of castration, limitation, and determination and to combat the insidious imposition of the images of the doxa.

Still a question remains: Where does meaning come from, if it is not guaranteed by the ordering of the symbolic, that is to say, by the orders given by "the name (the no) of the father?" Barthes is certainly seeking to escape from the imaginary into the symbolic, but this symbolic is still determined by an order that precedes each instance of textuality. One way around the impasse is to define the text as its own fulfillment: Barthes has just said that "text," tissue," and "tress" are all the same thing. Thus the fetishistic nature of the text is its meaning: the text is its own incarnation of desire. The text is the fetish in which the desire of the author is invested. But as the investment cannot take place in parcels of psychic energy but rather must occur through chains of signifiers, the signifiers as such are both the fetish and the invested desire. In that guise, the chains of signifiers of a text themselves occupy the position of the symbolic "Other" that defines meaning. There is no transcendental name-of-the-father with which to reckon, but rather a self-guaranteeing textuality whose rhetoric alone determines the flows of desire, meaning, and order in the text. One would think, then, that the text is a fetish that would seemingly be desired by the reader according to the desire of the author. Yet to submit the desire of the reader to that of the author is to enslave the reader and prevent him (or her) from cruising through the text as he (or she) wills.

Barthes proposes two positions to counteract the submission of the reader to authority. The first is a community; the second, a quasi-independent status to textuality. The theorization of the text as community property is rare in Barthes's work but it appears strategically in *Le Plaisir du texte*. Although he will eventually say that the text is the fetish of the mother's body, he says earlier that it is one's own erotic body: "The text has a human form, it is a figure, an anagram of the body? Yes, but of our erotic body" (*PT* 30). Is this the same body as that of the mother? It hardly seems likely, since for Barthes it is an inescapable conclusion that the text is the mother's body. Yet he mines the figure—he takes its riches and he explodes it—from the interior. Barthes would like to believe that the text is the body of the mother, but that will-to-belief is accompanied by the knowledge that this is not the case. To believe it would be to submit the text to the structures of the Oedipal triangle, whose castrating mechanism is safer than open (homo)sexuality. Barthes projects the rhetoric of the maternal as iconoclasm and as revisionist comfort in order to avoid the overt enunciation of the figure of his own sexuality. If the text is an anagram of one's own body, then that body is a collection of signifiers, letters organized according to a different grammar. Yet again, if the mother's body is the transcendental signifier of textuality, there is no independence from it and the anagramming of desire is diminished.

Clearly, for there to be jouissance there must be an escape from the dominance of the mother's body, viewed both as a whole and as a sign of itself in the form of a fetish. Barthes sees this whole as the transcendental image of the imaginary corresponding to the name-of-the-father in the symbolic. But in one case as in the other, the text must seek independence from this transcendental figure. The text must float as freely as a subject who has liberated himself or herself from his or her own family novel. Just as I desire the text in my cruising, it must desire me. The partial object that is a fetish must desire according to its own textuality: "The text is a fetish and *this fetish desires me*" (*PT* 45). The fetish takes on different forms; it is too easy to believe, as Barthes seems to do here, that there is a wholeness to the fetish. The nostalgic idealism of the whole, already discerned in the fragment, is present in this version in the text-as-fetish. Yet in the autobiography, the fetish marks its own divisions: "A taste for division: packets, miniatures, rings, brilliant precisions . . . the trait, writing, the fragment . . . the semanticist's realm or the fetishist's material" (*RB* 74).

Both in his discussions of fragments and in his discussions of the fetish, Barthes alternates between a concept that values the imaginary whole—constituted, for example, in the realm of the Lacanian imaginary—and an insistence that the fragment or fetish is a part that belongs to no whole, be it already constituted or not yet existing. The language of wholeness participates in the nostalgia that serves as a rhetorical device for Barthes. In contrast, the statements about fragments and fetishes send us toward a conception of the partial object, not in the sense originally given it by Melanie Klein, but rather in its re-reading by Deleuze and Guattari as part of no whole. Deleuze and Guattari (52–53) praise the "marvelous discovery of partial objects" by Melanie Klein, but they criticize her for not having seen the logic of these objects. In particular, they find fault in Klein's idea that partial objects recall a whole, be it an original one or one that has not yet been constituted.

Barthes's concept of the fetish posits a realm separate from both the imaginary and the symbolic that controls certain versions of textuality and desire, and he posits "writing" as the locus in which desire and textuality coexist without having to relate to transcendental signifiers and without the pressure of a whole brought to bear on the parts, for they are parts of no whole. It is a field where the flows of desire and textuality both occur: "The text you write must prove to me *that it desires me*. This text exists: it is writing. Writing is the science of the blisses of language, its Kama Sutra; there is only one treatise to this science, writing itself" (*PT* 13–14). This field is defined like no other, for its gaps are as significant as its markable figures. Composed neither of whole lines nor of broken ones, the field of the text, that is to say, the erotic field, has intermittence as its figure, simultaneously metaphor and metonymy. Like a series of incidents, the intermittent figures are arranged so that one reads a phantom whole from the intermittent parts. But the phantom whole is neither real nor valid:

> In perversion (the realm of textual pleasure), there are no "erogenous zones" (frankly a rather annoying expression); it is intermittence, as psychoanalysis said so well, that is erotic: that of the skin shining between two pieces of clothing (pants and a sweater), between two edges (the open shirt, the glove and the sleeve); it is the very flash itself that seduces, or the staging of an appearance and disappearance. (*PT* 19)

Barthes combines Proust's "intermittences of the heart" and Freud's *fort/da* into a single figure that arches over the combined realms of the textual and the sexual. So the figure of the text is both the dotted line and the whole line existing simultaneously as two borders. The whole line repeats the canon, gives the denotative meaning, and allows entry into the text. At a different level, this whole line gives the rules of cruising, the places to go, and the protocols to follow. The other line, the dotted line, intermittent, unseizable, fading as the subject, marks the loci of its own absences. Elsewhere, it is the cruising itself, the game, and the incidents that follow no rules except those of desire: "As textual theory says, language is redistributed. But *this redistribution is always done by cuts*. Two edges are traced: a wise, conformist, plagiaristic one . . . and *another edge*, mobile, empty (able to take any shape whatsoever)" (*PT* 14).

Superimposed one upon the other, endlessly struggling, the two borders give themselves up in a will to jouissance: "The text's *brio* (without which there is no text) would be its *will to bliss*" (*PT* 25). But will is not enough; jouissance is impossible as a guiding motif for textuality. Despite the rallying cry of Deleuze and Guattari, we are still imprisoned in figures of Oedipal textuality. Pleasure will have to be enough, since the text of jouissance is impossible (*PT* 37). It is an untenable and impossible text, out of reach of both pleasure and criticism. If it exists, it is "always already" premature; nothing can be done with it. Sign of death, the jouissance of the text is better glimpsed than sought: "The text's bliss is not precarious, it is worse yet: *premature* [*précoce*]" (*PT* 84). Alternating between his own precocity and his lateness, between premature ejaculations and latent textuality, Barthes produces a text and a sexuality that mutually define each other, that theorize each other, and that interpret each other: "it pearls, hails, caresses, shreds, cuts: it comes" (*PT* 105).[9]

9. For more on Barthes and homosexuality, see my *Alcibiades at the Door*.

Renaud Camus: Paris/Rome

Nouveau venu, qui cherches Rome en Rome
Et rien de Rome en Rome n'aperçois . . .
Rome de Rome est le seul monument,
Et Rome Rome a vaincu seulement.

Joachim Du Bellay, *Les Antiquités de Rome*

I. On (not) Being a Homosexual Writer

Since Renaud Camus is less familiar than the other three authors covered in this study, a quick overview of his work will be useful. His best-known book is *Tricks*, a series of short narratives about brief sexual encounters and one-night stands. The work first appeared in late 1978 to critical acclaim in some circles, though others found the book's frank and unproblematic amorality indecent. Equally scandalous for some was the fact that the book appeared with the imprimatur of the Nouvelle Critique. the preface was written by no less august a figure than Roland Barthes. In his introduction Barthes notes, undoubtedly to *épater les bourgeois*, that "Renaud Camus's stories are *neutre*" (*T* 15). Camus has liberated himself from the oppression of the doxa. It is not that he is thumbing his nose at the polite, yet hypocritical, bourgeoisie. Camus violates no laws of etiquette. It is rather that the stories of sexual escapades are told as if there were nothing, but absolutely nothing, wrong with sex, and a fortiori with homosexual sex. There is no apology, nor is there any titillation. These are simple stories simply told. Ultimately, the *neutre* stance is generic: this book is a series of narrated incidents unframed by the generic constraints of the confessional genre that one would otherwise expect. Missing are the posturing of John Rechy's *Numbers*, the narcissism of pornography in general (though *Tricks* shares the iterative quality of much pornography), the politics of betrayal of Jean Genet, and the confessional, apologetic, or explanatory modes of Proust and Gide. Never disguising its own comfortable amorality, *Tricks* is a text pleased with itself.

Aside from *Tricks*, the oeuvre of Camus currently consists of about a score of prose volumes that fall into a few broad categories. The earliest works are several experimental novels that seem to be partly autobiographical and partly fictional. These include *Passages* and *Eglogues*, whose experimental character, in the style of the post–*nouveau roman*, consists of a complicated *mise-en-texte* of imbrications, framings, and high degrees of self-reflexivity and self-consciousness, all of which have been discussed by Jan Baetens in his recent book, *Les Mesures de l'excès*. Second is a pair of historical novels, *Roman roi* and *Roman furieux*, that relate the history of a fictional Balkan nation and its rulers during the twentieth century. There is also a collection of lengthy prose poems, his elegies, currently five in number. The next group consists of collections of essays, notes, fulminations, musings, and autobiographical pieces that are acute observations of life and often subtle and wry commentaries on the subcultures of homosexuality, its social codes and behaviors, its semiotics, and its various manifestations in France and the United States. These works include *Buena Vista Park*, *Notes achriennes*, *Chroniques achriennes*, and *Journal d'un voyage en France*. They are the work of a *moraliste*, someone who observes and comments on morals and mores. Finally, there are the diaries, whose contents overlap the essays in many ways.

The *Journal romain*, a diary published in 1987, has been followed by several other diaries, including *Vigiles* published two years later, and the recent *Aguets* and *Fendre l'air*. The *Journal romain* is a lengthy diary of a two-year stay in Rome and is partly the Italian continuation of *Journal d'un voyage en France*, with commentaries on travel, culture, and gay mores. But whereas the earlier work takes the reader through France by means of a narrative whose structure comes from dates, days, and roads, *Journal romain* takes a distinctly different path. In subtle and brilliant ways, *Journal romain* is, to my mind, the meeting ground for the various genres with which Camus has previously dealt. Its text has a complicated rhetorical system that intertwines three strains of discourse: the discourse of history, here seen as the writing of Rome itself; the discourse of power, whose specific form is the discourses of and about homosexuality and hence the discourses by and against the doxa; and the particular personal discourse of the writing ego, including the forms taken by the author's writing. *Journal romain* is also the post–nouveau roman version of the writing subject: the structures and codes are as complicated as ever, but moved from the consideration of the object to the wrapping and unwrapping of the subject. Just as Barthes moves from examining structures in the sixties to considering the writing subject in the seventies, Camus moves from the experimental novel to the experimental subject.

This book is the story of the confrontation of a Frenchman and, metonymically, of French logic with Roman law. *Journal romain* faces off against the laws and discourses of Rome, sets them up against each other, and tries to resolve their contradictions, not the least of which is the opposition of the general to the individual. For example, Italy has not had laws against homosexuality since the implementation of the Napoleonic Code, so how is it possible, Camus constantly wonders, for almost every individual instance of homosexuality to be subject to an enormous amount of self-repression and self-censorship? How does one negotiate the gulf between this legal freedom and the simultaneous, stronger social repression? Camus's problem throughout is that he faces this question by relating it not to his individual situation, in which he is free to be homosexual, but to his craft as a writer. How can each individual instance of discourse be free? What constraints are placed on a discourse by genre and gender, or by Rome itself?

There is an additional wrinkle to this mise-en-scène, for, along with writing *Journal romain*, Camus is simultaneously writing a historical novel, *Roman furieux*, the sequel to *Roman roi*. So while the singularity of discourse is constantly subjected to the transcendental signifier of history and the laws of order thereby imposed by the narrative, Camus spends much of his time writing a diary of his life in Rome, a textual production as far away from the order of history as possible. It is soon clear to the reader that *Journal romain* is the "proof" of Camus's writing. It is both the display of the writer's consciousness of his craft and an autocritique of a discourse that has heretofore brought into question neither its own means of production nor its powers of discourse. It is not even the transcendental signifier of history that is causing a problem but its grandest synecdoche: Rome itself. Camus wonders and worries whether his writing will be sufficient for describing Rome adequately. And since it seems to be Rome that brings the very matter of writing to a head, it is to Rome that we will eventually turn in the second half of this chapter.

But before going to Rome, I would like to stay closer to home and look at the discourses of homosexuality, the role of the author as homosexual or as a homosexual writer, the possible incarnations of that author, and the kinds of texts that he might produce. All of these words and categories are problematic for Camus; one might say that Camus's major project as a writer is to investigate how these categories and problems all play out.

Like Barthes, whose pupil he was, Camus plays with the words he uses to make his point as he subverts and overturns meanings in repeated attempts to rid the text of the weight of the doxa. Let us take the best, most indicative example: the word "homosexual" has no meaning in and of itself for Camus. Alone, the word is meaningless; opposed to "heterosexual," the word "homosexual" becomes immediately subject to the doxa. Whatever meaning it may have comes from an implicit or explicit difference from its paired other, "heterosexual," but the latter word dominates the pair. Consequently, the meaning of "homosexual" is a marginalized, secondary one; its connotations are by and large negative. The meaning of the word and even the signifier itself are always dominated by the power grids, the doxa, and the discourses of repression that heterosexuality uses to perpetuate itself. Camus realizes one capital thing when it is clear to him that "homosexual" is always subject to a doxa: even within the dyad, the word can have no *intrinsic* meaning. The dominant member of the couple always exerts force on the marginalized member, engulfs it, and makes it parasitic on the definition of the dominant term.

This polemical position may appear to some to be an argument against a straw man, for it hardly seems reasonable to consider that heterosexuality is a unified monolith. But as we have already seen with Barthes, each instance of heterosexual discourse can be easily assimilated to the image of the doxa. Strategically, Camus needs to perceive heterosexuality as a monolith in order to underscore the a priori marginalization of his own type of discourse. Surely the word "heterosexual" makes as little sense as the word "homosexual"; the former term also gets its meaning from being part of an opposition. The difference is that heterosexuality is not parasitic on itself but tautological. At least on the surface, the doxa appears to serve as a support for almost every individual instance of heterosexual discourse. Heterosexuality is subject to its own doxology, and the tautology is just a more subtle way of forcing false identifications. For example, just as "homosexuality" covers two very disparate, general phenomena, desire between men and desire between women, heterosexuality includes both the desire of a man for a woman and the desire of a woman for a man. Surely no more disparate situations exist than this immoderate mixture that includes both desires by and for the "opposite" sex. One could hypothesize that the desire of a man for a woman is more similar to the desire of a man for another man than it is to the desire of a woman for a man. In other words, the various male structurings of desire are more similar than are the heterosexual male and female structurings of desire. But in order to attack the doxa iconoclastically, Camus has to start with the received definitions and those divide the world into heterosexual and homosexual, not into male and female desire.

Camus is a canny writer who needs the transparency of the argument in order to make us think more clearly. The straw-man argument about "heterosexuality" needs to be seen as such in order for him to reinforce the problems with and definitions and critiques of words like "homosexual." Without Camus's straw-man definitions of heterosexuality, even a sympathetic reader might be tempted to give a passing nod to the author's arguments while maintaining a view of homosexuality that is still implicitly subject to the doxa, and which thereby still maintains a marginality, albeit a more subtle one. In other words, because the argument about the monolith of heterosexuality is so obviously weak, we are led to question the aptness of any generic label, especially that of "homosexuality."

What can be said for the word "homosexual" can be said for "discourse" and even more so for the combination of the two words. Camus denies the possibility of giving meaning to the phrase "homosexual discourse," since it is not at all clear who would do the "giving" in this bestowal of meaning. The definition of "homosexual discourse" by a largely heterosexual world sees that discourse as being *fundamentally* oppositional. On the other hand, while Camus clearly acknowledges the act of repression by heterosexuality or heterosexual discourse and constantly rails against that repression, homosexual writing is only *secondarily* oppositional for him, as a result or by-product of the confrontation of textuality with a doxa that "always already" marginalizes homosexual discourses. But this opposition is no more intrinsic than it would be in a heterosexual text; homosexual discourse is different, just as every heterosexual discourse is different.

Camus's position is a strategic mixture that includes the straw man of monolithic heterosexuality and a faux-naïf protestation of the innocence of his work. Certainly, in the ideal textual world the difference of his text would be the same kind of difference that subtends any heterosexual text. In the practical world of heterosexual definitions, where the dominant discourse wields accreted power, the difference is inseparably seconded by an oppositional or political difference. Any erasure of that second difference would place his text in the Arcadian realm of shepherds and bucolic catamites, far from the very self-aware position from which he writes. For all its self-proclaimed innocence, *Tricks* is hardly Camus's written version of "Et in Arcadia ego." Again, the strategy is transparent: Camus certainly gives a value and a meaning to his own writing projects which are, to say the least, fully informed by the questions of homosexuality. Why else write?

For Renaud Camus, the subject of homosexuality is endless, constantly changing, and ubiquitous. When he says that "it writes itself [*il s'écrit*]" every day (*CA* 9), we should understand this, too, not merely as a reflexive verb substituting for a seldom-used French passive, but as a verb in the middle voice. The writing of homosexuality is the inscription of homosexuality as the subject and object of discourse, a constant spinning of language and not merely something separate from language, something that one just writes about. The writing of homosexuality changes each day as the subject changes, as it changes the subject in its own production. What might appear serious to Barthes becomes playful to Camus since this discourse of homosexuality, that of a constantly changing subject, is also the writing of desire, as desire is filtered through the consciousness of a writing subject.

Writing a constantly changing, ever-desiring subject means not casting the subject within the prison of a doxa. The easiest way to maintain the necessary playfulness is to use forms that avoid the processes of totalization. Though the early novels have numerous formal, self-reflexive structures, they are punctuated by endless imbrications, shifts, quotations, and internal references. The complication of the game effectively prevents the constitution of the subject as a whole. When discussing homosexuality thereafter, Camus preferentially uses genres that guarantee more formlessness than form, more mutation and metamorphosis than structure. Camus chooses fragments and diary entries as his preferred forms; strung together by loose parataxis in the former case and by the neutral chronology of a calendar in the latter, the fragments remain signs of a constantly changing discourse and subject. Sometimes the form chooses him: the chronicle proposed by the editors of *Gai Pied* is seductive because it combines the writing of desire at the core of Camus's writerly project with a desire that is "fooling around [*désir en baguenaudage*]."

Each bit of writing is a trick, as is each act of reading, for this performance definitely occurs on a two-way street. The reader's act "cannot be entirely placed under the superego of value and conscientious deciphering. He has the right—and even if he didn't he'd take it—to wild appropriation, to phantasmic investment, to uncontrolled transposition" (*NA* 114). Nowhere is the trick more in evidence than in the aleatory adventures of this writing subject. Roland Barthes chooses the terms "seduction" and "cruising" as metaphors for his writing; Camus goes one step further, as the metaphor is carried out and through into its accomplishment as a trick, an action that demetaphorizes the metaphor. Each fragment, each note, and each daily chronicle is an anonymous trick with his imaginary readers who then may or may not go on to form stronger bonds with the text. The reader's desire magnifies the anonymous relation into "something *beyond* the trick: affairs, friendships, sexual camaraderie, superficial and deep relationships, marriage. The trick would thus be the minimal degree of a relation in this realm" (*T* 20–21).

In the ideal world of free-floating desire, homosexuality would be on an equal footing with heterosexuality: the two would have absolutely equal rights. Obviously this is not at all the case, and if it were, Camus probably would not be the remarkable writer that he is. As it stands, however, there are three aspects of the doxological dominance of heterosexuality that provide a target or ground for Camus. In a certain sense, Camus needs heterosexuality for his writing, but he does his best to minimize that need: he takes on the doxology and he deconstructs the opposition. Finally, he stakes out a territory for the subject based both on those two negative moments of opposition and deconstruction and on the positive flow of the individual's desire.

First of all, for Camus, heterosexuality uses its accrued power to dominate with its doxa. Not content with simply being the category for the sexual orientation of the majority, heterosexuality presents itself as having precedence, as having priority, and as being transcendental over each individual instance of (hetero)sexuality: heterosexuality reproduces whereas homosexuality is nominally sterile. Camus does his best to combat the orthodox ideology of heterosexual dominance by showing its prejudices, its hypocrisies, and its smugness, doing so with the very tools of dominance: "I rise neither against society nor against morality, but on the contrary, I rely on them, ideally, to criticize society and morality where they stand" (*NMT* 104).

Second, Camus constantly underlines that for him, both heterosexuality and homosexuality are fictional categories whose presumed monolithic nature should be deconstructed along with the opposition that sets one against the other: the pair homosexuality/heterosexuality is not an elemental binary. Moreover, each individual act (of writing, of sex) should be nominally free of the constraints of genre and gender. Third, as a writer Camus needs to remark his own singularity through his writing: he must thus use various means to refuse being pigeonholed as a "homosexual writer" merely writing for a like-minded reader caught in some discursive, linguistic, and social ghetto. This complicated rhetorical mise-en-scène of his project as a writer allows Camus to question all the preconceived oppositions taken as received knowledge, while not for one moment falling into the trap of believing his own position is somehow one of absolute truth.

Camus shows that he is acutely conscious of the fictionality of every position. After a long paragraph on freedom, for example, he writes: "I thought we'd never get out of that and that I was going to have to imitate Origen" (*FA* 123). Then, as elsewhere, Camus uses a strategy of false naïveté to get where he is going: one might say that the master trope of his work is sincere irony, its master emotion ironic sincerity. Camus often says that he is doing nothing different or strange but rather something completely innocent and wholesome. Such a remark usually comes after he has just told his reader about having spent a night in anonymous tricking in the parks of Paris, in a back room in a Florentine bar, or on the hills of Rome.

Most of the time, Camus takes a stand and refuses the traditional discourses about homosexuality, as liberal as these discourses might be. Even in the most generous case, Camus believes, it is specious to argue that homosexuality is a variant of the dominant discourse or the dominant sexuality. As well as rejecting the secondary status accorded to homosexuality by its critics or even a number of its apologists, Camus rejects a situation whereby heterosexuality is considered to be the zero degree of a situation in which homosexuality is the marked variant. It is simply not enough for the doxa to be generous, liberal, and understanding when faced with homosexuality. Commenting on a review in *Pariscope*, a weekly guide to cultural events in Paris, Camus remarks the magazine's use of the expression "homosexual film." Like "black film" or "feminist film," such labeling does not advance the cause of equality because it is only the marginalized member of a dyad that is marked, however generously that may be: "What might a 'heterosexual film' be for *Pariscope*? Those words are meaningless" (*CA* 177).

Homosexuality should therefore not be considered as the marked variant of a neutral, zero-degree discourse that passes invisibly because of its ubiquity. The omnipresent discourse of heterosexuality maintains its power through its diffusion into every available space, except for the marginalized ghetto space it allows for homosexuality and its discourses. And of course that very ghetto space is circumscribed by heterosexual discourse and power: that is precisely what makes it a ghetto. No matter how much freedom is allowed within the ghetto, be it geographic or discursive, Camus feels that the division must be overcome. If this ghetto space is part of an eventual dialectic, some resolution or synthesis must be reached, for the antithesis that defines the ghetto space is always minor: "The ghetto stage is indispensable, but it is necessary to go beyond it" (*CA* 34).

The only valid categorization for discourse or behavior that Camus accepts is that of the "sexual," in which homosexuality and heterosexuality are not versions of one another but two equally possible subcategories of sexuality. If the discourse of the "sexual" and not that of the "heterosexual" were all-pervasive, heterosexual discourse would lose its primacy. Does this really exist? Of course not. But for his purposes, Camus can hypothesize a general sexual discourse that would not necessarily be determined by its object, be it real or ideational. He has gone part of the way toward this general discourse since the primacy ascribed to heterosexuality has already disappeared, if it ever was present, for Camus as reader and as writer. Heterosexuality has no prestige in his eyes, since there is nothing *intrinsically* valuable about it. Moreover, Camus bears ill will toward those with an attitude of noblesse oblige, an attitude that dominates in certain heterosexual circles and which is subtly emulated in the realms of homosexuality. Camus sees no virtue in adopting any of the models and values proposed to homosexuality by heterosexuality:

> Sometimes I think that I am the only queer who likes queers, and for whom heterosexuality as such, even that of an eventual lover, is completely without prestige. A more or less liberal, adventuresome, frustrated or drunk heterosexual who would "allow" me to do this or that to him means nothing to me. I have no desire to be "accorded" anything, as in old-fashioned heterosexuality. (*CA* 12)

In providing the dominant mode, heterosexuality has made certain assumptions about its own naturalness and about the behavior patterns associated with it. Camus does not accept the "give-and-take" behavior associated with heterosexuality, which is raised by that dominant behavior and discourse to the status of being considered "natural." By refusing to accept the corollaries of heterosexual behavior and by insisting that homosexual behavior is absolutely equivalent, Camus attempts to undo the current divisions of the "sexual."

By removing all aspects of the opposition between heterosexual and homosexual along with the attendant protocols, then, Camus hopes to propose a new way of looking at the world. If space were filled with an undifferentiated discourse of the sexual, the very categorization of space or text based on sexuality would soon disappear: "The sexual would not demand any particular discursive status or any independence for itself. It would deny itself as a category and would promise its own destruction" (*CA* 34). The only way for a sexual discourse to continue to function as a mechanism of power is for it to separate and label its various manifestations as ranked categories and marked and unmarked varieties of sexuality and discursivity. Again we seem to be in the throes of a straw-man argument. Camus is positing the dissolution of the patterns of dominance associated with the dyad of heterosexuality and homosexuality. Instead of that dyad, he proposes "the sexual" as an undifferentiated amalgam or conglomeration. Obviously, without differentiation the category as such would have no discursive power and thus would disappear as a means of decision. At the same time, one could think of the argument as a means of making the division between sexualities into nothing more intrinsically meaningful than a range of hair tints or eye colors. Camus needs a straw-man argument in order to point to the deep-rooted dogma, belief, and protocols that surround the division of "innocent" sexuality.

As we have already briefly mentioned, the word "discourse" is problematic for Camus because it entails both a freedom and a constraint. Certainly the "accepted" discourses of homosexuality evince a certain tendency toward incompletion because they tend to be fragmentary. Their constantly marginalized status pushes them toward the aleatory, the random, and the "tricks" of life. But in opposition, there are discourses that remove the freedom of the aleatory even more easily than it is attained. The problem is that a certain discourse of "wooden language" and of stultified systems of prose completely misses the object of desire:

> I have a problem really respecting a discourse that I recognize as a discourse, that is to say, as a constraint and not as a freedom; one that has obviously been forced on the speaker, one he has not chosen; and one that, as soon as I have figured out its premises, I can easily—and more rigorously—complete myself.[1] (*NA* 104–5)

For desire to be realized there can be no constraints on its vehicle, nor any limits imposed as a system of choices that exist before desire finds its form in language. If the possibilities exist before language, the discourse that eventually comes to be used is a parasitic text reproducing a discourse of power that marginalizes, separates, and determines the parameters of the subject. No longer free to make his own choices as a gay writer/desirer, the subject has his place usurped by one of two discourses of power or

1. Barthes says the same thing in a fragment entitled "Predictable Discourse": "The boredom of predictable discourses. Predictability is a structural category, as it is possible to give the modes of waiting or connecting (in short: of suspense) of which language is the scene (it has been done for the story); a typology of discourses could be founded relating to their degree of predictability. *The Book of the Dead*: the text as litany, in which not a word can be changed.

"Yesterday evening, after having written that: in the restaurant, at the very next table, two individuals speak, not loudly, but clearly, cleanly, mellifluously, as if an elocution school had prepared them to be heard by neighbors in public: everything they say, sentence after sentence (on some first names of their friends, on the last film of Pasolini), everything is absolutely in order, predicted: not a flaw in the endoxal system. The agreement of this voice that chooses no one and of the inexorable Doxa: that is *the gift of the gab* [*jactance*]." (*RB* 152)

even both of them working together repressively. The more obvious of the two is the discourse of heterosexual power that marginalizes an authentic homosexual discourse or reduces that voice to a secondary, even parasitic status. Less obvious, however, is a ghettoized homosexual discourse that accepts its marginalization because there is a certain free play within that eccentric space. For Camus this is not authentic free play: the rules limit the game and the wall protecting the ghetto is always erected from the outside. Chosen before the subject, the object of desire or of language is a product of this unacceptable ghettoization.

On the surface, then, the phrase "*écrivain homosexuel*" has no inherent meaning for Camus but functions instead as a constraint on his discourse. Calling Camus a "homosexual writer" is to label him in a way that excludes his being, for example, a writer from the Auvergne or a writer who reached the age of majority about 1968 (*NA* 138). More significant is that this label maintains the marginality of the writer in a category determined for him by the dominant discourse: thus there are "black writers," "feminist writers," and "homosexual writers." It behooves all of them to play by the discursive rules of the space allotted to them by male heterosexual writers who, in addition, determine the quotas for each category.

Such "minority" writers may choose not to play by the rules of the game. Some, though not Camus, choose an act of revisionism that reorders the space of writing, reverses polarities, and promotes its own secondariness as an intrinsic value. In such work, marginality itself is ironically celebrated as a central value; the fringe status of the writing becomes the defining moment of the work of outlaw writers. In the realm of the "homosexual writer," obvious examples are William Burroughs, John Rechy, and, perhaps most notably, Jean Genet, whose homosexuality, for Camus, "resembles too much the one imagined and depicted by his worst enemies" (*NA* 132). If, for Camus, the expression of "male heterosexual writer" is ridiculous, then any similar expression is equally meaningless: Genet's well-documented, even caricatural version of Sartrean bad faith in becoming a "male homosexual writer" is anathema to Renaud Camus.

This does not mean that Camus cannot take advantage of the codes and games already in place, even if he believes in the need for their ultimate disappearance. The codes of homosexuality serve as an act of liberation that engenders a discourse that helps free him from the doxa: "homosexuality was my moral lucky break" (138). Homosexuality has allowed him to escape from a stultifying cultural envelope, not merely the heterosexuality of the majority but the oppression of the dominant discourses of Catholicism and the bourgeoisie. Having escaped "the incomprehensible animosity, the segregation, the violence, and the humiliation of racism" (*NA* 138), Camus feels that he can know them. How does this knowledge come to him? It is a combination of the discourses of dominance and the dissemination of these discourses through a power grid.

Once again Camus uses exaggeration for effect, for "racism" is perhaps somewhat of an exaggeration for the purposes of his argument. Though in a white, male-dominated society one can never be invisible as a woman or as a black, the case of a "homosexual" is different. Subject in France to local, if not legal, repression, homosexuality can still be "invisible." As Tony Duvert ironically remarks, there is a "*bon homo*" who "respects laws, the majority, the minority. . . . He does not cruise, does not masturbate, keeps his anus closed, disdains penises, especially when erect." For Duvert (67), the good "homo" is nothing but a "conservative and sexually modest heterocrat."[2] The possibility of being simultaneously visible and

2. The reader interested in Duvert's ironic descriptions of good and bad "homos" is referred to another essay in the same collection, entitled "The Seven Deadly Sins" (133–58). Camus and Duvert are not always in agreement, but Camus certainly agrees with Duvert's critique of "heterocracy" (*NA* 93).

An anonymous reader's report for this manuscript stated that I should tell my readers that Camus and Duvert are the same person. Without some inside knowledge, there is no reason a priori to think that they are one and the same, but there is a confusion in names that leaves the answer a bit murky. Aside from *Tricks*, many people are familiar with Camus through the pages about him in the special issue of *Yale French Studies* devoted to contemporary French fiction. In their introduction to Camus, Pierre Force and Dominique Jullien (288) credit Tony Duvert with being a pseudonymous coauthor with Camus of the latter's early work. Perhaps Force and Jullien know this; perhaps they were led to that belief or to that typographical error by the name game of some of Camus's early work, which includes *Travers*, by Renaud Camus and Tony Duparc and *Eté (Travers II)*, by Jean-Renaud Camus and Denis Duvert. Yet on the next page, Force and Jullien list the titles and "authors" correctly.

So are they or are they not the same person? There seems to be confusion on both sides of the Atlantic. As far as I know, Camus has always written about Duvert as if they were different people, though that is obviously no guarantee. For example, in the latest volume of the diaries, *Fendre l'air*, in response to a question from Pierre Léglise-Costas, who had heard that Duvert and Camus had lived together for a long time, Camus says that this was not at all the case (*FA* 385–86). In fact, Camus dislikes Duvert's *Abécédaire malveillant* and is not at all favorable to the prose "of someone who dragged me through the mud." So it would seem that they are different people and that they are not even friends. But in the same volume, Camus twice mentions the article in *Yale French Studies*, and calls it a "nice, long article" (*FA* 298) and a "long, favorable study" (*FA* 390). Since Camus is usually extremely particular about factual details, one might assume that the so-called misprint of "Tony Duvert" in *YFS* is getting his tacit approval. In a personal letter to me (Feb. 18, 1993), Camus writes as follows:

> I completely missed the misinformation contained in the article of *Yale French Studies*. I think it is a typographical error, quite excusable insofar as, among Denis Duvert, Tony Duparc, Denis Duparc, and Tony Duvert, people, and I among them, truly tend to get mixed up. But, once again . . .
>
> Not only are Tony Duvert and I certainly not the same person, nor even friends, but also, as far as I know, we have never met.

In any case, I am going to assume that these two names refer to different authors, whether

invisible and of playing in a phantom zone that is imperceptibly beyond the "good" realm of heterosexuality is precisely what allows for an understanding of both power systems from within. The "homosexual" writer whose homosexuality is only spelled out in invisible ink can still participate in a dominant culture. By virtue of the fact that the writer is never invisible to himself, he can begin to understand that dominant discourse from outside, without *necessarily* being in the position of writing an oppositional discourse. Seated ultimately in both camps, the homosexual writer "beset by signs," as Harold Beaver (104) notes, is able to subvert a sexual dialectic between homosexuality and heterosexuality and substitute a parallel discourse for that dialectic.

The specificity of Camus's "homosexual writing" is found in the parallel aspect of that discourse and not in some presumed oppositional practice. For if he does not see what "homosexual writing" might be (*NA* 138), it is precisely because he determines a position for his writing that is neither secondary to nor parasitic on heterosexual discourse. Although for Camus the phrase "heterosexual writing" is as meaningless as "homosexual writing," the effects of the power of heterosexual discourses are hardly negligible. Heterosexual discourse fills the space of the world and disseminates its power therein; at best, it allows a margin within which homosexual discourse might operate. Since he sees the discourse of homosexuality as something that at least potentially coexists with the discourses of heterosexuality by occupying the same space and marking the same world, Camus continues to refuse that marginality.

How then does one explain the relation between homosexuality and heterosexuality here? More precisely, what is the relation of their discourses and their power grids? If homosexuality is posited as equipotential with heterosexuality, both as a practice and as a discourse, the discourse of homosexuality potentially describes the same space as that covered by heterosexual discourse. It is as if there were two maps of the same territory, or two speeches, one in French and one in English, that described the same object. Certainly, the discourses are neither globally nor locally exactly the same, but there is an approximate equivalence between the two.

---

or not they inhabit the same body. One could, I suppose, argue the contrary, as was the case for the person who argued that Wanda Landowska, Isak Dinesen, and Edith Sitwell were all the same person, since no one had ever seen a photo of all three of them together. One of Camus's own favorite authors is the many-named Portuguese author Fernando Pessoa. Still, Camus himself seems to distinguish between "Renaud Camus" and his various pseudonyms on the one hand and an "other" person named "Tony Duvert." Since my interest is in what "Renaud Camus" writes, I shall leave "Tony Duvert" to other critics.

The absent object can be described in either discourse just as desire can be effectively communicated in either. Yet if the two discourses are alternatively possible, they are not simultaneously compossible either within the individual producer of discourse or within the space of discourse in general. A discourse can be either homosexual or heterosexual but not simultaneously both; it can alternate, even within the same sentence (as is often the case in Sade), but at any given moment there is only one possibility. From within the walls of omnipresent heterosexual discourse, the reader perceives homosexual discourse as being other and elsewhere: "Homosexuality is always elsewhere because it is everywhere. It always has another face because it has none of its own" (*NA* 24).

There is a distinction to be made in the relation of the words "homosexual" and "writing." On the one hand, there are the expressions "homosexual" and "heterosexual *writing*," as fixed, closed fields of language in which homosexuality constantly reinforces its own marginalization and thematization and in which heterosexuality constantly reinforces the doxa. On the other hand, there are open discourses, not fixed *langues de bois* but rather languages whose power relates to their own means and acts of expression. Still, *as a category*, "homosexual writing" makes no sense to Camus because it is predicated on two false assumptions. First of all, the concept presumes some essence to homosexuality that preexists discourse. Second, it presumes that this essence is translatable into writing, as if the signified of homosexuality could be directly reflected in a set of signifiers. But there is no essence to homosexuality; it does not precede the codes that (re)define it each day, be they externally imposed or self-generated: "Homosexuality does not preexist as an unchangeable territory that one would only have to recognize once and for all in all the details of its eternal truth. New with each new glance and with every word, it is what we make of it each day" (*NA* 11).

The intellectual filiation from Sartre through Barthes to Camus is manifest in such postexistentialist definitions of homosexuality. Though the situation of a "pederast" during the Occupation was necessarily more closeted than Camus's post-1968 freedom, part of Jean-Paul Sartre's initial discussion of homosexuality in the chapter on bad faith in *L'Etre et le néant* could still be applied to Camus's own perception of his homosexuality. Sartre (100) says that the homosexual would be correct in saying that he is not *a* homosexual in the following situation:

He would be right if he understood the sentence: "I am not (a) homosexual [*pédéraste*] as "I am not what I am." That is to say, if he declared: "To the extent that a series of behaviors are defined as the conduct of a homosexual, and to the extent that I have behaved in that way, I am a homosexual. To the extent that human reality escapes all definitions by behavior, I am not."

Sartre goes on to say that such a person would be in bad faith if he continued to believe that he was not a pederast *en soi*, that is to say, if that given status of being homosexual were refused. Obviously, Camus would part from Sartre here, much as another Camus had once done, because Sartre's concept of the *en soi* of homosexuality (where heterosexuality would be constituted as a *pour soi*) does not allow, at least for Renaud Camus, the infinite variety of being described by his constantly changing engagement in the world.

Finally, then, for Renaud Camus, the only valid definition one can give to homosexuality relates to its encoding and not to its signified. All one can do is deal with the various codes that frame sexuality: "Homosexuality has no natural mode of existence. It has only codes that it chooses, invents, or undergoes" (*NA* 164). The great difference then can be simply put: heterosexuality believes itself to be natural; homosexuality, at least in Camus's eyes, knows that heterosexuality is as unnatural as homosexuality. Camus's recent remark on the "natural" brings the point home: "I never have spoken of a *natural* innocence of sexuality, even if I spoke of absolute innocence. I even took care to indicate that, for me, innocence, just like the *natural*, was a long and difficult conquest" (*FA* 122).

If there are only codes, the point is not to have an additional discourse on homosexuality, but to determine what language can be used by the writer-who-happens-to-be-gay. Camus wants to be able to "choose" or "invent"; he wants to be able to refuse forcible submission to the discourses of the other. For whatever voice homosexuality might have and whatever styles with which it might write, be they shared or not with the dominant discourse, the writer must first free the discursive praxes and their contents from the system of dominance. That too is "a long and difficult conquest" because there is a tendency to let oneself go toward the multifarious incarnations of the doxa, as many seem sweet and seductive. But all reflect a position that involves the revitalization of a marginal and secondary status for homosexuality. Thus, acceding even to the most seductive of doxological positions means, *en fin de compte*, giving in to a measure of self-loathing, to a definition of the self from a totally alien position.

Camus categorically refuses the internalization of this image that Sartre would call the bad faith of the *en soi* or that Althusser would call interpellation:

Being disgusted by homosexuality has an echo within homosexuality itself, relative to everything that designates it. It is thus endlessly confronted by the same eternal vocabulary problem: take up the enemy's words as a challenge, words stained with his disdain, with his ignorance, with his stupidity, or invent other words. (*NA* 72–73)

Any sign of this interpellated image is to be combated. Thus Camus professes himself shocked at gay men who define themselves as "*vicieux*" in graffiti, personal ads, the Minitel, or on the *téléphone rose*, the phone lines used for making sexual contacts. Even though the word "*vicieux*" does not mean "vicious," but describes someone who likes "vice," that is, sex, there is still a slippage in connotative meaning from what Camus sees as the innocence of sex to the sinfulness of vice. Thus, as far as Camus is concerned, the word "*vicieux*" is a vestige of oppression by the dominant discourse: "a good example of how the opinions of others are internalized to reflect on your own practices" (*NA* 33).

Still, as one might suspect, the example of "*vicieux*" is not as simple as Camus would have it for the purposes of his arguments. As we have already seen, Camus's examples are seldom as innocent as he would like his readers to believe. Clearly, he does not want to see homosexuality as "vice"; yet in common parlance the word "*vicieux*" applies to "vice" of the homosexual and heterosexual varieties. To drive home the difficulty of extricating oneself from the insistence of the doxa, Camus provides a choice between two unacceptable possibilities. The first sees "*vicieux*" used as an erotic stimulant, for in its naming of itself it names transgression. The very fact of transgression, as Georges Bataille (77–103) would say, adds immeasurably to the jouissance of the act itself. Though not usually a fan of Bataille, Camus (*ES* 244) would agree with this assessment: "But perhaps those given over to it, victims, as are so many others, of the picky erotics of transgression, really need to see themselves as *vicieux* in order to come?" (*NA* 34).

The equally unacceptable choice is a definition that is vapid and/or wrong: "Maybe, in their mouths and minds, '*vicieux*' has nothing of its traditional meaning, and only means 'enterprising,' 'original,' 'inventive [*recherché*],' 'out of the way'" (*NA* 34). Camus needs a word, but it is not there. No other word in French comes close to describing in a more neutral fashion what this word "*vicieux*" connotes. Discourse does not exist in a utopia and a catachresis or dead metaphor may arise in a less than innocent fashion. The development of such a catachresis maintains certain elements of a power grid and thus of a doxa. No word is ever free from the discursive power that engendered it and that continues, in part, to provide its connotations: there are always "leftovers" from another discourse that mark the word for other users. This situation of the *usage* of words, use and abrasion, a usefulness or utility that is always shadowed by a ghost discourse of the doxa, is avowed in *Fendre l'air* (158–59). Railing against a remark of Danielle Darrieux, who speaks of her own "modesty" [*pudeur*], Camus notes that it is impossible to say honestly of oneself that one is "frank," "sincere," "modest [*pudique*]," "naive," "natural." Having entered into a doxology of innocence, the words have become frayed through overuse. Such words, along with "*vicieux*," among others on the other side of the coin, have lost their impact, meaning, and validity.

Camus knows full well that language is never innocent and his polemic, once again, as is the case for his other straw-man arguments, forces us to examine the thrust of his reasoning more closely. The argument makes more sense when we look not at a word but at an individual: not the "good *homo*" whom Duvert describes, but a "bad *homo*." As we have already noted, Camus is fairly strong in his objections to the behavior, writing, and rhetoric of Genet, the most notorious example of the homosexual who lets himself be defined by the discourses of the other. Camus categorically refuses the mantle of notoriety associated with Genet, whom he does not see as a pioneer in gay liberation. Camus is distressed that, like theft or assassination, homosexuality for Genet is no more than a way of provoking hated bourgeois society. Against Genet, but also against various other kinds of apologists and antagonists, Camus makes a simple assertion: "Homosexuality has nothing to do with Evil. It is not a provocation. . . . Quite simply, it just is. It is on the side of pleasure, joy, amusement, affection, and—if we must, we must—love" (*NA* 137). Although there is no real innocence, one can continue to strip language of a number of its noxious effects until a less oppressive discourse emerges, not through law-breaking but through joy.

Thus the demarginalization of homosexuality is a plural event: there must be an examination of the discourses in which it has been encoded in order to liberate it from the image forced on it by dominant discourses. No other action, however politically correct it may be, can reach completion if the discourses already in place are not investigated: "Instead of one more discourse on homosexuality, one should try to recognize existing ones, 'pinning them down,' as Barthes would say" (*NA* 45). By playing discourses off against one another, by finding the secret agenda hidden in the very fact of dominance, an agenda that is often nothing more than self-perpetuation, Camus is militating for a reevaluation of the distribution of power and received knowledge. One might be tempted to think then that Camus is simply going through the motions of revisionism: that having liberated homosexuality from the discourses that constrained it, he finds nothing else to write, no other codes, and no modes in which to talk about this pleasure, joy, or amusement. It would naturally follow that the codes used would be the same as those used by heterosexuality to discuss its own pleasure, joy, or amusement.

Is there a choice then? Or is there a set of invented discourses or chosen textualities in Camus's written realm? What Camus defines as the realm of encoding involves the openness of the textual praxis, its constant reinvention, and its refusal of closure. Like Proust and Barthes before him, Camus uses the floating signs of homosexuality as interpretants for the world. Camus chooses a textuality in which each individual instance of enunciation adds to the code and modifies it. Homosexuality is constantly redefined by every additional homosexual event or act. Concomitantly, homosexuality continually redefines the world, both by forcing the world to recognize the validity of homosexuality and by questioning the assumptions hidden in the semiotic structures of the dominant discourses. In homosexuality, there is no pretension to constructing a whole; every rhetorical move is intended to underline the fragmentary, tricklike nature of the discourse that is constantly in the process of inventing itself:

> The note, the fragment, contradiction, repetition, the "fictional," autobiography, the subjective, quotation, the nuance: thus homosexuality cannot be pinned down as *discourse*, as doctrine, under the illusion of being exhaustive or definitive. Since it is existence before being essence, it is invented every day for everyone, through every meeting and every word.
>
> On the other hand, one could also say, by playing on words, that "homosexuality" is *only* discourse, and hence very recognizable, easily demarcated, and historically and geographically situated (beginning with the term itself, in 1869). (*NA* 26)

Camus's rhetoric is thus doubled: the insistence on the fragment is a way of refusing the image that accompanies the internalization of a dominant discourse while simultaneously creating an encoding of homosexual behavior that is never complete and always partially self-consciously ironic.

One way for this irony to develop is through the invention of a new vocabulary, untainted by the power grid or the repression already in existence. Again, by using a word that is strictly devoid of prior connotations to define a constantly changing category, Camus infuses his definition with irony. Camus invents the word "*achrien*" as an equivalent for the American and now international word "gay." The neologism first appears in his novel *Travers*, published in 1978. He suggests taking seven words "chosen automatically, the first that come to mind" (*Trav* 94). The words are: *Diane*, *archer*, *marque* (mark), *échange* (exchange), *transe* (trance), *signe* (sign) and *vol* (flight or theft). He then picks the seven letters that appear the most often in these words. Making the various possible anagrams, Camus comes up with "achrien" as the neologism of choice. The irony of the situation is readily apparent and is due to the purported idealistic belief that this neologism can banish the other, inadequate words. Obviously this is not to be the case, for even when a new word has been defined, all the other words formerly or concurrently used still seem to be hanging around. The neologism is not invented to describe something new, but to supplant words that are already there but inadequate to the task of describing Camus's perception of homosexuals and homosexuality. The other words do not disappear; ghostlike apparitions, they still remain readable in every use of the new word.

Even the random technique Camus uses to come up with the word touches an ironic note or two. In this scene of automatic writing, he echoes the act of liberation that the Surrealists, and especially the "gay Surrealist," René Crevel, saw in that very process of gaining access to an uncensored psyche. At the same time, the uncensored psyche is anything but random: the uncensored words that appear are rather less than haphazard. If this is true automatic writing, we have gained access to Camus's unconscious mind; if it is a fictional verisimilitude, the words are no more random than before. Once again, there is less innocence than is implied. If the automatic side of the game opens the discourse of consciousness up into that of the unconscious, we can begin to map out the imaginary realm in which this new word occurs: taken together, "Diane" and "archer" recall Saint Sebastian, the early Christian saint martyred by being shot with arrows. Penetrated by the arrows after their flight (*vol*), the body of the saint is marked for all to read. As is the case in the famous Mantegna painting of the saint in the Louvre, Sebastian is usually depicted in a trance, as he is beatified by his martyrdom. In any case, Sebastian passes for being the patron saint of homosexuality.[3] And as for "*échange*," aside from its use as the title of an earlier volume in the series of novels of which *Travers* forms

3. The references to Saint Sebastian in gay literature are legion. Mishima (38–47) relates how his first orgasm occurred as he fantasized about Guido Reni's painting of Saint Sebastian. Later in life Mishima went so far as to have himself photographed in the position of Guido Reni's St. Sebastian. In a completely different realm, though one as theatrical as Mishima's posed photograph, there is Derek Jarman's film *Sebastiane*, which has the distinction of being the only soft-core gay porn film whose dialogue is in Latin. As far as I can tell, there is only one reference to Saint Sebastian in the *Recherche*, where Legrandin is called "a Saint Sebastian of snobbishness" (1: 127).

a part, for Camus the text is the locus of the exchange of flesh for text, of flight for penetration, of hunter for hunted. Site of an eventual sacrifice of the body in favor of discourse, Camus's text is always in the process of defining its own jouissance by explaining the encounters of the writing subject.

Even the letters and pronunciation of the neologism are signs of the texts to come. If the "h" is silent—for Camus intends the word to be pronounced with a hard "c"—all of the author's efforts will be used to make this silent "h," for "homosexuality," speak. On the contrary, if the "h" makes the "c" soft (as in "krach"), something plausible if not intended, the word sounds like "*ache rien*," that is to say, "'h' nothing."[4] Again, the role of the author will be to make something of this nothing and make homosexuality speak in its own voice. But most important, what comes out of a proposed deciphering of an innocent neologism is this: in the realm of sexuality, few words, if any, escape partial determination by a vocabulary with a degree of built-in repression or condemnation. There is no full release from the doxa, and a renaming of parts, though an effort in the right direction, cannot fully change the insistence of the doxa. Even if the word "gay" has gotten general acceptance both in English-speaking and non-English-speaking cultures, it comes at the price of the standard dictionary definition of the word in English.

Not surprisingly, Camus is inconsistent in his militating for or against certain forms of language. The true battle is not there, in the act of nomination. His neologism "*achrien*" never catches on to find general usage; Camus himself eventually uses the word "gay" more often than not. If he rejects repression through words, he does not do so at every turn. As has been noted, he rejects the word "*vicieux*," because of its negative, repressive connotations. But he has no trouble with another word promulgated by *Gai Pied* that is no less repressive in its origins (*NA* 46). He likes their use of *pingouins* ("penguins," in this case male) and the invented *pingouines* ("female penguins") to describe male and female homosexuals respectively. Perhaps he likes these words for their puns. Like the very title of the review that is a play on words between "*gai pied*" and "*guépier*" (wasps' nest), these are a play on words on *gouine*, which means "dyke." Why is *gouines*, which means "dykes" and which comes from the name Nell Gwynn, who

4. In an unpublished interview (May 18, 1988) with me, Camus said that he meant the "h" to be silent. Still, compare *Le Côté de Guermantes* (2: 816): "'—I shall willingly compare the Emperor,' continued the prince, who, not knowing how to pronounce the word 'archaeologist' (that is to say, as if it were written 'kaeologist') never missed an opportunity to use it, 'to an old archaeologist' (and the Prince said arshaeologist) 'whom we have in Berlin.'"

was suspected of that "vice," any less damaging than "*vicieux*"?[5] The difference may be in the ironic turn, a tongue-in-cheek use of the word that defuses the hatred and dissipates the doxological power.

So I would say that the most effective tool Camus finds is the touch of irony that makes language move off the mark of the definite into a realm of ambiguity. Certainly this irony is almost always close at hand in Camus's writing. Even when he is attempting to write a whole book—that is, one not composed of fragments—a historical novel such as *Roman roi*, the text proffers an ironized code. For example, the first three epigraphs in his novel *Roman roi* are attributed to "Odradeck Melin," a book by "Ossip Dork" entitled *Le Cousin de Proust*, and a certain "Landor Thesbar," a transparent anagram of "Roland Barthes," noted by Philippe Roger (36). *Roman roi* is certainly less overtly self-conscious and metaliterary than the flashy earlier novels; it nevertheless remains under the sign of its own self-conscious modernity as an heir to Kafka, to Proust, and to Roland Barthes. Camus's epigraphs are written tongue-in-cheek and intended to be read that way, but in that very play is situated the irony of literary referentiality. In the first case, for example, "Odradek" is the creature in Kafka's tale entitled "Die Sorge des Hausvaters"—that is to say, the cares or worries of a "father/head of the house" (157–58). From that questionable literary paternity, we move to a "dork" who writes about the cousin of Proust and then to the anagrammatic Landor Thesbar, in whose book, *Points d'interrogation* (Question marks) one finds the following definition of a gesture: "Something like the supplement to an act."[6]

Camus writes his novel in the literary space of supplementarity as he invents a geography of the imaginary country of Caronia, abutting on the Black Sea and occupying the area the "real world" allots to Moldova, parts of Ukraine, and Slovakia. This fictional country is precisely a country of fiction, with a city named "Proust" and another named "Silas Marner," written, of course, by a woman named George. The imaginary country also has an area named "Le Horla," a river named "Léda," and a city named

5. For that matter, according to one critic, "dyke," which is a pejorative term, has a "good" etymology, a fact (or supposition) which has not helped one iota. For Grahn (136), the word "dyke" (from "bulldike") comes originally from "Boadicea," a Celtic queen "remembered . . . as the leader of a major Celtic revolt in A.D. 61 against the Roman conquest of the tribal people of Britain." History and etymology guarantee nothing.

6. There are also references to a certain "Denis Smadaj," which, like many other overdetermined words in Camus's work, could be read as an anagram of "Den(n)is J. Adams," but also as an anagram of "Smadja" (*RR* 111). After 1947, Albert Smadja was the part owner of *Combat*, a fact that reminds us of Albert Camus. It was a name familiar to Barthes, and thus, one may assume, eventually to Renaud Camus as well, after Maurice Nadeau invited Barthes to write for *Combat*. See Calvet 104–5.

"Maalox." Another approximate anagram for Roland (Barthes), "Landsor," is the maiden name of the consort of the king of Caronia. Camus uses fiction to highlight the possibility of the free play of discourse within a world that he himself has structured. Through this ludic text, one sees that the theory of fiction for Camus is the same as his theory of "real" existence, and it reminds us of the interpretive model of *Le Côté de Guermantes*: a world can be structured by a set of rules, be they geographic, legal, discursive, psychological, or even the rules of etiquette, without the possibilities of behavior and expression in that world being limited by an automatic insistence of the doxa. Camus's version of freedom is a combined fictional and real version of the social contract, which he opposes to the palpable constraints on freedom imposed by various discourses and power structures.

Ultimately, then, Camus's rejection of "discourse" is itself rhetorical. It is a way of refusing the patterns of oppressive and repressive behavior, which are often self-imposed in what is called "internalized homophobia." These patterns come with the interiorization of a discourse into one's private theater. Camus would be the last to deny that homosexuality gives rise to certain forms of writing. But for him it is important to note that while this writing falls under the generalized sign of inversion, to reaffirm freedom, it must be marked by irony. In Camus's writing irony takes various forms: false naïveté, a tongue-in-cheek attitude, a *préciosité*, a splitting of hairs, and especially "bathmology," which, in a general sense, is the textuality of irony.

In his early book *Buena Vista Park*, Camus is guided by a comment of Roland Barthes's relating to a game of degrees in discourse called "bathmology." Bathmology is a discourse of gapes, gaps, and gazes. Like the gap of a piece of clothing that Barthes sees as the most seductive of poses for the body, the bathmological text for Barthes and for Camus (*BVP* 24) is a difference that measures an opening to a more subtle version of discursive truth and reality. *Buena Vista Park* is a collection of verbal "tricks," heterogeneous fragments relative to instances of discourse by which paradoxes of degree are constituted. The task of the bathmologist, who is defined only insofar as he (or she) is writing, is to remark a degree of difference in discourse; the practice of bathmology clearly takes place in the middle voice. Thus for the bathmologist, discourse has the inherent capability of marking a fourfold difference: an ontological difference from the world it seeks to describe and thus an ontological difference from the *discourse* that is supposed to describe the world; and an epistemological difference from the truth redoubled by the same epistemological difference from the *discourse* of truth.

For Camus, writing is imbued with its origin, the point from which it issues, not merely the objective qualifications of the subject: homosexual, Auvergnat, white male, and so forth, but also the desires, impulses, and drives that do not define a whole subject. Correlates of the desiring machines of *L'Anti-Oedipe*, these drives or desires underlie the discourse or the writing of a subject. The rhetoric of sexuality of that subject undergoes the impact of the various forms of these partial desires: part of me (a desiring machine) desires "X" and that desire is translated into a rhetoric whose focus is the recounting or explanation of the desire. Equally important, however, is that this rhetoric of sexuality can work in nonsexual situations. For example, one can conceive of a work in which the sexuality of a writer remains invisible. But for Camus, such writing would be antiseptic, for "all writing worthy of the name is perceptibly worked upon by drives and desire" (*NA* 139).

The rhetoric that informs an author's own reading of his sexuality informs other processes as well. An image is created from these partial desires, an internal image posited not so much as an identity that says "I am *that*," but rather as a nontotalizing whole, as Deleuze and Guattari would say, that provides a vehicle for integrating desires. This nontotalizing whole operates as its own machine on nonsexual writing, just as various other desires—social, cultural, poetic, political (*NA* 139)—work at both sexual and nonsexual levels. Just as being gay might inform a political comment made by Camus, being politically on the left might inform a sexual comment or action.

Freed from imprisonment in a false paradigm of dominance and marginality, Camus, as a "homosexual writer" or as a producer of a discourse imbued with homosexuality, can submit his writing to a multiple rhetoric in which homosexual desire is one component among many. Does it dominate? It dominates only to the extent that heterosexuality dominates a heterosexual discourse. The heterosexuality is only interesting insofar as it operates as a discourse that produces unexpected effects. Otherwise, it passes invisibly before the eyes of the reader who participates in the same system. So homosexual desire does dominate in Camus's work, but not as we once thought it would. Homosexual desire and its figuration in discourse, paralleled by the channeling and formation of desire by language, dominate Camus's text without a subjection to doxa. Almost Sartrean in inspiration, Camus's homosexuality and his writing are condemnations to freedom.

Up through *Journal romain* Camus had maintained a rather hopeful and idealistic view of homosexuality. He had seen it neither as a problem nor as part of a binary *opposition* with heterosexuality in which homosexuality would be an acceptable alternative to the mode of sexual orientation of the majority. Such a role would place homosexuality in a position secondary to, and determined by, an institution and its power (*NMT* 104). Camus's idealism, seen as much in his conservatism as in his writing about homosexuality, does not allow him to accept being second-best. Thus homosexuality should not be subject to the power system described by Foucault. To Foucault's assessment of the discourses of sexuality, Camus prefers the *flou* of Barthes or the nonseparation of Deleuze and Guattari's desiring machines. Camus does not accept the possibility of a discourse that establishes its own domain, either properly or improperly. Even if there is an undeniable semiotics of homosexuality, it is for Camus subject to its own undoing.

Again we see the remainder of a certain existentialist thought pattern in Camus's views of homosexuality: he refuses to grant an essence to the discourse of homosexuality and he promulgates a tropics of irony to combat any conscious or unconscious emphatic reassertion of inherent power, validity, or propriety in the discourse of another. His rhetoric undoes the power base of the discourse of the majority. And while not marginalizing his own discourse as such, he stresses that the discourse of homosexuality is as proper as that of heterosexuality. If discourse is marked by a dominant other, it is only within the terms of the discourse of power that thinks the term by starting with its own false propriety. Within its own discourse, homosexuality undercuts its own position by a remarking of the fictions of its own semiotics. Hence, for Camus, homosexuality has its own inherent trope of irony in every situation: to be homosexual, to talk about homosexuality, is necessarily to be ironic. Perhaps Roland Barthes sums it up best with the following comment, read and commented on by Camus himself. Barthes comments—without explaining—on Camus's irony: "Renaud C. passes, completely blue, eyes and shirt; I don't know anyone less metaphysical—that is to say, more 'ironic' (with the slight unpleasantness that that implies)" (*I* 93). Camus comments in return: "Less *metaphysical*, he is not wrong; although . . . I would say less *religious*, but after all, that is not my diary. And too bad for the 'slight unpleasantness'" (*Vig* 18). Camus, by the way, lets us know that he is on the toilet when he comes across the comment by Barthes. The irony never ceases, and there is often a smile at the most serious moment. It is that smile that will keep Camus going through his adventures in Rome.

II. Urbi et Orbi

Let us turn now to what may be Camus's most problematic work, the *Journal romain*. It is problematic because the definitions, systems, and strategies that served him heretofore in his "achrien writing" seem to fall short, to be inadequate, or to lead him astray in his Roman text. Awarded the "Prix de Rome," Renaud Camus comes to Rome in 1985 for a two-year stay in the Villa Médicis where he completes a novel, *Roman furieux*, that is ostensibly his main work while in the city (*JR* 165). It is also the continuation of his earlier novel *Roman roi*. The diary is initially presented as merely a product of the author's graphomania; it is secondary to the project of the novel. We soon realize that neither of these suppositions is wholly correct. *Journal romain* is neither a marginal text nor a parasitic one. In its own right, and more consistently than any of the author's other works, it engages the problematic of discourse because discourse is everywhere a problem. The work is not just a scribbler's private diary, for *Journal romain* starts out as a column for the French magazine *Gai Pied*, a publication geared toward an engaged, left-leaning, middle-class, male homosexual readership. Such readers would presumably be well-disposed to the belles lettres of a writer like Camus.

As a running column for *Gai Pied*, *Journal romain* has a public face as a travelogue and guidebook to Rome as accurate as and often more perceptive than a *Guide Bleu* or a *Guide Michelin*; *Journal romain* is an updated gay version of Mme de Staël's *Corinne*. Given the particular interests of the readership, there is another aspect to this public face, which is the record of sexual encounters. In addition to being the diary of various cultural and social events and observations, the book catalogues Camus's sexual activity in Rome, with detours to Florence and Paris. Since the framework of the discourse is the open discussion of homosexual relationships, encounters, and events, the sexual *récits*, new tales of Italian tricks, form a part of the *public* domain of the text. But there is a private face to the work hidden behind the seemingly facile prose. The book is a chiaroscuro record about the very activity of writing: the book is a very personal and subjective record of a gay consciousness trying to write in and about Rome.

Were the book merely the transcription of a set of weekly columns for a French magazine, it would still be interesting for the perspicacity of its observations and the "pleasures of its style." Yet the book continues long after the initial raison d'être disappears: the editor of *Gai Pied* writes Camus to let him know that the weekly chronicle is to be discontinued. Mention of the letter is made on page 146, but the writing of the *Journal romain* goes on for about another three hundred pages. Freed from the exigencies of immediate marketing and from writing for his select audience, Camus writes something both more revealing and more complicated than the public travelogue of the first part of the book. In its state of minimal censorship and in its active exploration of an individual consciousness writing in and about Rome, *Journal romain* is the record of a conflict and conjunction of discourses to which Camus's consciousness is subject and with which he must come to terms.

In *Journal romain*, Camus finally has to face the discourses that have preceded him; and neither irony nor bathmology provides the comfort they once did. Two of these discourses loom large: first, the personal and sociological discourses of homosexuality that we have already examined at length. As Camus notes in retrospect (*FA* 109): "Rome and the Villa Médicis, when I lived there, appeared to me like a belvedere from which I could see below my entire past, my entire youth, all the places that I'd been [*toutes les contrées que j'avais été*]". But here, added to the discourses of homosexuality, are the multiple, conflicting, eternally present discourses of Rome. The combination of these two will challenge Camus's ironic idealism. Rome will no longer allow Camus to avoid conflict, to produce parallel texts, or to refuse opposition.[7] Rome is discursively conflictual, not because of an imposed doxa, but in its very being.

Camus's discourse on Rome has numerous literary and historical antecedents, from Mme de Staël's novelistic guidebook *Corinne*, to Freud's urban geography at the beginning of *Civilization and Its Discontents*, from Stendhal's Italian disease to the illness that Edith Wharton calls "Roman fever." Despite the fact that Rome has served as the touchstone of innumerable texts and that, therefore, any author who approaches Rome risks repeating past writing, the singularity of the Eternal City is necessary for Renaud Camus. No other spot, not even Paris, will allow for such probing of the act of inscription; no other spot will test his power as an author quite so conspicuously. It has long been a literary commonplace to be disappointed in one's visit to Rome; Camus is no exception. For example, he says that he has always been disappointed by his visits to the Sistine Chapel (*JR* 154). The traveler seeking "the grandeur that was Rome" is faced with a mass of ruins, dilapidated old neighborhoods, and fragments of former luxury, but few signs of the grandeur he or she hoped to find.

7. Obviously, Camus continues to write a parallel text, *Roman furieux*. But the novel fails to convince; it is seen as a critical failure, or as a work to which the critics will remain indifferent (*Vig* 17). And I think the reason is that the battle that occurs in *Journal romain* makes *Roman furieux* rather an inert, tame, or indifferent text in comparison.

The monuments that have remained intact belong to Christian Rome and not to classical Rome. These Renaissance edifices, such as St. Peter's and Santa Maria Maggiore, are obtrusively present and marked with an autoreflexivity that calls attention to their own wonder and monumentality. Such is the case for the ostentatious gold ceiling of the church of Santa Maria Maggiore, which is itself remarked by a sign about a miraculous summer snowfall having occurred where the church stands. Though Camus does not mention the snowfall or the ceiling, he does note the need to see the church lit up and he finds that its functions as a religious institution interfere with his aesthetic appreciation (*JR* 341). Such is also the case for the embracing wings of the colonnade of St. Peter's or even the point of creation in the ceiling of the Sistine Chapel, there to be remarked, seen, and read: "It is not a question of a calm reading, but of a feverish consultation, in search of a lost truth, of a definitive *aleph*" (*JR* 156). They do not merely indicate a religion whose glory they celebrate, but also a semiocentrism that indicates the work of art as a glory unto itself.

In Rome, the sign indicates itself, what it signifies, and what was once signified. The churches of Rome signal a phantom classical Rome that stood on the very same sites, but now that Rome is found only in texts. More or less aware of the world he is seeing, the visitor to Rome is both delighted and frustrated by the juxtaposition of three Romes: classical, Renaissance, modern. Even if one ignores the disappointment of the present, the fragments of classical ruins and the plenitudes of the Renaissance that replaced other fragments are side by side in the Roman map of the mind. The juxtaposition undercuts any possible reign of the sublime by the insistence of the whole on an order of temporality and change in which the sublime has no place. This juxtaposition has itself given rise to a set of literary texts that consist of figures of walks, maps, layers, puzzles, and solutions. Rome is viewed as a text to be deciphered, sign by sign and bit by bit. Strange juxtapositions are the "proper" figures of Rome, and its metaphors and metonymies are the very stuff of which Rome is constructed as a text. Its truth is not in a Greek temple of absolute beauty and knowledge but in a map that is never completely readable. To come prepared to Rome is to come prepared to read something that is never fully coherent but which one still hopes is readable. To come to Rome prepared to write is to come prepared to assimilate what one has read and add another layer to the bibliographic map of the Eternal City.

On the surface, Camus would seem to be discursively well-armed for his writing of Rome: he has the knowledge necessary for seeing "Rome in Rome," and the comprehension for understanding Renaissance Rome as a self-proclaiming sign of itself *urbi et orbi.* Not incidentally, he also has the flexibility that comes from a bathmological reintegration of his own marginalized discourse of homosexuality. Bathmology does not return his discourse to a center, but to a decentered discursive grid that now bears only a few traces of the preexisting discursive impositions of the majority. Finally, for there still must be some laws in this idealized universe, Camus returns repeatedly to a law of mutual understanding, tolerance, freedom, and politeness: in short, to civilization.

As a project then, the *Journal romain*, even given its quondam raison d'être, becomes the personal semiotics of Camus's stay in Rome. The book takes the measure of Rome by means of a theoretical discourse and a modifying praxis backed by knowledge. Theory and praxis are filtered together through a consciousness that distills its observations into an ordered text. In the first part of the book, that is, from the beginning through the mention that the obligation toward *Gai Pied* has ended, there is a set of thoughts about the Eternal City in which Camus attempts to fix a certain vision of Rome. As if he were a scion of Henry James, Camus reflectively reads in the city a set of words, given to the world by this city, that define both Rome and the human world: city, civilization, civility. These words should help define and redefine a semiotics of Roman urban and urbane behavior. Almost despite himself, Camus starts out searching for a new set of definitions. The rules by which he has lived and the usual modes of production of discourse have become so banal that all subtlety and difference have fallen by the wayside. Rome will perhaps be the release from what Camus perceives as the suburbanization or Americanization of France and the false concept of democracy that touts a flattening out of differences instead of a recognition of multiplicity. According to Camus, even in Paris there has been a misguided zeal that sees democratization as equalization instead of as plurality. What passes for civilization has for Camus become lamentable and disappointing. As he ironically notes, "sincerity, frankness, the *natural* being supreme values, nothing is more praiseworthy than having only one language, to speak the same way to anyone at any time" (*JR* 26). Rome, he hopes, will help him fight the trivializing of civilization, a battle which he sometimes feels he is fighting alone.

Yet Camus does not turn to Rome with some false hope of Romantic renewal. He knows that Rome will not provide a permanent answer to what he considers to be nothing less than the decline of Western civilization. For this or any other view of Rome is limited by the fact that Rome is always inscribed, has always previously been written, and cannot be approached without the words of a predecessor. Rome cannot be seen before it is read through the words of another: thus there is always, for Camus, a danger of interference from the doxa. Even if Camus chooses the gay guidebook, *Spartacus*, instead of the traditional Baedeker (*JR* 55), Rome still must be read in someone else's words before he can apply his own. If the *Spartacus* tells the reader that the Monte Caprino instead of the Janiculum is "worth the detour," it is a change due to a difference in criteria and not to some new epistemological or doxological order. This new sort of guidebook still must be read before difference can be determined. As one might suspect, Roman semiotics becomes a reading of signs of others who have already read Rome.

It comes as no surprise, then, to the reader that in addition to the *Spartacus*, Camus has another textual vade mecum. This one is literary: Stendhal's *Promenades dans Rome*, which functions as a pretext and as a *point de repère* for Camus in literature. As is well known from his autobiographical writings, Stendhal made much of his amorous conquests in Italy. Stendhal's success is the literary precursor for what Camus hopes will be his own success both in writing and in sex. His choice of the very heterosexual Stendhal is one more indication of the way Camus refuses the false dichotomy that splits the world a priori into heterosexual and homosexual realms. Yet when Camus reaches an impasse in both literary and sexual endeavors, not even Stendhal can provide much help: Camus notes that he has been reading Stendhal for over two months and has not read a quarter of the work (*JR* 165). It will take him a full six months to finish the book (*JR* 229). There is no way to overcome one's antecedents without having worked through them. So even the failure to read Stendhal becomes significant for Camus as a sign of the impasse he faces in Rome.

Later, when Camus is beginning to see his way around this impasse, Stendhal's text again serves as an index. This time, however, it is as the substrate for the text of another: Camus comments on del Litto's edition of Stendhal, in which, through copious notes, del Litto "corrects" Stendhal's exaggerations and tells the reader where Stendhal might be lying (*JR* 194; 229). We must not, however, jump to obvious conclusions, for as banal as del Litto's remarks might seem to Camus, their very presence signals Stendhal's success at having been published and republished. Despite Camus's previous successes and his current, continued graphomania, he seems to fear the possibility of a noncontinuation of his text, both this diary and the project of *Roman furieux*. Hence, he underlines overcoming the impasse with this redoubled reference to Stendhal.

Over and over, *Journal romain* is concerned with the very possibility of continuing to write. How can Camus write when his previous theories of his own middle-voiced writing seem to vanish into thin air as they face the arcana of Roman semiotics? How can he justify going on? In *Journal romain*, Camus is involved in justifying, explaining, and theorizing his writing to and for his readers. My hypothesis therefore is that if this were merely occasional writing, Camus would not have to develop such an extended and elaborate theory for it. Occasional writing needs no inherent theory nor any resolution of discursive conflict. Even the occasion of writing a diary as a daily habit is the only explanation of textuality that is needed. But literary theory is necessary if the writing is to go beyond the occasion and if that writing is to have some internal consistency. *Journal romain* will justify both itself and Camus's continued writing of the conclusion to his novel. More specifically, *Journal romain* will seek justification for the ongoing practice of writing in general in a world that understands little and rewards less. Hence Camus's repeated appeals to the truth: he categorically states that there are no lies in the journal, and only, perhaps, a few sins of omission, such as sliding over a case of crabs (*JR* 194). Stendhal's text will not give the answers, nor will it provide permanent succor. It does, however, serve to reassure from time to time: another French literary mind once conquered the slippery heterogeneity of Roman semiotics of text and of sex. With that assurance and hope, Camus can forge ahead.

III. On the Monte Caprino

To understand Roman semiotics, Camus searches for a point at which the reflection of the subject can meet the elusive object of his reflections: Rome itself. He seeks a point at which there is the reflection both of Rome in Rome and of the ego's vision of itself as pure subjectivity. The point, Camus tells us in his own elements of semiology, is the *punctum*, the term used by Barthes in his book on photography, *La Chambre claire*: the punctum is the point in the photo that piques one's interest (*CC* 48). Willingly trying to read the other, Camus remarks the punctum in Gauguin's paintings (*JR* 33), as if to tell his reader that there is a point that reflects the subject even within the most obviously other, be it the overtly exotic subject matter of Gauguin's work or the equally exotic subject matter with which he, Camus, is faced: Rome.

For quite a while, Camus seems to believe that this defining punctum will be found in the ludic sexuality of the Monte Caprino. The transcultural free play of gay sexuality has served him well before and he has no reason to believe that this system of ludic give-and-take will not work in Rome. Although this capital spot for gay cruising should be a pivotal locus for understanding Rome, the Monte Caprino turns into a locus for stylized patterns of disengagement. Instead of the free play Camus expects, the Monte Caprino is filled with one-way actions, taboos, and ritualistic reaffirmations of heterocratic sexuality. Italian men who go there for gay sex seem, as often as not, not to want to be gay and not to want to know who they might be. Standing in the shadows of classical Rome, these men seem to deny that past and present have some continuity and that their own present behavior is not just a one-time chance occurrence. What these men affirm to Camus is a discontinuity of behavior, of thought, and of semiotics. They have affirmed only one thing, the internalized figure of the self proffered by the other, the picture of the "faggot," "*pédé*," "*frocio*." The barriers set up by the words of the other allow no reading of Rome, for in hearing the words of a dominant heterocracy, Camus cannot hear Rome talk to him. The free sex of the Monte Caprino comes wrapped in garb of self-loathing. He cannot risk contamination by this new version of "Roman fever." Decidedly, this will not be the point of reflection needed as an entry into Roman semiotics.

A point is needed to fix both a view of the outside and a nonalienated view of the self, an image of the self unmediated by the impositions and orders of the heterocracy. Finding it is not a simple task, for it is the entire city, he soon realizes, that is problematic. Rome is always askew, "*de guingois*" (*JR* 43): "This city was devoted to the Baroque, to cut-off perspectives that repeat and invert, to false axes" (*JR* 156). At times it would seem that there is no point that can encompass both a view of Rome and a definition of self because one simply cannot get the perspective right. One does not know where to stand, one is eclipsed by the anamorphosis of the spot. Or, one cannot assume that one's stance is centered, focused, even transparent: on the Monte Caprino, Camus notes, one is always asked, eccentrically, to play a role, be an organ instead of a subject. In Rome, it would seem ec-stasis can come only from eccentric positions.

What does one do when nature is awry? First of all, one writes, especially if one is Renaud Camus. The more he is frustrated by an inability to solve his Roman problem, the more he writes about it. In the first place, in a kind of self-reflective feedback, he fetishizes his own semiotic systems, inquires about his own writing and his own ideas, and wonders if he has himself become other to himself. He will write where there is no sex; his text will become a fetish and sign of an absent sexuality. And, if he cannot meet Rome directly, he will substitute a sign for that absent, impossible meeting point; he will seek a fetish. What Naomi Schor has pointed out in *Reading in Detail* (91) concerning Barthes's work holds also for Camus's

Roman text: there is a relation between the point—the punctum—and the fetish: "The Barthesian detail is always supplementary, marginal, decentered. . . . the detail which draws and holds Barthes's attention is like the fetishist's fetish, a detail which, camouflaged by its perfect banality, goes unnoticed by others."

In the absence of a focal point that is the synthesis or at least the meeting point of outside and self, Camus posits an artificially determined point: a fetish invested with the desire that there be a point. Rome, endlessly demanding, requires a fetish of local origin, *made in Rome*. Of course, we can already see this: a fetish that is *made in Rome* will still somehow resist use and interpretation. In Rome, the fetish encompasses the fragment or ruin whose whole comes from the investment of desire in (and of) vision. The Roman fetish also includes the essential figure of the Baroque, Rome's own style, the detail separate from the whole. Not unexpectedly, the Roman fetish corresponds to the various toeholds or *disjecta membra* of the semiotic system whose bits and pieces are available in lieu of the whole. The idea of the Roman fetish thus is the artificially chosen meeting point that associates the fragments of a city that can never be captured whole with a concept of homosexuality made of a few body parts behind which the Roman himself can never admit his wholeness or normality as a homosexual. Because Camus can determine neither the heart nor the essential point, he is willing to allow the artifice of the fetish to substitute for the missing point from which he could have said that he saw a symmetry. The fetish becomes the focal point, though by its nature it refuses focus in perspective.

In practical terms, this means settling for partial pleasure instead of total satisfaction and accepting a trick for the teleology of an orgasm instead of for the individual behind the body parts. In fetishizing Rome or, metonymically, the body parts and appearances of its citizens, Camus can still operate a bathmological reversal: the artifice of the unessential though purely existential detail can be substituted for some perfect but unreachable perspective in which self and other are seen. Necessary, however, to the validity of the fetish is the possibility of bathmology, by which a reversal by degrees is effected. Yet once again, Rome refuses to allow the fetishism to enact a tropic substitution. Rome does not permit reflection to occur; in fact, reversal is refused at every level. Within fetishism, there is an ideal that may be theoretically attained, though admittedly this occurs with difficulty because the desire is difficult to satisfy: "First, the object of the fetish in question must be found and that is not always so easy. Then the possessor of this object-fetish must not only allow you to get off on it, but also—and this is the best—seem to find as much pleasure as you in your use of it" (*JR* 67). Within fetishism there is a reciprocity, albeit a bathmological one; yet the manners of Rome allow neither this reciprocity nor any symmetry whatever. In the realm of the sexual, Rome stays resolutely askew: "Nothing is further from the homosexuality I like—strictly, literally defined, completely symmetrical—than these one-way cruisings like passes usually made at women" (*JR* 63). Roman homosexuality refuses to escape from the shackles of the heterocratic world order. Gay Roman men behave as if they were macho heterosexual men who are not gay but who would deign to allow themselves to be serviced. Alternately, these Roman men seem to be playing at their antithesis: coquettish female virgins who have to be wooed. For Camus, coming from a Paris of reasonably open gay relations, the alienation of the Roman homosexual is, more often than not, too much to bear.

One might very well think that the problem of Roman homosexuality is sociological. For various reasons relating to the structures of home life, city life, and local culture, gay Roman men live under the yoke of closeted behavior, self-loathing, and self-deception. That is, as far as it goes, a perfectly correct assumption for Camus. But, as I have hypothesized, the Roman fever of this work makes of it something far more significant in Camus's writing than an *étude de moeurs*. This volume reflects a crisis in writing, a crisis brought out by Rome itself, a recalcitrant handmaiden who nevertheless points the way. The unique combination of fragments and self-reflection that is Rome brings the adept, or even the awkward, reader of Rome to a point of thinking about his or her own activities. Rome provides a focus even if, or especially if, one cannot get Rome itself in focus.

The problem of Roman semiotics is always a general one. Even if it starts out here as a sexual question, it is gradually broadened to be a general disorder of signs. Rome, origin of much of our received doxa, is the spot that upsets the doxa. Every law of the doxa must present itself as if it were transparent, original, self-identical, and self-evident, yet in Rome, every sign (sexual, social, historical, cultural) is both the mark of the thing and the sign of its opposite, absence, or past. In Rome, the sign is the figure of a paradox but with a complete absence of irony: "this attitude of an untouchable virgin, ready to be seduced, seems to be taken for manliness here" (*JR* 63). Strangely, then, for Camus, the semiotics of Roman homosexuality reproduce the improprieties of an official discourse and enthroned power that are eternally proclaiming their own innocence. Instead of the sublime point of realization of self and other that sees both symmetry and difference, there is a parasitic system of one-way streets, power differentials, and systematized abuses, like those of *The Barber of Seville*—except in this live production, all the gay men of Rome play Rosina (*JR* 65). Such a parasitic message system is anathema to Camus because it distorts any free play of the subject and it eliminates the possibility of his language ever being anything but an acquiescence, an opposition, or at worst, a part of the improper system of discourse. Camus's personal Baedeker has led him to discover a Rome that should be his, but the semiotics of Roman homosexuality already in place seem to form an immutable block. This impediment prevents the author from realizing the pleasure of finding his Roman discourse, his own combination of fragments and auto-reflexivity in his Roman columns.

When Camus no longer has to write for the readership of *Gai Pied*, it is as if he has been released from having to observe the laws of writing with reason. Thereafter, nothing justifies these pages except a will to write that translates a desire to know Rome, to understand it, and to conquer it. But every attempt at understanding Rome, we have already seen, becomes in part a reflection of the writing self. Almost despite himself, Camus realizes that there is no justifiable reason for insisting that Roman semiotics be grounded in some transcendentally valued vision of Rome. Though this realization is never announced as such, within twenty pages of the announcement of the discontinuation of the columns for *Gai Pied*, Camus discovers an arbitrary nature to the sign in Rome. He realizes, for example, that "the ideal of the Italian homosexual or at least the Roman homosexual is to be invisible" (*JR* 146). It is already clear to the attentive reader of *Journal romain* that the Roman homosexual would willingly or ideally exempt himself from being read and thus from having a significance in the eyes of the other that is not determined by his own stereotyped sign system. But it is only at this point that Camus seems to become aware of it himself.

Recognition does not mean acceptance. Camus is still unable or unwilling to accept that this sexuality refuses to be an engaged discourse for itself or a visible and comprehensible semiotic object for another. These qualities, present in Florence and Milan, seem somehow to have disappeared when the invisible border is crossed between Tuscany and Latium. It is not that Camus is looking for some fixed, doxological meaning. It is rather that he is seeking in vain what I would call "meaningfulness," which I would define as the possibility of meaning(s), the potential for sense, and the plurality of possibilities. Meaningfulness results from the constraints inherent in a semiotic system confronted by, and acting together with, the free play of the signifier.[8] Meaningfulness is not the one-to-one correspondence of signifier and signified, nor is it even the range of connotations offered within a standard encoding. Meaningfulness depends on the undeniable point of subjectivity, the punctum in the photo, or the jouissance in the text.

And it is unacceptable to Camus that meaningfulness should have disappeared from Rome of all places, even if this same meaningfulness has itself disappeared elsewhere, vanished in the theatricalization of communication. For example, Camus notes with displeasure (*JR* 145) that the entertainment industry in Paris has become affected by an auto-reflexivity that he sees as an impasse. Paris may fail him but Rome *should not*. Again, in Paris, he deplores the constant misuse of language; it is not that he seeks an absolute meaning, but that he sees in that misuse a negation of the possibility of meaning: "The relation of the adjective to the noun it modifies is vaguer and vaguer" (*JR* 181). So Camus is not erecting French meaning, logic, or clarity as a model against which the will to invisibility or the parasitic nature of the Roman system is to be measured by a disparaging evaluator. The auto-reflexivity of one part of the French system is just as parasitic, in the form of hollow, self-destructive feedback, as the system of Roman homosexuality. It is rather that Camus cannot accept this sterility in the domain in which he least expected it. If it has appeared in institutionalized communication, the vulgar use of language, or even current social manners, he can suffer it by writing against it. But in the matters of Rome, of sexuality, and, a fortiori, of Roman sexuality, writing itself is not strong enough to combat the problem.

Camus objects to a perverse leveling of language or manners because such an action reduces the plurality within meaningfulness: "Bad manners are seen everywhere in Paris nowadays. I am convinced that they come from ignorance and from the breakdown of secular codes, that is to say, languages" (*JR* 181). As an author, Camus can fight this breakdown of language with language: he can do his work, he can write his novel *Roman furieux* (165). But he cannot use language to combat the devaluing of a sexual semiotics that turns the meaningfulness of sexuality into a theatricalized version of male and female signs, with no free play or foreplay whatsoever.

8. I am thus giving the opposition between meaning and meaningfulness a somewhat different definition than that provided by Chambers in his article "Meaning and Meaningfulness," found in his book of the same name. Chambers (135) writes: "the *meaning* which is the product of a text's semantic and formal structures is not identifiable with the *meaningfulness* the same text derives from its being apprehended in a context."

This insistence on sexuality, even as it reaches impasse after impasse, does not diminish, but finds its way instead into this text as fuel for the writing. Willfully eschewed within the so-called principal writing, that of the historical novel (for *Roman furieux* is probably the most chaste of the author's books up to that point), this sexuality becomes a central, integral part of the writing of the journal. In fact, the intensity of the *Journal romain*, which links his interest and insistence on sex and his graphomania, threatens to overwhelm the project of *Roman furieux*. Camus spends so much time on the *Journal romain* and the sex that fuels it that he has no time left for the novel:

> Almost six in the evening; it's dark and I haven't gotten back to *Furieux*. It is I who am furious, with myself. The whole afternoon, from two to eight, has to be kept for the real work, the novel, and the diary can only have whatever other time may be found. The advantage of this rule will be that it will control my biographomania a bit. (*JR* 188)

For Camus, the true work remains the novel, for in it he can control the semiotics in which he is immersed and which he himself knowledgeably uses. The transcendental signifiers of history and the clarity of his organization of the signifiers provide a welcome relief to the confusion detailed on every page of the diary. Yet the *Journal romain* is not at all marginal; on the contrary, its passion tends to invade the space of literary production and overwhelm that space. Even if he cannot make the connections between sexuality and textuality that will enable his understanding and manipulation of the local code, Camus fills his text with the sexuality that seems to be missing in a more carnal sense. The more he writes, the more the writing itself becomes a fetishistic substitute for sex. Oddly enough, the Romans become correct in their perception of the dangers of sexuality, as he shows us at one remove how it threatens to consume his writing.

By this point, Camus has at least sorted things out: if we read *Journal romain* as the record of a consciousness coming to terms with its actions and frustrations, we are aware of the moment that Camus consciously figures out the distributions of functions and signs in the various realms of writing and sexuality. We now know in detail why the *Journal romain* is far more than an unmediated diary of a two-year stay in Rome, though it is certainly a record of that stay. And it is more than a traditional coming to terms with Rome by writing commentary on certain cultural aspects of the Eternal City, though it is that coming to terms as well. Nor is it only a realization of what the author perceives as various kinds of sociopathic behavior, whether such behavior is found in the sterility of the French mass media, the vulgarization of linguistic and behavioral codes in Paris, or the perverseness of the semiotics of Roman homosexuality. *Journal romain* is all of these but it is also the record of their realization; it is this record that provides a theory of textuality for those behaviors. It is only when Camus has realized what drives him to write that he is finally able to come to terms with the foibles of Roman homosexuality. When he realizes that the failure to enjoy the system is itself an erotic drive, he turns this eroto-criticism into text as he accepts that his pen finally becomes his phallus: "I pushed a table in front of the large French windows that look out over the city. I now have all Rome under my pen [*plume*]" (*JR* 227).

Able to frame his renewed concept of Roman homosexuality, Camus can determine the elements of Roman sexology. This Rome steadfastly refuses to present an objective system of laws. Instead, it proffers a series of one-way streets endlessly violated by the Romans themselves. If the rule seems to be one of invisibility, Camus respects it until a Roman himself ignores it. This particular example is all the more problematic since for once the Roman code and Camus's own code seemed initially to converge: "His one mistake was to be a bit shapeless, though he was bulky, to chomp on strawberry chewing gum, and to have asked me to suck him, something which, in my book, is not asked for" (*JR* 217). But Camus's use of language tells a different story from what he seems to be saying: he says there is one mistake (*son seul tort*) and then proceeds to list three things that are wrong with the Roman in question.

By this point in the book, nothing could go right. So even when the author understands the code, it seems to disappear before his eyes in a paradox of endlessly self-violating laws by which, for example, it is wrong to show one's desire, even narcissistically, except when one wants to show one's desire. Unable to make head or tail of the system, he ensures that he will not understand it by consciously looking for problems; this curmudgeonly attitude appears in subsequent books. Camus is irked beyond measure by an inconsistency in the system, a caprice that seems so un-Roman as to put the very Romanness of the Romans in doubt, since these "supposed heirs of the Romans have no true feeling for the law" (*JR* 248). At one bathmological remove, he has become the traveler who perceives "rien de Rome en Rome."

Still intently looking for a law that will be applicable, Camus does not yet consciously seem to realize that the space of the law is negative. Instead of being an organic or logical continuity, the paradigms and rules of the various discourses, including Rome itself as their sum, endlessly give way to their own negation. The space of the law in Rome is precisely that space from which the law is endlessly retreating; the law itself falls apart. And thus a discourse like that of Roman sexuality can have only two forms, neither of which corresponds to Camus's idealistic polysemy with maximum communication and engagement. On the one hand, there are the institutionalized mechanics of a communication system, with channels that are unavoidably present: even on a one-way street, one can go only one wrong way. In terms of the channels of homosexual communication, "these Italians are all terribly genito-anal: jerking off, blow jobs, fingers up the ass, and attempts to butt-fuck, beyond that they are neither very knowledgeable nor curious" (*JR* 263).

Along with such narrowly defined channels of communication is what Camus perceives as Roman men's endless retreat from engagement, as if the Italians themselves realized the possibility of a plurality of discourses within a code of flexibility based on mutual respect, but refused to act upon it. Faced with possible plurality, the conscious Italian voice or the purveyor of discourse retreats to leave a void. It is as if, for Camus, stereotypical truisms about Italians found a truth at the level of sexuality and its discourses. Either there is a narrowly defined path of action, a true Roman classification, or there is an anarchy of a centrifugal discourse: "Eros and desire are always discounted, even in the supposedly intellectual class. A book that speaks of them immediately loses some prestige" (*JR* 275). The heirs of Petronius and Boccaccio have abandoned ship.

No possibility of free play appears. For Camus, free play usually takes two forms, but both of them seem to be absent from Roman consciousness. First of all, there is the polysemy of signs within a system. Accepting a series of channels, Camus seeks to explore all their ramifications as well as the unchanneled spaces they define. To this end, he would provide a renewed code of behavior that determines the rules of the game but not the actions of the players. His would be a game that allows for polysemy, as he proposes making up "a written chart of what is tolerated in the realm of the flesh" (*JR* 254). The remark goes for his writing as well: he seeks freedom in writing even more than in the realm of the flesh. That Camus is at this point proposing to write sex, as opposed to writing about it, shows that his Roman fever has uncovered the intimate relationship that exists for him between writing and sex. Is it possible that his graphomania is both the supplement and the complement to a permanent sexorama? That is to say, the more he has sex, the more he writes about it; the less he has sex, the more he writes about it. In *Fendre l'air*, after a long discourse on innocence and nature, he remarks: "I thought we'd never get out of there and I would have to imitate Origen because of a fatal concern for logical coherence" (*FA* 123). Sex, graphomania? Sometimes the difference is barely perceptible.

Accompanying the free play is the supplement to Camus's system, its *Witz*, that remains for Camus something far from gratuitous:

> Italians endlessly ask me in sexual situations why I smile, which seems to concern them greatly. For them, making love is something completely serious—for me too, but not in the same way—and even a bit "dramatic," where any humor is only out of place. (*JR* 277)

Camus has established what he perceives to be the possible bases for action or discourse, be it his own or that of the Romans. But what he wants never happens in Rome; it exists elsewhere, in Paris or Florence, for example, and in his books. Still, despite his very evident frustration with the situation, he can continue with his real work, since sexual activity was, after all, a supplement to the writing. We would continue to presume that the real work is the writing of the novel, yet just as he is realizing how free play and supplements are not acceptable to the Roman system, he makes a remark that surprises: "Is this a diary? No. Its individuality is due to its origins. I had promised the jury of the Academy of France to write a 'Roman diary'" (*JR* 273). The reader initially believes that Camus's work for the Prix de Rome was the novel and that the *Journal romain* was itself supposed to be a marginal text for a review. Only the writer's own admitted biographomania lets him continue to write these pages after the contractual raison d'être, the columns for *Gai Pied*, disappeared. The reader now learns that this *Journal romain*, a series of fragments and necessarily a self-referential work, is, at least officially, one of the basic texts of the enterprise.

Within the literary artifact there is finally a statement, taken either as a fragment or as a mark of autoreflexivity, that allows the reader to assemble the various strands of the text that are simultaneously process and reflection, activity and discourse, action and critique: Rome, homosexuality, the meaningfulness of text, and writing itself. And this is accomplished without having to rely on the fiction of a unified ego that writes or a unified textual subject like the historical novel, for example, which would be guaranteed by chronology and a coherent time line. Traditionally, the coherence of an autobiographical text comes from the presumed integral nature of the writing subject. Even if a theoretical critique makes the faults of the subject evident—even if within whatever critical mode is used, a split in the subject is seen—the text itself is read as a suture of that split. A strict parallel then exists between autobiography and occasional writing. Autobiography solves its problems by relying on the integral nature of the author, the sutured subject. Occasional writing relies on the integral nature of the event. In neither case is the fundamentally referential nature of the text ever seriously put in doubt.

Yet this suturing, if not the referentiality, is a fiction; when examined critically, even the referentiality seems doubtful. Certainly, Renaud Camus is a real person, but his identity as an author, like that of any writer, is less clear, even aside from the merry-go-round of authors' names found on the covers of his books. Like each sexual or textual incident for Barthes, each new text changes the quondam definition of the author; each new reading modifies the polysemy of the whole. Hence, the suturing by text is itself an act of fiction and *Journal romain* no longer appears to be simply a diary whose backbone comes from the physical reality of Renaud Camus, the civil identity of the same individual with a *carte d'identité*, or even some Kantian categories of space (Rome) and time (1985–86). Camus states that "it was then decided to publish this rather quickly as a volume" (*JR* 273). Despite such factual disclaimers, which invoke a minimum of reflexivity, the identity of the author of the text comes from the polysemy of every aspect of the text itself. This includes more than the strands that Camus has consciously determined: a logology of fetishism, a grammar of Roman homosexuality, a personal Baedeker, a diary of the production of a novel, and a reflection of a two-year stay in Rome. It also includes the double act of fragmentation and autoreflexivity that comes from a juxtaposition of these strands in and as text unsupported by the preexisting excuses of identity and contracts.

If the text is then a literary object and not an explication, even when it tells the truth, it is literary because its multiple discourses are marked with the desire to tell themselves, to seek their own object of knowledge, and to describe that object fully. Instead of a certainty enunciated without rhetoric, there is a degree of recursion of the text on itself that is the sign of its own literarity. The infolding of the text at the point where the author has assented to the unfoundedness of his own position is the reflection of the message given to him by Rome: no position is that of the truth or of the whole. Not coincidentally, this infolding corresponds to the author's own infolding as a human subject: "Aside from Italophobia, the clearest effect of Italy on me will have been to start me anew in a habit neglected for two decades, masturbation" (*JR* 297). This act is both autoreflexive and fragmentary, since it is an incomplete sexuality for Camus, yet replete with lost babies from the Auvergne: "What a number of Auvergnat babies can get lost between the floorboards, under my desk, in my house in the woods!" The ultimate masturbatory status of the text is reflected in the theory of textual production that could never be arrived at or deduced from an irresolute French logic that is never askew.

The observer is now caught in the unsolvable nexus of flights from meaningfulness, negation of understanding, and the necessity of having writing communicate, if only in an autoreflexive fashion. If Camus is at sea, the reader is even more displaced from the text, in which the author continues to say that he does not understand. Things are not getting any clearer for the author: "the syntax of this city, its use, its package directions, continue to escape me" (*JR* 333). Not until *Vigiles* will he allow that he has finally mastered that syntax: "I know the places, their use, their syntax well" (*Vig* 30). Moreover, even when understanding occurs, it means getting caught in a double bind. It is no longer a question of appearing or not appearing, but of both at the same time: the Italian homosexual's ideal "is to force the other to express his desire, without showing any oneself" (*JR* 362). For Camus, the Italian homosexual seems somehow stuck in a role that comes straight out of nineteenth-century novels, Balzac's in particular. There, in the Vautrin cycle, such a law of desire is the general law of the literary universe: the strength of a text comes not from the imposition of its force or power, but from the invisibly coerced desire that there be expression. The Italians may want to live like Balzac's characters, but Camus stays resolutely in the twentieth century. He seeks multiple meanings, plural voices, and parrhesia.

Not surprisingly, the effect of *Journal romain* will have been to turn itself into a text that resembles the contradictory discourses of Rome itself, Baroquely pointing to themselves, discourses that are endlessly fragmentary and autoreflexive but never integrally whole. The uncanny flight from meaning seems even to invade sacrosanct territory where once fiction was guaranteed by a certain order and logic. Even the author's own reading of his novel seems to reflect this as he realizes that the truth of his writing experience in Rome is not the act of closure of his two-volume historical novel, but the imperfect openness, meaningfulness without meaning, of his Roman columns:

> I finished writing *Roman furieux* this afternoon. Good, something done. But when I recently had to reread certain passages, sometimes they appeared presentable and other times, mediocre or worse. . . . My opinion depended on the time, mood, light, fatigue, and the kind of reader I imagined in my stead. (*JR* 415)

So Roman aporia, Roman fever, Roman communication systems, and Roman skullduggery have all invaded *Roman furieux*. And the former pleasures of the text, the fail-safe measures of literary self-consciousness that worked in the past, seem to have faded from view, blocked as they are by the ruins of Rome. Forced willy-nilly to accept the inevitable, Camus has to rely on the anarchy of ruins and one-way streets that is Rome. The truth of Camus's literature depends not on the permanence of past text but on the absent point, the negativity that has come to replace the Baedekers, the *Spartacus*, Stendhal, Barthes, or Camus's own texts, fictions, and being.

The final strength of Camus's *Journal romain* is that it provides the reader with a new version of intertextuality in the world of the maps, guides, and endless texts on both the ruins and monuments of Rome: the function of the intertext is to disappear and enable an absence. Only then can a new text come in its stead. It is no wonder that in the book published after *Journal romain* and *Roman furieux*, entitled *Elégies pour quelques-uns*, which, not coincidentally, is made up of earlier texts only now assembled and edited, the author finally notes that absence: "books always recall other, *absent* books, words, other sentences, illusions, other hopes, blanks on a page, other silences, other dreams, misunderstandings, God" (*EPQ* 80).

It remains to be seen how the documenter of *Tricks*, who is also the author of *Journal romain*, builds on this newfound but quite dangerous and frightening negativity. For the moment, the most recent publications do not seem to indicate that Camus has conquered this negativity. *Vigiles*, *Aguets*, and *Fendre l'air* continue in the mode established in *Journal romain*, yet they lack the problematic that is at the heart of the diary: the complicated questioning of writing, of the position of the self, and of the relation between doxa and individual discursive liberty. In *Esthétique de la solitude*, Camus seems to be branching out into what is new territory for him: that of the writer absolutely alone with his thoughts. Since the sexual and social dimensions are almost completely absent, there are fewer cavils than before. Alone with his thoughts, he is less of a *renaudeur* (or "bellyacher"; *ES* 218) and more of a meditator. Camus without sex is something new; one can only wait to see where this new chastity leads.

Tournier's Double Discourses

SURIN: A city well known for its annual roundup of elephants, whose number can go up to 200. Parades, shows of strength, etc. Many tourists, but especially Thais. The spectacle is also in the street.

Philippe Gloaguen and Pierre Josse,
Le Guide du routard. Asie du Sud-Est

I. Recuperation and Plenitude

Michel Tournier's novel *Les Météores* is a reflection on how homosexual desire is inscribed in the world, in communication systems, and in social structures. Since this desire occupies an indeterminate locus in a specular view of the world, as we have already seen to be the case for the beginning of *Sodome et Gomorrhe*, the status of this reflection within a fictional text is not easily grasped. To see the import of this inscription of desire, we must explore the relation of a theory of homosexuality both to the text in which it is found and to the world it purportedly reflects. Our understanding of Tournier's use and explanations of homosexuality necessarily informs our comprehension of the novel. This understanding, however, partly depends on recognizing the communication system that transmits the message to the reader. Despite the apparent transparency of the system, the model is not as simple as it initially appears, so it may not immediately be apparent that homosexuality has as major a role as I am claiming.

Much standard Tournier criticism centers on models of repetition and twinning, on a system of return, on the reinscription of identity, and on a text that returns to origins. Orthodox readings of Tournier allow for, even demand, a recuperation of the whole. The text may appear strange, but it will ultimately keep the promise of a return to origins. What if, quite simply, we eschew that safe teleology? I am suggesting that there is another reading, more disruptive and less reassuring than the standard one, a reading of differences, be they heterological, centrifugal, or homosexual, among others. In this reading, the text is sooner or later perceived as being an unnegotiable alterity in which difference cannot be reduced to zero. I am proposing a reading in which identity itself is based on difference and nonrecuperability; the return means the recognition of irreducible otherness within the displays of difference and pretensions to identity. I argue therefore that the recognition of this difference is a powerful means by which to read Tournier's work, despite the author's stated intentions, directions, hints, and strategies, which always seem, at least superficially, to point the reader toward the recuperation of plenitude. I argue that the return to plenitude is, often as not, a half-hearted fiction that seeks to reduce the author's and reader's ambivalence, discomfort, and ambiguity. As soon as we read further, we realize that Tournier is never so confusing as when he is directing his reader; he is a master at what magicians call misdirection. Under the denotative interpretations and beyond the forthright indications lie vacillation, difference, displacement, and the irreducible other of text and being.

First, let us look at the models of recuperation that take teleological plenitude as a basis. Tournier's writing wavers between stability and movement, between same and other, and between totalities and lack of closure. Such readings of Tournier would reduce the second member in each pair just mentioned to the errant and finally recuperable variant of the first. As early as his first novel, *Vendredi ou les limbes du Pacifique*, the recapitulation of Daniel Defoe's *Robinson Crusoe*, Tournier seems to be setting up his basic model of recuperation. Consider the import of Defoe's text: by reinventing England, Defoe controls and orders the anarchy of a desert island to make it a new England. Moreover, the gestures embodied in the individual novel, *Robinson Crusoe*, whose text invents a world, parallel the development of the novel in general, whose generic thrust is to proffer verisimilitude as a viable construct.

In repeating Defoe after two centuries, Tournier acts like Borges's Pierre Menard, a new author of old material. Tournier can seem therefore to flirt with movement and play as he releases Defoe's original from its Puritanism and its moorings in the exchanges of a mercantile society. Accidents brushed aside, within the text Tournier stresses a return to origins, unity, and a womblike plenitude. Moreover, this whole novel can be perceived as a nostalgic return to the origins of the novel as a genre. Tournier's novel flirts with Vendredi, his difference, and his kite that is the figure of free play, but the text returns to Robinson to repeat the myth.

As early as *Vendredi*, we thus find the basic figure of recuperation in Tournier's writing. In *Le Roi des aulnes*, he calls this figure or movement "*phoria*"; the neologism comes from the Greek word for "carry" or "bear."

The phoria is inevitably accompanied by the sense of return, given as the goodness of the one borne or the message carried. On the surface, phoria is inherently good; it is always euphoric: "The euphoric individual is the one who carries himself with happiness, who bears up [*se porte*] well. But it would be even more literal to say that he simply *carries* with happiness" (*RA* 132). The ultimate version of this phoria is divine; it is christophoric: "this fundamental idea of carrying, of *phoria*, is also found in the name Christopher" (*RA* 133).[1] While the movement away from the whole underlines difference through its transporting, there is inevitably an insistence on the presence of the whole and on the maintenance of the safe recuperation of that whole. Linked to a christology, phoria reinscribes the whole as a return. Phoria recuperates, brings back to plenitude, and reveals its move toward completion as it traces a path and finds its bearings. Bearing an evangel of redemption, phoria reorients with every step and re-marks any difference within a unity that includes division. Through the phoria that marks a return to a capacious unity, the whole, "more than the sum of its parts," is seen to include any possible splits, differences, clinamens, and *différances*, precisely because it is the whole.

For example, phoria recuperates the difference of twinning by capturing the duality within a whole: in other words, twins are part of one whole and indicate that whole. Hence the reader is not surprised to find that quite often in Tournier's writing there is an insistence on myth as a regenerative and recuperative force for modern textuality. For Tournier, it is possible to read through Jungian archetypes and to write about the topoi of bisexuality and twins, for these are perceived as unifying and recuperative. Recuperation becomes a double phoric movement, a voyage out and back: it corresponds to a search for, discovery of, and insistence on stability. The double movement then returns toward a whole that was, quite obviously, always already there.

Concomitant with the insistence on stability, recuperation, and return, there is an attraction to and a seduction by movement itself. For Tournier, the promise of redemptive recuperation is always matched by an unavowed loss that occurs through movement: recuperation never returns every bit of difference. There is an additional wrinkle: as the reader knows, no matter how much Tournier is himself seduced by irrecuperable difference, he will sooner or later tear himself away from that seduction and abruptly insist on the need for return. Tournier single-mindedly intends to maintain the primacy of stability in his writing. Seduced by movement, drift,

1. Bougnoux (538) proposes reading "phoria" in the context of a Freudian structure of infantile sexuality on the one hand, specifically as a sublimation of the oral stage, and, on the other, a Hegelian *Aufhebung* of the same system.

and difference, he recalls his intention and pulls himself back to an original position, as if he himself were Defoe's Robinson Crusoe intent on rebuilding a world at a pure point of origin.

The draw and seduction of otherness are sooner or later chastened by a quashing of the other, so that the self can be simultaneously content and continent instead of being an island of desire set adrift in a murderously ambiguous sea. As Tournier writes in *Journal de voyage au Canada*:

> For many people, travel is a singular occasion to escape from their structuring environment and to give free reign to their passions, especially sexual ones. . . . For me, it is exactly the reverse that is true. . . . Sexually, I am an inveterate homebody, and, in this matter, travel can only be a form—eventually an interesting one—of continence. (*JVC* 59–60)

While insisting on the comfort of his own figurative bed, Tournier returns time and again in his writing to outbound movement, a phoria of sexual discovery, and to an exploration of otherness which he abruptly cancels at a convenient, belated moment. Despite it all, Tournier is seduced by movement. In movement there is a will to ambiguity, as if somehow the recuperative model did not provide the promised redemption or as if he knew that the redemption, in order to be just that, had to exclude something: difference itself. I would like to examine a few of these ambiguities, which turn out to be sexual, for that, the reader will have guessed, is the crux of the matter.

The vacillation between stability and movement is clear in the very title of a book of short, disparate pieces: *Le Vagabond immobile*. The fragmentary nature of this book's writing contrasts with the elephantine novels, *Le Roi des aulnes* and *Les Météores*, where the very length of the novels is part of a strategy to recuperate the whole by mimetically repeating it through a gargantuan representation of it. *Le Vagabond immobile* presents no whole and, much like Foucault in the parrhesia of his interviews, Tournier allows himself a liberty in these short pieces that is checked in *Vendredi*, *Le Roi des aulnes*, and *Les Météores*. One fragment from *Le Vagabond immobile* can serve to illustrate the ambiguity that is often occulted in the longer texts in favor of a stabilizing mythology. Tournier reports a conversation he had with Pierre, an eight-year-old boy, who is looking at a copy of *Playboy*. Pierre asks Tournier, "Have you ever seen a real naked woman? [Tu as déjà vu une femme nue en vrai?]." The expected answer comes: "Of course. At my age, it would be upsetting [Bien sûr. A mon âge, ce serait inquiétant]" (57). But what exactly would be "upsetting"? We know he means "not to have seen a naked woman"; we silently supply the missing words. The text is more ambiguous: unless we impose some sense of "normality" on the text, as we "know" that it would have been quite singular for him *not* ever to have seen a naked woman, it is just as possible, grammatically, for it to have been "upsetting" to have seen a nude woman. As I think will become clear in the pages that follow, there is a pattern to Tournier's grammatical ambiguity.

Again, there is an indicative example in the essay "L'Enfant coiffé," in *Le Vent Paraclet*. Tournier makes an ambiguous analogy between a tonsillectomy and circumcision. He describes a tonsillectomy as "an anti-erotic mutilation—a symbolic castration," after which "fellatio becomes impossible, or at least so laborious that it loses all its charm" (*VP* 18). Since circumcision is used as a metaphor for a tonsillectomy, should we see the tonsillectomy as an oral castration, or better yet, as a castration of the throat in which fellatio occurs? In his answer about having seen nude women, there was a syntactic ambiguity; here the ambiguity is conceptual. One would assume that the impossibility of fellatio is in the supposed diminution of pleasure for the fellated individual, but the reference to the laboriousness of the exercise ascribes the impossibility of fellatio to the fellator. Drawing a conclusion is not so easy. Reminding us of his story "La Mère Noël," Tournier himself says that the *pater nutritor*—the nourishing father—is frustrated at not being able to become the *almus pater*, or fostering father, the complement to the *alma mater* (79). Yet the point of view immediately shifts: "Fellatio does not compensate for this infirmity, despite the obvious affinity of sperm with milk." If the first half of the sentence relates to the point of view of the irrumator, that is, the fellated person (Adams 125–30), the second half relates to the fellator

So there is a choice deferred, a decision pushed off. One pattern coming from the novels valorizes the whole and the integrity of the mythic model. The text is recuperative, as it brings back the disparate parts to a purported unity. When we turn to *Les Météores*, we find that much is made of the mythic dimensions of twins: their unity, their completeness, their wholeness, and their ideality. At the same time, the other point of view, which is that of the homosexual uncle Alexandre, stresses openness, marginality, and incompletion. The incomplete individual is marginalized by the metatextual commentary, and by the structure of the novel as well. Though central to the novel, Alexandre is shunted aside to make way for the twins and the theory of twins; he is killed off two-thirds of the way through the text in a brusque departure that leaves the reader with questions about the structures of the novels.

Despite the intense, complex structurings of Alexandre, the disquisitions related to the character, and the Weltanschauung presented as that of the character which one suspects is the author's own position, Tournier wants us to believe that the focus of the story is the twins, not Alexandre. By way of explanation, Tournier offers the following story, yet another in a series of misdirections in his work. He explains that he has received a fan letter from a set of twins who have read the novel and in it the writer goes into detail about their behavior as twins. Tournier says: "That is why the two homosexuals of *Les Météores*, Uncle Alexandre and his friend, Abbé Thomas Koussek, are only secondary characters, despite the blatant outrageousness [*l'éclat flamboyant*] of Alexandre" (*VP* 250). But the explanation is illogical: the letter is a fan letter received after the publication of *Les Météores*. The reason Alexandre and Koussek are secondary characters could not possibly be a fan letter written after the novel was published. Unable to directly state the will to otherness, unwilling, I think, to focus on the margin as a margin that rings no center, that is, to accept that the whole world is ec-centric, Tournier needs to justify the somewhat schizoid text with a banal and transparent rationalization.

In a later text such as *La Goutte d'or*, things change somewhat, as I have tried to show in an article about the incorporation of theory into the narrative structure ("Tournier's Theoretical Pretext"). Tournier seems willing to abandon his own fetishized idea of plenitude—or at least he no longer feels compelled to insert a fictional return to plenitude, even when there is still some nostalgic rememoration of a moment and a locus *ab illo tempore*. In *La Goutte d'or*, plenitude is left behind in the mythic wholeness of the desert. We are led to believe that those who do not participate in this plenitude are marginalized, so the protagonist of that novel, Idriss, is a marginal figure in his own text. But such is the case for every figure, every character, and every scene of the novel after the initial exposition. If Idriss is marginalized, we are all living, like him, in a Baudrillardian world. Like Idriss, every subject of action always falls prey to an external, imposed figuration of desire. His desire is given to him, without will, by the other; desire is imposed from the outside. What is different in *La Goutte d'or* is not this postlapsarian position, but the loss of faith in the return to a prelapsarian state.

In the earlier *Les Météores*, however, Tournier makes recuperative gestures to harmonize the center and the margins or the whole and its/the parts. He proposes a coalescence of the whole with the marginal through the development of a textual christology, whereby plenitude is discovered in the spelling out of the text. Both marginal, as a scapegoat, and whole, as a paternal God, the Christ figure repeatedly appears in Tournier's work as an explanatory mechanism. The clue for understanding this christology comes once again from *Le Vagabond immobile*. Jesus, who is physically beautiful (*VI* 109), reveals himself to three male followers, Peter, James, and John. Yet Jesus is unapproachable because he is transfigured. Too beautiful to approach even at the moment of the Passion, Jesus gives way to the undesirable, but equally pure, desirer. Of all the passages in the gospels, Tournier chooses the following from the Gospel of Mark: "And there followed him a certain young man, having a linen cloth cast about his naked body; and the young men laid hold on him: And he left the linen cloth, and fled from them naked" (14:51–52). Tournier comments:

> That young boy was you, Mark, and that is why you are the only author of a gospel to relate this discreetly erotic and amusing episode occurring at the most tragic moment in the life of Jesus, his arrest in Gethsemane. Everyone else fled, and you, naked beneath a sheet, you remain alone with Him. (*VI* 27)

The desirable one remains pure after the fact because even as an adult he is not sullied by any debasing desire; he stays unattainable. In turn, he is desired by the one who is pure before the fact, the one who maintains the innocence of a child. Tournier's christology is unabashedly and unapologetically homosexual. It would seem that for him the patterns of earthly desire repeat that homosexual desire of the child for the unattainable pure other of the Christ. Yet if Christ cannot be reached by Mark, Tournier seems to say, then here and now, every desire must fall far short of that perfect and ideal position. Thus, once again, by the very example of redemption, we see that the recuperation of the whole is unattainable. Moreover, the problem is inscribed in the form of desire itself understood as homosexual. In Tournier's view, homosexuality is difference, and is given a priori as the nonrecuperable point. Hence the endlessly reproducing figure of continuity and stability in Tournier's work has as its ultimate meaning a homosexual christology in which both transcendental and immanent meaning comes from the excluded difference, the excess, the un(re)productive.

But, that aside, the christology is still never a complete solution: in fact, if the synthesis between whole and disparate parts were always guaranteed, the novels would have little interest. The textuality is constantly renewed, with new themes and variations being explored and with repeated indications that the solution is neither in the mythology of the whole nor in some promised christology or eu-phoria, but rather in the playing out of oppositions. Instead of the ultimate failure of a redemptive christology, of far greater interest is the line between difference and the same, between a recuperative mythology and a different language, or again, between a recuperative language and a signified of difference. I shall concentrate, then, on the interpretation of the line between difference and the eternal return of the same. Sexual in *Les Météores* and, for that matter, in *Le Roi des aulnes*, this figure is in fact repeated, more or less asexually, in *La Goutte d'or*, which draws the same line between determination and free play, or sameness and difference.

Les Météores is a study of the inscription of desire in the world as a means of interpreting that world and as a figure of the desiring subject. Its focus, as I shall argue, is on homosexual desire and its inscriptions. And even its christology, as we shall see, is homosexual and similar to the one just discussed from *Le Vagabond immobile*. Yet as visible as homosexuality is in *Les Météores*, it is far more difficult to seize there than in the works of the three other authors discussed. Tournier does not specifically make any of the *rhetorical* functions of the text homosexual: no part of the enunciative system except the character of Alexandre has an explicitly homosexual component. For that reason, it may be easy to compartmentalize Alexandre as a figure whose presence has no import for the rest of the novel.

But from all the evidence I have already marshaled, I would argue the contrary: the marginal figure in the text is, and must be, at the centerless center of interpretation. Tournier's ambiguities, his misdirections, even his statements of belief, all point us, in a roundabout way, to making that fundamental hypothesis. In short, Tournier makes homosexuality the operative model for the reader's understanding: it is the source of sexual theories, the origin of textual poetics, and the vehicle for the inscription of desire within the novel. But that figure is not a comfortable one. Far more overtly than a recuperative heterosexual model, this homosexual model stresses difference at its core and the need, already intimated in many a move by the author himself, of expelling that difference. Tournier sacrifices difference so that a misnamed plenitude seems to come into being.

The alienation that is intrinsic to desire is paralleled by an alienation of textual motives and reasons: to indicate the alien, the other, or the different, Tournier makes a gesture that expels that difference. The difference within sameness is never made clearer than in the realm of the sexual, which is the Janus-like figure of desire and of theory:

> But nothing is as good as sex for interrupting loneliness. Without sex, I don't really see whom I might need. An anchorite in the desert, a stylite standing day and night next to his column. Sex is the centrifugal force that chases you out. Get out of here! Go screw outside! That's the meaning of the prohibition of incest. None of that here! Daddy's monopoly! (*Mét* 85–86)

The novel is a meditation on the impossibility of ever fully determining same and other and thus of bringing back the different to the realm of identity. As Anthony Purdy has shown, there is a recognition of the need to develop a heterology, the epitome of which is in the realm of the sexual, but there is a simultaneous recognition of the impossibility of that development. Will the Oedipal crisis as Tournier understands it—the prohibition of incest—be a reproduction of the same or a means of generating difference? Will the wayward child come back only to repeat the paternal order or will he maintain his status as outsider? Such is the dimension of what is at stake in an understanding of Tournier's theory of sexuality.

In a parallel vein, as sexuality and textuality echo each other in this work, the novel is a study of the alien nature of fiction. In specific, what Tournier demonstrates is how fiction keeps a fundamental difference from what it describes, despite any strategies of recuperation or appropriation and despite any mythologizing of the whole. These two perspectives are in fact aspects of one program, the meditation on the indeterminacy of same and other, figured as both sexual and textual difference. I would like to propose the term invented by George Bauer in "Sartre's Homo/Textuality" (in Stambolian and Marks, eds.): the *homotext*. Following Bauer's reading of Sartre in light of the combined figures of textuality and sexuality, I would pragmatically define the homotext as the locus in which a theorization of a different sexuality, that is to say, homosexuality, is joined to a theorization of a different textuality, this novel. In *Les Météores*, then, Tournier proposes a doubled redefinition of the world, based neither on the separation of sexuality and textuality nor on the definition of either of those as a figure of identity. Rather, he conflates the two and places that conflation under the sign of alterity.

Now, in using the word "homotext," I am aware that neologisms often have lives of their own. The term has been employed by at least two critics, who each related it to the specific author whose work they were studying. In an article about Roland Barthes, John O'Neill (in Shapiro and Sica, eds., 172) defines "homotextuality" as a matter of style; for him, homotextuality is "the corporeal bond between the man and his text." Even if I were sure that this "man and works" approach were valid, O'Neill's definition cannot be usefully applied to Tournier, because, as we already know, he constantly absents his body. Whereas in works such as *Fragments d'un discours amoureux* and *Le Plaisir du texte* the literal body of the author comes into play, Tournier is quite ambivalent (as in *Le Vagabond immobile*) about enlisting his own body or his own sexual being into the text.[2]

My criticism of the other use of the word relates to a generalized

2. In fact, the presence of Tournier's body is a somewhat rare event. Fernandez (288) notes that Tournier could hardly be called a gay militant. He seems to admire Tournier for not being a model as much as he seems to execrate Barthes for not having been a model.

problem, one that we have seen throughout this study. Emily Apter (viii) uses the word "homotext" to describe the "rhetorical codes governing 'the lover's discourse'" and as "a theoretical construct in the context of Gide's explicit politics of gender."[3] What I would like to do is return to a more generalized integration of text and sexuality, since I believe that the four authors examined in this study all make homosexuality a generalized, as opposed to a local, interpretant. In line with the view that homosexuality can be used as a textual interpretant in the general sense and that, as a transcendental signifier, it is not restricted to local gender politics, I shall return to the more broad-based use of the word proposed by Bauer. In the homotext, the hermeneutics of interpretation are determined by homosexuality, independent of the experiential stance of a given author. For me, the term describes something more general: the homotext is a whole textuality that goes beyond the specifics of sexuality and gender politics to provide a reading both of the textual and of the sexual.

Still, the figure of the homotext seems compellingly to reach for a definition by negation, one that the reader will already have guessed, and will have considered as applicable to the three authors previously studied: in such a definition, the homotext is a text in which the structures of heterosexuality are not given primacy. Obviously, if neither homosexuality nor heterosexuality is considered as originary, then a heterosexual text could be just as profitably plumbed through the positing of this simple axiom as could the homotexts I have been examining.

In *Les Météores*, Tournier defines the world of the homotext through the character of Alexandre. As Alexandre develops into the means of theorization, a concept of sexuality and textuality appears as a semiosis of unanchored signs floating in a decentered system. Neither the series of emitted signs nor the system to which they somehow belong is stable. This instability has proven problematic for the author as well as for critics, and many readings of Tournier rely on the author's own view of mythology as the basis for his work, giving a totalizing or even a Jungian reading to the novels (Merllié; Bouloumié). In the realm of the sexual, such critics emphasize the whole or recuperative nature of bisexuality over the difference, marginalization, and nonrecuperative category of homosexuality.

3. Apter adds, "I am, of course, aware that there is no way systematically to define the term. In using it, I have been conscious of its value as a kind of omnibus signifier referring to dimensions of the relationship between Greek codes of ideal love and what the early sexologist Edward Carpenter would characterize as a 'homosocial' epistemology, to displacements and indeterminacies of narrative voice and gender, and to the fluctuating semiosis of a sexually suggestive textual silence."

In contrast, I believe that the phoric movement separated from its christological fulfillment in bi- or omnisexual return to totality is more fundamental to an understanding of Tournier's writing than the recuperation of the whole. In other words, there are productive ways of looking at the phoria without *necessarily* engaging in a strategy of recuperating wholeness. Moreover, not only is Alexandre homosexual and not bisexual but also the concept of bisexuality is an idealization, far from the perfect recuperative system indicated by some critics. Bisexuality could just as easily be considered a set of two incomplete, partial sexualities instead of some idealized, hermaphroditic psychosexual totality. Because I doubt the efficacy of using a recuperative whole as a model for reading, the strategy used here depends on the difference of nonrecuperative homosexuality or pederasty. The injunction "Go screw outside!" (*Mét* 86) must be followed as a guide to reading, even if the road "outside" never turns back to find its origin. As Tournier remarks: "the natural, irrepressible vocation of the book is centrifugal" (*VV* 10); in that it is undoubtedly like the "centrifugal" force of sex mentioned in *Les Météores* (*Mét* 85–86).

The reader must choose a point of view. The advantage of the model of the homotext is its ability to discuss desire; the disadvantage is that the last third of *Les Météores* is not nearly as interesting as the first two-thirds. The twin model recuperates that last third, but with the concomitant loss of ability to explain the constitution and production of difference in the first two-thirds of the text. In an interview, Tournier himself suggests that the work is a composite text: "In *Les Météores*, Koussek is the remains of the novel I would have liked to write" (Hueston 404). Thus at least one of the homosexual characters of *Les Météores*, whom Tournier sees as the figure of the unwritten theological novel, is part of an attempt to write a novel that never was.

Had Tournier succeeded in his project, the combined figures of Koussek and Alexandre would have formed a more obvious counterweight to the twins than they do now. Even in its incompletion, the novel tells us that it cannot be read as a story of twins, despite the rhetoric of the twins, despite the promises made. The work is really two stories, not twin stories: the story of Alexandre and the story of the twins. It is, after all, a text of difference, where the monstrosity of difference must be tamed. The novel itself is monstrous in that it consists of two anomalous parts that will never be joined in an organic whole. Since the story of Alexandre does not seek to exile monstrosity but to bring it back, it is now, more apparently, the locus for a description of the homotext. By naming monstrosity with an *appellation contrôlée*, by making an appeal to monstrosity and an appeal to the reader, by making monstrosity appealing, the text reduces the terato-logical to the phono-logical, the lexico-logical, and more precisely, to the homo-logical.

The central ambiguity of recuperation versus difference can be seen in the way in which *Les Météores* uses intertextuality, a process that implies both recuperation of a past textuality and a difference from it. There are two kinds of intertexts in this novel and I shall deal with each in turn. There are references to Tournier's own work as well as references to Tournier's literary forefathers, Gide and Proust. Each kind of intertextuality illuminates an aspect of Tournier's writing for the reader. References to two of his own previous novels, *Vendredi* and *Le Roi des aulnes*, are found within a forty-page span of *Les Météores*. Signposts for the reader, the two intertextual references recall two exiles, two epistemologies, and two aesthetics.

Le Roi des aulnes is the story of a monster who reflects the monstrosity of World War II as well as a difference from it. As is the case in Günter Grass's *The Tin Drum* and, for that matter, the story of "Beauty and the Beast," a surface monstrosity hiding a general goodness is contrasted with the deep monstrosity of many cloaked in the banality of evil. In the world of Abel Tiffauges, the only meaning that is available is produced reductively: the monstrous third dimension of reality dissolves into the two-dimensional world of the photograph. The world of the photograph denies depth and makes any inner being invisible. With a camera slung around his neck like a large sexual organ sheathed in leather, Abel Tiffauges can reflect and seize this world by reducing its format, scope, and parameters (*RA* 167). Tiffauges, the monster pariah, reduces the world's own monstrosity by capturing it in a trap of endless reproducibility, a rhetorical strategy that will reappear in *La Goutte d'or*. In that novel, the constant reproduction of the signifier and thus its banalization are engaged in the textual motifs relating to photography and to Idriss's job as a model for mass-produced mannequins. Tournier repeats a technique that tames the other by making it appear to be of a different order: the same is presented as real and three-dimensional, the other, as a two-dimensional copy.

When Tiffauges is glimpsed in *Les Météores*, the same thing happens to him that transpires with his reduction of the "other" in *Le Roi des aulnes*. Wrenched from the political world of *Le Roi*, Tiffauges reappears in *Les Météores* as a two-dimensional version of his former self, as if he had finally been captured by his own camera. Tiffauges appears in a scene (*Mét* 195) in which he serves as the sign of the singular, the portent of separation, and the index of monstrosity. For Paul, Tiffauges is the epitome of the world of violence, of murder, and of the crime that is called History (*Mét* 196); for him, only twins are completely innocent of this violence. Born in plenitude, always fulfilled even before they start, twins are complete *ab ovo*: "Tied to my brother-likeness in an ovoid position, my head held between his thighs, as a bird hides its head under its wing to sleep, surrounded by an odor and a warmth that were mine" (*Mét* 75). The intertextual reference to Tiffauges as aberrant other, like Alexandre as aberrant other, seems to capture that other to make the text safe for the approach of plenitude.

Excluding this other, reducing him or it to a marginal figure, allows Tournier and his twins to pretend that wholeness can come on the scene. And though Tiffauges's presence is an index of that axiomatic plenitude, Tournier does not rest on that pat assumption. In fact, as I have pointed out, the last third of the novel, relating entirely to the twins, does not fall under the sway of the homosexual model. Still, the development of this part of the novel occurs just when the twins are separated, when plenitude is not there. The last third is a search for a return to a whole. The elaboration of the story of Jean and Paul is found in this last third of the novel, which consists of Paul's search for renewed fulfillment after their separation.[4]

In both works the marginal other, Alexandre or Tiffauges, is excluded to produce a fiction: though the focus of much of the novel, Alexandre is marginalized in the author's theorizings and killed off two-thirds of the way through. Metonymically, Alexandre's intertextual alter ego, Tiffauges, becomes the repository for things that do not comfortably fit into the model of a dyad resolved into unity. Recalling the intertext rejects its difference, yet in that recalling, we remember that it is the gesture of expulsion—of Tiffauges from his world, of Tiffauges's violence from the world of *Les Météores*, of Alexandre from his own text, of homosexuality from the paradigm of completion—that allows the model of identity to function. At the same time, we realize that it is precisely that act that gives us a picture of the novel as homotext: a work in which the act of expulsion always leaves a trace.

The second intertext is *Vendredi*, which is used to underline the development of an aesthetic position. Alexandre makes the most of difference by demonstrating how it is both named and maintained through language:

4. As will become clear below, a religious discourse in *Les Météores* subtends part of the theoretical arguments. One already sees evidence in the naming of the twins and in the difference between them that comes from these names. The plenitude mentioned is incarnate in Paul, the follower or the one who comes after (Saint Paul); it is not present in Jean, the precursor or the one who comes before (Saint John the Baptist).

"I have a dog. I have to find him a name. Robinson called his man 'Friday,' because he adopted him on a Friday" (*Mét* 226). Tournier reinscribes desire and difference through language and, with the counterpoint of self-referential intertextuality, he capitalizes on that difference in *Les Météores* to reach aesthetic ends. The presence of the two intertexts allows for two possible readings of the world and two ways in which desire is inscribed in language: a theory of twinning and a theory of difference. But despite Paul's reiterated insistence, the two views are not two related schematic or analogous views of the world. The views are not even fraternal twins; they are as different as teratology will allow. Because it is not truly recuperative, the monstrous twin model spews ever-increasing untamed difference.

To capture difference, Tournier resorts to a functional act of nomination, with an insistence on the milestones on the Canadian Pacific railway in a reference that farcically recalls Michel Butor's *La Modification*. But Butor inscribed desire and difference and capitalized on the means of inscription to generate his text. In contrast, through an inscription of difference, Tournier turns naming, calling, and the taming of desire into indifferent sterility: "Milestone 1405.9 Winnipeg. . . . Go to Winnipeg to stay locked in the compartment to read the page of the guidebook about Winnipeg" (*Mét* 565). Just as he has reductively inscribed Tiffauges, Tournier does the same for the writing subject by making Paul nothing more than an amanuensis. And Paul, in turn, inscribes the outside world by reducing Canada to milestones and to words in a guidebook.

Having long before disposed of Alexandre and that character's attempts at taming desire by exploring it, Tournier can offer no solution in the last third of the novel other than a functional nominalism that cannot say anything about desire. When difference and desire are explored, when the homotext openly flourishes, the work spins centrifugally toward a dissemination of the parts. Since Tournier seems to need to recuperate, he stops that dissemination, draws the character in, and kills him off. And yet, with Alexandre's death, desire has no language in which it may be couched. It would not be unfair to say that the real end of the novel comes with the death of Alexandre, because that is the death of desire. When the multiply pierced avatar of Saint Sebastian, the corpse/corpus of Alexandre, is found among the dark warehouses, black spots on/in the whiteness of the city of white houses, Casablanca (*Mét* 386), that is the end of desire and of its incarnation as fiction.

Now if the signs of self-referential intertextuality bring us to an understanding of the simultaneous expression and refusal of Tournier's homotextuality, allocentric intertextuality frames the clear, unambiguous inscription of difference at the very heart of the same. Tournier may propose a recuperative model, but every homotextual gesture points us toward the alterity of the text. In *Les Météores*, Tournier blatantly appeals to the readers' intertextual memories of the *topos* of avuncularity, a subject that will continue to fascinate him in *La Goutte d'or* (Merllié 110). Avuncularity is the reduction of the question of relation to a very simple conundrum: Is one related to one's uncle? Is the uncle the repetition of the same family pattern or the destruction of this pattern? Is the uncle the one who brings about difference to avoid the eternal repetition of the same?

Obviously one is related to one's uncle, but the obvious is a screen. If we consider the concept of relation as meaning both the blood line and the perpetuation of the structure the case is not so simple. Certainly uncle and nephew are related by blood, but the position of the uncle may in fact guarantee difference in the system, may help the nephew escape from the pressure of the tautological reproduction of identity by the Oedipal triangle. The uncle's very existence is the encouragement the nephew needs to "screw outside"; the uncle helps reduce the tyranny of the reproduction of identity. Certainly this is the message of both anthropology and literature. The message of difference through avuncularity is a standard structure of homosexual literature: the *Recherche* has both "Oncle Adolphe" and "Tante Léonie" for the narrator and the pair of Charlus and Saint-Loup; *Les Faux-Monnayeurs* has Edouard; Patrick Dennis has Auntie Mame, and so on.

Form illustrates contents here: as befits the inscription of the concept of difference central to avuncularity, the intertextual references to avuncularity are outside Tournier's own oeuvre. We no longer look to *Vendredi* or *Le Roi des aulnes* for an explanation, but rather to Tournier's own literary uncles, Marcel Proust and André Gide. Tournier's comments in the interview with Penny Hueston (402) are worth mentioning:

> I have an infinite liking for Gide, particularly his life style. He led a truly admirable life. . . . Proust I admire greatly, but I detest him. . . . as a person, as a writer. None of that interests me. His salons, his aristocrats, that enormously long sentence that looks like an octopus.

So we know that we need first to look at Proust. For Proust, both Oncle Adolphe and Tante Léonie are the figures of avuncularity for the young Marcel in *Du côté de chez Swann* (Mehlman 20–64). But as Proust continues to write, he extends the family drama of avuncularity to a full-blown hermeneutic of homosexuality. Proust turns the relation into the "discovery" of similar sexual natures in an uncle and a nephew, the best example being the case of Charlus and Saint-Loup. As Proust says in *Sodome et Gomorrhe* (3:94), "one could thus make a whole portrait gallery, whose title would be the German comedy *Uncle and Nephew*, and in which one would see the uncle jealously watching and waiting (though involuntarily) for his nephew to wind up resembling him." In *Les Faux-Monnayeurs*, Gide also insists on a special relation: Oncle Edouard combines avuncularity with a voyeurism tinged with signs of incestuous desire. Oncle Edouard surreptitiously enjoys the act and recognition of transgression as he watches his nephew, Georges Moulinier, pilfer a book and then put it back (*Romans* 998–1003).

The references to Proust and Gide in *Les Météores* continue to underline the expression of heterological, homotextual difference in Tournier's work. At the same time, and this should come as no surprise, Tournier once again tries to minimize the appearance of fundamental difference. Though avuncularity is fundamental to *Les Météores*, in a move that is contrary to the production of difference Tournier carefully severs the avuncular connection that he overtly implies with his intertextual references. It is, for example, not coincidental that Tournier chooses the name "Edouard" for the *father* in *Les Météores*. Tournier cannot allow the reader to repeat the connection between uncle and nephews in a similitude that implies difference, for that would undercut the primacy of the twin model on which the author is endlessly insisting. Furthermore, an outright reference to the canon would undercut the solipsistic project of self-sufficient homotextuality. If Alexandre is forced to parody Gide's Edouard by following his (Alexandre's) nephew around Casablanca, as Gide's Edouard had done in Paris, contact is precluded between uncle and nephew. Moreover, the event occurs too far into the novel to make a structural difference. The recognition of the relation, which should be simultaneous if it is to be valid as a *cri du sang*, is deferred until death has intervened. In fact, Alexandre recognizes his nephews (*Mét* 385), but Paul remarks his/their uncle *qua* uncle only after his murder (*Mét* 386–87). The meditation on avuncularity returns us to the nonavuncular within the avuncular: the nonrelational within the related and the difference within the inscription of identity. The theorization of homosexuality in this novel is tantamount to the search for difference within the realm of the same, that is to say, the heterological within the homotext. At the same time, it is the determination of the *flou* within the inscription of desire. Finally, it is the rejection of an other textuality imposed from without.

Current literary theory would do well to reconsider the problem of intentionality. Why do certain authors seem to invite readings that depend on bringing the question of authorial intent to the fore? One hypothesis would be simple and straightforward: the complex texts of authors like Mallarmé, Flaubert, or Proust need help, and the intentions expressed in the author's correspondence or criticism might illuminate the work. Another hypothesis would be that intentionality provides comfort. If we know what the author meant, we are clear as to how and where to look for meaning; at the same time, we can discount what he or she "did not mean." But there is another degree of comfort: intention clears up the uncomfortability, the dis-ease of the text itself. This is the appeal of the intentional argument in reading Tournier. Knowing what Tournier means allows monstrosity to be circumscribed and impurity to be brought back into the fold as part of a cosmic circle or cycle. Thus the model of sexuality in this universe is bisexuality. We can understand Robinson's body smeared with feces, with the excrement generalized into a general slime (*VLP* 37–38), Abel Tiffauges's shit-shampoos (*RA* 73–75), and Alexandre's position as king of the sewers. These are all negative poles of a universe that includes the *yin* and *yang* of every situation.

If it were just a matter of critics rehearsing the intentional fallacy, it would not be worth discussing. But the singularity of Tournier's discourse comes from that fact that he seems to want us to believe that his extratextual remarks are gospel. He seems to *intend* his intention. Such a rhetoric cannot be dismissed out of hand. Before proceeding any further, we would do well to note Tournier's intention for the character of Alexandre. In *Le Vent Paraclet* (*VP* 255–56), Tournier assures the reader that the model for Alexandre was partly Louise Falque, a woman of his acquaintance, and that the rest was "a bit like Barbey d'Aurevilly, a bit like Maurice Barrès." A little research tells us something different: from Alain Corbin's study of smell, *Le Miasme et la jonquille*, and from Charles Bernheimer's excellent study of the representation of prostitution in nineteenth-century France, *Figures of Ill Repute*, it is clear that Tournier modeled Alexandre at least somewhat on Alexandre Parent-Duchâtelet. Parent-Duchâtelet noted six different odors in the sewers of Paris and, as Bernheimer (10) comments, Parent-Duchâtelet "enjoyed descending into the city's lower depths, smelling its odors, meeting its people, sharing their food, listening to their stories." The question is not so much why Tournier omitted the justly named "Alexandre Parent" as the avuncular origin for his own "Alexandre," who is still a "*parent*," the French word for "relative," but why such an explanation would itself be inadequate.

We have seen that the archetypal model is inadequate for an understanding of this text and that the biographical model is also not the solution. There is another type of intentionality, however, lexical in nature, an example of which is the name "Surin." Critics such as Merllié (89) and Bouloumié (51) have pointed out that the name is a slang word for "knife." In that, they are following Alexandre's own musing projection of the real, and not the rhetorical author, concerned with making things, as Proust's Françoise would say, *de la même parenthèse*: "His name will be forgiven in consideration of the admirable and quite rare first name that makes him my close relative [*parent*]: Eustache and Surin both mean an evil knife in underworld slang" (*Mét* 103–4). We already know that Surin is the name of a city in Thailand well known for its elephant roundups. Given the various references to elephants, given the name of Sister Gotama, with her name referring to Buddha and thus to the religion of Thailand, this reading cannot be excluded.

If I had to choose between Tournier's explanation for the model for Alexandre or for the origin of the name Surin, I would always choose the answer he omits, since that repressed reasoning seems far more consonant with other problems in Tournier's texts. Tournier's intended intentions and willful misdirections are, in fact, the indicial signs of the acts of exclusion of practitioners of homotextuality. Tournier's excluded explanations give reason to the excluded others; the act of forgetting or excluding those explanations parallels the very topic and focus of the book. We can see therefore that Tournier's book is founded on negativity, absence, and exclusion. At every level and at every moment, there is an illustration of this act, and language itself, along with what it represents, is the simultaneous sign of that exclusion and yet another exclusion itself. Would one be going too far in saying that for Tournier, literary language itself, or at least his own, is at its very heart homosexual?

The undecidability concerning the determination of certain characters in Tournier's novels is part of a founding negativity. It is to that founding negativity, the product of the indeterminacy of origins, that we now turn. Alexandre's theoretical determination of the world begins as a negativity that defines his relation to it. In essence, this negativity is the foundation of all emotional and intellectual attachments that Alexandre eventually forms. Clearly, this negativity is the acceptable version of the figure of homotextuality that for Tournier cannot be directly enunciated. The negativity is initially determined as an absence or a fault within the relational system. Alexandre is attracted to waste disposal because he was "seduced by the negative aspect, I'd even say the *inverted* aspect of that industry" (*Mét* 36). Each human activity, no matter how intimate, leaves a "trace," a set of paper or paperlike signs of the action or relation: "A cigarette butt, a torn letter, a peel, a sanitary napkin" (*Mét* 36). Thus, although sexual relations are the determining factor for Alexandre's existence, a situation that is not without echoes of Foucault's discussions of sexuality, they initially exist as the trace of their own nature and as one relation among many. If sexual relations are to be distinguished from other human activity, there must be a special sort of trace. With this trace, sexual relations become metarelations as well, the signs of all other types of congress.

Though all human activity produces waste, it is sexuality that is especially indicated by Tournier's invented signifier for "household garbage [*ordures ménagères*]": *oms*. This new measure, the measure "of man [*de l'homme*]," is the crystallization of the liquid—or more precisely the nonsolid, the *flou*. Tournier sets up his world through a simple paradigm: the solid having disintegrated and the *flou* having appeared, the world of objects can be re-related through the processes of meaning, naming, and calling. Man (*l'homme*) gives a name (*un nom*) to what he has produced and to what can be traced in the homotext: *oms*. The text calls to itself, reinscribes itself, and rewrites the world as the traces of the homologous, the home, the homophonic, and the homosexual.[5] Taken as the language of desire that appeals and that recalls, language returns the rejected and brings back the excluded: oms, homo.

For Tournier's Alexandre, only homosexual language, given in the form of the homotext (*l'homme au texte*), works in this way. The language of heterosexuality is produced in a realm that has two absolute prerequisites for production. The language of heterosexuality insists on the homogeneous at the point of discourse: there must be a consistent, fixed spot, identical to itself and to power, from which to speak and write. Each individual instance of heterosexual discourse is presented as a synecdoche of the whole. Second, the discourse of heterosexuality simply expels the other: it rubs out the signs and inscriptions of difference. René Girard's comments in *Des choses cachées* (358) on the homosexual basis of heterosexual desire are especially pertinent here, since they explain that expulsion is necessary to heterosexuality because it is a way of eliminating its underlying homosexuality, given the fact that "the model-rival, in the realm of sex, is normally someone of the *same* sex, due to the very fact that the object is heterosexual. Every sexual rivalry is thus structurally homosexual." As Girard shows, the discourse of heterosexuality is subtended by a struggle for unique power, a process to be accomplished by the expulsion of the other (the rival), who marks a difference by his very presence. Thus the

5. This last term can be read within the paradigm as: "homme ô/au sexuel." See Purdy's comments (36–37) on the prefix *homo*. "Oms" can also be read as the mystic syllable "om" that is part of a mantra in Hinduism.

maintenance of the fixed center *as* center, or the erection of a center of power, a symbolic phallus of prohibition, is the mark of male heterosexual discourse. This discourse seeks to institutionalize desire through a system of prepositied relations that themselves are neither links to (a) desire, traces of (a) desire, nor calls to (a) desire. The attempt to institutionalize desire is a fiction intended to hide the fact that there was an act of usurpation, that there was a difference, and that there is a lack of authenticity.

The marks of homosexual desire are the signs of a wandering discourse in a decentered system: rather than being a fixed mark, the point at which discourse occurs is itself constantly different and centrifugal. It is the sign or trace of the different within the same: "For me, sex has always been a centrifugal force that throws me toward the faraway, illuminated by my own desire, like a lighthouse at night" (*Mét* 333). Between Tournier's concept of the prohibition of incest (*Mét* 85–86) and this latter lighthouse effect, one can detect a shift that relates to the concept of a homotext. Although the position of the father remains anchored to the symbolic phallus at the point of origin in the homotext, the locus of enunciation is drawn to the imaginary phallus, not the symbolic one, and calls to this imaginary phallus in order to bridge and remark difference as such instead of expelling it.

The imaginary phallus acts as a beacon for homosexual desire and for the accomplishment of this desire or its remarking through the homotext. In the homotext, the realm of negation and prohibition (and not of negativity, which is the realm of the symbolic) disappears. The imaginary becomes more "real" than the reality grounded in the negations and prohibitions of heterotextuality:

> He turns around and faces me. The light just allows me to see that his unbuttoned fly unveils his genitals. In any case, the exhibition follows so logically from the situation at hand that, in the dark night with my eyes closed, I would have guessed it, I would have seen *it*. (*Mét* 127)

This *phoric* power attributed to the phallus of the other within the realm of homosexual desire is present from the beginning of the novel. It is initially a diffuse presence that impregnates the air with eroticism; from the beginning it fills the space of the textual imaginary. It thereby creates both a real and an imaginary situation in which the discourse of desire can operate: "From the first day on, I was seized by an amorous giddiness in penetrating the laden atmosphere of the awakening manhoods of the prep school" (*Mét* 42). The beckoning of desire or its call to presence operates within the realm of the same by means of a phoric call that bridges the gap of desire. Whereas expulsion occurs within the dynamics of heterosexuality and its incarnations, an expulsion of the other and of the homosexual, no such action occurs within the homotext. In it, likes attract and a community is formed in which only rejection itself is rejected. One can imagine the electricity, the magnetic attraction, the very gravitational pull of the other in Tournier's description of the moment of contact:

> Pushed forward and soon stopped by the students ahead of me, I had to admit that I was grasping with both hands, through the thin material of his trousers, the erect penis of the student behind me. In moving my hands, in removing them from this offering, I would have, with a mere imperceptible gesture, rejected the move made on me. On the contrary, I answered by stepping back, by opening my hands wide, like shells, like baskets to gather the fruit of furtive love. (*Mét* 43)

In spite of the attraction, the presence of the phoric phallus "feminizes" Alexandre by reducing him to a vessel or receptor, which, in a phallocentric view of the world, is associated with the feminine. The genitals in question having been proffered anonymously, Alexandre becomes the receptacle, basket, or shell for this wayward male member. By opening his hands, he demonstrates that he does not participate in the altrilocal system of heterosexuality. Sex is here and now, though at an ec-centric position; the gap between the two participants is filled by the phallus and its inscription.

In order to be a full-fledged member of the select group of homotextualists that Tournier baptizes the Fleurets, Alexandre has to be at the male position. Unlike the fixed systems of heterotextuality, the sexual politics of the homotextual discourse allow a free-flowing mutation from one pole to another. In other words, though Alexandre is initially feminized, it is not an essentialist framing of him. Since sex is here and now, since there is no altrilocal model to force essence and expulsion, he can change positions at will. And though Tournier approaches overt misogyny at times, the female position is not simply denigrated. Rather, the female position is defined by an altrilocal system: one is not born a woman but becomes one, as Simone de Beauvoir says. For Tournier this becoming takes place within the model of allocentric, altrilocal sex. In that being a woman depends on an enforced otherness, for Tournier this female position cannot bridge desire.

In the text's own metaphoric order, female sexuality does not have the requisite quality of male sexuality: the ability to encapsulate or solidify a liquid. This is a rare case in which Tournier's phallocentric discourse is ironically supported and reinforced by the subtending mythology of the wholeness of the text. Alexandre's hands may very well be a receptacle at first, but they are not a container. His genitals, however, *are* a container; they embody the bridging of liquid desire through the imposition of solid form:

> At first, I had been deemed barely "edible" because I was thin, but Raphael, the authority in erotic matters, had rehabilitated me by praising my penis, which, at the time, was relatively long and plump, and whose silky sweetness, said he, contrasted with the dryness of my thighs and the aridity of my belly stretched out like a canvas between the bony projections of my hips. "A bunch of juicy [*juteux*] grapes hanging on a sunburnt stake [*échalas*]," he asserted.[6] (*Mét* 45–46)

Alexandre's nickname "Fleurette" (*Mét* 45) is the feminine version of the name of the club, *les Fleurets*, which itself means "fencing foils," and thus echoes one of the orthodox meanings of "Surin." Aside from the floral connotations of the words, "*fleurette*" is a culinary term for "sweet cream," as opposed to *crème fraîche*; it is also, in the phrase *conter fleurettes*, the "sweet nothings" whispered in the ear of the beloved. So in the orthodox view of naming, Surin and the Fleurets represent cutting, difference, division, and indeed, castration: thus, in the official version, they represent a lack, an absence, and an expulsion of the other. Like Proust's disquisition on Sodom, the homotext resonates with the vegetal imagery of flowers and grapes. Tournier recuperates a vocabulary of symbols of the feminine, a cache of words that define the other, and turns those words into a homotextual vocabulary. In the meta-phoric version of the text, the homotext of sexual and textual identity, the descriptions vibrate with the sexual, liquid imagery of sweet cream and the juiciness of the grapes, described as "*juteux*": "*jute*" is a slang word for seminal fluid (i.e., cum). And the very same key word, "*juteux*," appears later in the novel as Alexandre looks for a room at the "Grutiers"; the solidity of his phallic power has allowed him phorically to bridge the gaps or absences created even within liquid desire and he expects "some rather juicy [*juteuses*] experiences" (*Mét* 110).

For Alexandre, the heterosexual experience is a system of simple, bivalent logic, limited in scope, and depending only on the concept of exclusion for its continuation. Certainly it represents both multiplication and fertility, but only within a binary system of zero and one. No other points are possible and no other combinations can occur. In contrast, for Alexandre, homosexuality is neither imprisoned nor expelled. It is not subject to a system of bivalent logic and it allows for an ever-increasing, though lin-

6. The word *échalas* means the stake or prop that supports a vine, but has the figurative meaning of a "bean pole," that is to say, a tall, thin person.

ear and nonfertile, arithmetic daisy-chain to occur, a chain of production and not of reproduction. If heterosexuality is the endless reproduction of same and other, homosexuality becomes an arithmetic progression where numbers are added one to the other and where nothing is excluded (*Mét* 237). Heterosexuality generates the chain of binary numbers, branchings, logical attachments, choices, and exclusions. Homosexuality generates a linear, decimal system, but an "open-ended" set that does not exclude. Never complete and never fulfilled, the decimal system is the tally and the tally-ho of the hunter, the notched count on the bedpost, and the rousing call to action: "my hunting mood led me toward the Bois de Vincennes because of its well-known cynegetic possibilities" (*Mét* 122).

Beyond being a possibility of individual desire, homosexual desire is phorically placed in two figural fields. One is properly metaphoric, due to its tropic nature; the other is rather metonymic, as it names what is unnameable and encloses this unnameable through the process of naming. Homosexual desire seeks to bridge the gap of desire and difference; it seeks to remark difference by closing the space between self and other. The homosexual's genitals are thrust forward toward fulfillment just as they are figured in their own metaphor in Alexandre's sword-cane, a magic walking stick and a scepter of power. The homosexual's genitals bridge the gap of difference and flout heterosexual laws of exclusion as well. Homosexual desire also covers the *flou* by transforming it into something tractable; the desire solidifies the liquid and thereby forms the amorphous. The pure, omnidirectional flow of desire is channeled through the imposition of a homosexual modeling system. Bridging and containing desire, this system remarks both difference and the undifferentiated within the process of reinscription that is the homotext.

As omnidirectional and undifferentiated flow, the unmarked state of desire resembles nothing more than unbridled animal behavior, like the eruptive defecation of elephants provoked by the sounds of love (*Mét* 130–31). For Alexandre, this unbridled behavior is doubly reflected in the world. Uncontained in heterosexuals except by exclusion, heterosexual desire is a capitulation to the basest urge of all, the cannibalizing of the world through a simultaneous consumption and expulsion. In other words, in that it does not exclude the other, homosexual desire, for Alexandre, is a play of differences, whereas heterosexual desire, depending as it does on the exclusion of the other, is a banal repetition of the same and the undifferentiated. So for Alexandre, the eternal repetition of the same that marks heterosexuality leads to the most nefarious and villainous ends: Hitler's arrest of the Jews and their subsequent imprisonment in concentration camps is an expression of all that is bad in the nondistinguishable and the undifferentiated. The horrors result from the attempt to eliminate difference: "Of course, heterosexual rabble [*racaille*] says nothing [*ne pipe mot*] about this collective crime. Stupid bastards!" (*Mét* 120).[7]

So Tournier's irony is in his reversal of the accepted order. Normally, one would see heterosexuality and not homosexuality as the field in which differentiation occurs, because heterosexuality involves two different, "opposite," sexes. But that is not at all the case here. Far from the iterations of the heterosexual, Tournier's version of homosexuality develops the play of differences in the homotext of which Alexandre and his activities are the focus. Far from this collective defecation of the world, Alexandre's garbage is a tesselated and varied system of differences that he alone can discern, read, and absorb. Along with his insistence on difference from the "heterosexual rabble" comes a parody of that world. Alexandre introduces his brand of difference as an imitation of their insistence on identity. He proposes translating the collective herd mentality of the heterosexual rabble into an exquisite betrayal, fulfillment, and parody, glossed with a degree of sadism: "He who is often constipated says that he would be cured if he had the face of a heterosexual to shit on each morning" (*Mét* 141).

Alexandre's theorization and practice of homosexual desire are not the only versions of homosexuality and textuality that Tournier proposes in the novel. In fact, he posits two other systematizations of desire. One comes from the twin model; the other, from the unwritten theological novel already mentioned. Paul's position is given as a postmortem on his uncle and represents the nephew's attempt to fit homosexual desire into his own paradigm of twinning. Whereas for Alexandre the division of the world comes about through the difference between heterosexual and homosexual desire, for Paul cosmology, ontology, and epistemology are all bound together in a theorization of twinning. For Paul, the self-contained totality of twins, represented in a reciprocal act of simultaneous fellatio, is the refusal of the dialectics engendered in the world by the "*sans-pareil*," the same dialectics that Alexandre attributes to the heterosexual. For Paul, twinning is fulfillment, completion, and the bridging of difference:

> The communion of twins places us head to tail in the ovoid position of the double fetus. This position shows our determination not to get involved in the dialectic of time and life. On the other hand, the loves of a nontwin—whatever the position

7. Under the words "*racaille*" and "*pipe*" an amateur of cryptonyms could see the hidden expression "tailler une pipe," that is to say, to perform fellatio. Beyond the out-and-out disgust with heterosexual evil, Alexandre may be indicating that such people will not or cannot fellate others and that it is their loss.

used—put the partners in the asymmetrical and unbalanced attitude of a walker taking a step, his first step [*le premier pas*]. (*Mét* 387)

For Paul, following the Platonism of the *Symposium*, the homosexual seeks to overcome the dialectics of the *sans-pareil* by searching for his missing half: his missing "twin." On the other hand, the homosexual is an inverted version of Julien Sorel looking for completion after he has taken "le premier pas."[8] Despite the posited plenitude, Tournier ironically overturns this theory in the last third of the book: in searching for his missing twin, Paul repeats the gesture of the homosexual always searching for his partner. Thus, untwinned, Paul becomes a homosexual seeking his missing other. Untwinned, Paul as homosexual goes beyond a functional definition of homosexuality determined according to the genital conformation of the individual with whom one is having sex. In fact, by this point of the novel, the question of physical sexual relations is tangential to the real question. As an untwinned twin who follows or conforms to his own theorizations, Paul becomes a homosexual epistemologically, ontologically, and narratologically. Tournier does not allow his whole theorization of the homotext to crumble because of the exigencies of plot. As the imitation of an imitation, according to his own theorization, Paul is in fact subject to Alexandre's theoretical view of the world in the uncle's theory of imitations. When related both to the strained vicissitudes of the plot and to the strong arguments developed for the homotext, the concept of twinning, through its enactment of homosexuality, seems more and more a "closeted" metaphor for a general theory of homosexuality valid for the whole novel.

Because, in some senses, Paul's theory is the negation of a negation, it is incapable of producing a homotext in which sexuality and textuality are immediately intertwined. Rather, Paul's version is like a revisionist position that returns homosexuality, after the fact, to a central position. But that return comes through the mediation of another sexuality, the sexuality of twindom, which is not a direct, immediate, or accessible sexuality like the one described by Alexandre for the Fleurets. Paul's vision of homosexuality is an uncomfortable, forced intimacy far different from Alexandre's game of unmediated desire, whose dynamics come from a play of excluded difference.

Similarly, the final theory of homosexuality is incapable of producing

8. In a famous passage at the beginning of *Le Rouge et le Noir*, Julien Sorel finds a piece of printed paper "spread out as if it were meant to be read." The paper gives the details of the execution of one "Louis Jenrel," that is, the anagram of "Julien Sorel," his twin. On the back of the torn paper are the words "le premier pas" (Stendhal 240).

a homotext. Unlike Paul's theory, this last one is fulfilled and proven in a spirituality that serves as a leitmotiv for part of the novel. This is the theory for the novel Tournier did not write, the religious novel about Koussek, the scarcely developed character who seems at times to have floated in from another novel. This theory starts more or less simultaneously with that of Alexandre and both realize the intrinsic nature of difference within homotextuality. But whereas for Alexandre sex is used to bridge difference and to mark the continuity of inclusion, Koussek turns his back on these included others and refuses to venture into the world to bridge difference. Alexandre develops an aesthetics of homosexuality that intertwines beauty, talent, and action. Aside from his own physical charm, he notes, he developed "a talent to suck long and hard, which came from the taste I have always had for seminal liquor" (*Mét* 46). In contrast, Koussek is interested only in the spiritual side of any situation and action, as he develops a spiritual aesthetics of nonaction: "As for that taste, Thomas had it more than any one of us, but he rarely satisfied it in our direct manner with a straightforward blow-job" (*Mét* 46).

So Koussek's view of Alexandre's activity is far different from Alexandre's own. In the religious terms Koussek proposes, Alexandre's version of homosexuality is like an act of communion. It is a Eucharist that bridges difference through the remarking of the same. There is no need here for a transcendental, redemptive christology; the Eucharist is the immediate present of identity internalized. Through the medium of this spiritual figure, Tournier seems to introduce a movement of phoric dimension even to Alexandre, who consistently refuses that redemption in its various guises. Tournier does not stop there, for Koussek refuses the act of taking the body and making it one with oneself. Even the bridging of that infinitely small gap between self and other is too much for an absolute view that requires pure immediacy, instant transfiguration. While postulating exchange and redemption, Koussek shows that there is loss, even in the very act of redemption.

Undoubtedly like the mythic construct of the author himself, Koussek is far from that act of communion. Unlike Alexandre, Koussek "rarely satisfied" the communal exchange. Tournier quite pointedly gives Thomas over to a specific action that does not translate, (ex)change, or share:

> The dry run [*coup sec*] consisted—as its name indicated—of a complete orgasm without any flow of sperm. To accomplish that—or to have that accomplished by one's partner—a great amount of pressure is needed from one's finger on the furthest reachable point of the spermatic canal, that is, at the front edge of the anus. (*Mét* 48–49)

Thus, for Koussek, homosexuality becomes a sterile sort of autoeroticism. The antithesis of a "*juteux*" homosexuality, Koussek's version replaces the imaginary with the transcendentally symbolic. But in its insistence on the presence of difference in the here and now, the world of the homotext has no room for the transcendental. And without a metaphysics of transcendence, Koussek's version is mere solipsism. For Alexandre, who serves here as the rhetorical figure of the author, Thomas's *coup sec* is alien to the project of building bridges and channeling desire because it is imprisoned in "a sort of closed circuit that seems to me to imply the refusal of others" (*Mét* 49).

For Koussek, the container is always there, the desire is mastered, and the orgasm, even though present, is superfluous; he produces a transcendental christology of homosexuality for himself. It is only in Thomas's later discourse on the subject (*Mét* 146–48) that Tournier finally anchors the spiritual discourse to the homotext and its ancillary commentaries. He does this through the interposition of several intertextual reference points that appear both in Thomas's disquisition and in other places in the novel. The intertextual references are shared by the competing kinds of textuality in the novel; through this mediation, Koussek's observations are related to other parts of the novel with which they had seemed totally incommensurable. For example, Nazis appear again at this strategic point; in an odd juxtaposition, Molière's Monsieur Jourdain appears as well, only to reappear in Paul's disquisition on the same subject (*Mét* 387). For Koussek, the heterosexual is like Monsieur Jourdain, whereas for Paul, it is the homosexual who resembles him.

Thus, in retrospect, though Koussek's version of homosexuality seems to start out as the spiritual complement to Alexandre's direct phenomenology, by the end of the book we realize that Koussek's view of the subject is more like Paul's: both are derivative. In either case, one could say with Monsieur Jourdain that all that is not prose is poetry, or all that is not heterosexuality is homosexuality. Contrasted with Alexandre's theorizations, Paul's conception of homosexuality as well as Koussek's are points of view that ultimately define homosexuality according to the laws of heterotextuality. In other words, their starting point is implicitly that of an outside world that views homosexuality as an aberrant function of heterosexuality. Thomas's transcendental *coup sec* repeats the heterosexual prose of the world, for the same pressure of the majority "thrusts the homosexual into the skin of a faggot. What is a faggot? A homosexual docilely accepting working-class prohibitions" (*Mét* 148). One is not born a *pédé*, one becomes one.

Spiritual nephew of Naphta in Mann's *Der Zauberberg*, Thomas represents the thetic position of the christological sacrifice. Despite the absence of a real *last* sacrifice in this world where Alexandre's death ends nothing, language itself is placed under the sign of the mocking INRI that is erected as a *sign* of the last sacrifice. In Thomas's version, homosexuality becomes a spiritual version of mimetic behavior (*Mét* 152), a repetition of castration with a reference to Abelard (*Mét* 153), and finally, the Pentecostal explosion (*Mét* 155). In a world where transcendence is possible, transfiguration and miraculous fulfillment accompany the Pentecost. For Michel Serres, who writes brilliantly of the Pentecost in *Le Parasite* (57–67), the heart of the Pentecost is the Paraclete. But in *Les Météores*, neither the christology of the Eucharist nor the Paraclete of the Pentecost provides a valid final source of meaning for Tournier. Instead of being the fulfillment of the spirit, the Pentecostal explosion in *Les Météores* results in a *ruach* that mimics the defecation of the elephants:

> *Ruach* is the Hebrew word traditionally translated as "wind," "breath," "void," or "spirit." In the old Semitic South, *ruach* meant something vast, ample, and open, but it is also an odor or a perfume. . . . One of the first *ruach* of the Bible is the evening breeze in which Yahweh walks in Eden, when Adam and Eve, who have already sinned, hide from his sight. (*Mét* 156)

Once again, what Tournier omits is as important as what he includes. His gloss on the word *ruach* omits that the very first (as opposed to "one of the first") *ruach* in the Bible, the one of which all the others are in part a repetition with difference, is in the second verse of Genesis. *Ruach* is the vague spirit moving over the waters; it is the unchanneled and the *flou*. It is precisely that aspect of *ruach* that Tournier must omit: it is an impossible theoretical model for the construction of a novel. Without that aspect of *ruach*, Thomas's theory is a possibility, though a rejected one; with it, the point of view is impossible. No novel can be built on the *flou* without there being a transcendental position to organize it.

In *Les Météores*, the *flou* is organized only within the channels of the homotext and not through a transcendental figure of faith. In a world where the language of the Pentecost, the true transcendental *logos*, is lost, Thomas has to choose faith over text; he picks the antinovel in which he is separated from Jesus as from a twin (*Mét* 160). In this world of the novel without faith, a world that is only text, such a solution seems to be "the craziest" (*Mét* 160). If certain illuminated figures can go directly from the *ruach* to the Pentecost (*Mét* 160), the miraculous model cannot be used in all situations. Tournier encapsulates Thomas's disquisition on homosexuality to give the reader an alternative to Alexandre's view. But the transcendental faith and spirituality of the former are rejected in favor of the phoric textuality of the latter.

In sum, Tournier makes homosexuality the operative model for the reader's understanding of the text. At times, because of the author's implied willingness to have the reader participate in committing an intentional fallacy, a twinning model seems to be an equally valid point of view. But in the twin-couple of Jean-Paul, Jean almost always remains a silent partner. Paul's search for Jean is subsumed under the homosexual model of desire. The homosexual model is the basis for both parts of the plot, the source of textual theories, the origin of textual poetics, and the generator of metaphors and metonymies. Finally, it is the source for parameters of interpretation for characters' psychologies and their interpersonal relations. It would seem to be a totalizing model for the whole novel.

II. Toward Textual Autonomy

In this last section on *Les Météores*, I should like to turn to an examination of some final figures related to the intertwined discourses of sexuality and textuality. Whereas the theory of the homotext accounts for the deployment of difference and its exploitation, it is the commentary on masturbation as autoeroticism that explains Tournier's figures of self-identity, whence come his concepts of authority and autonomy. Enunciated most notably by Flaubert, who wanted to write a "livre sur rien," the old dream of producing an autonomous text surfaces in this novel. What is sought is a text that is self-identical, one that does not depend on the banality of the real world, one that is its own argument and foundation. To produce an autonomous text, one would need a theory founded not on a difference to be bridged nor on a substance given form, but rather on a self-sufficiency. For Tournier, turning his back on the world of heterosexuality, and even turning away from the cynegetic hunt to bridge difference through homosexual union, autonomy relates to a transcription of autoeroticism. That text would undoubtedly be Koussek's; yet it would, at the same time, undoubtedly be a Trappist text of silence.

As Koussek's immediacy and self-sufficiency cannot become a text, except as set off against other textualities (those of Alexandre and Paul, for example), Tournier must look elsewhere. He posits a model for sex and writing that seems to have the requisite independence of the other and the world, even if it does not have the perfection of immediate form and moment that he might find in a novel constructed solely of silence: "The sex organs, the hand, the brain. A magic trio. Between the sex organs and the brain, the hands, mixed, intermediate organs, little servants of both, caress due to the sex organs and write under the brain's dictation" (*Mét* 88). Autoerotic masturbation is distinct from strict homosexual desire; masturbation does not posit an external object to be attained by overcoming difference. It does not even internalize an imaginary or real other in a process analogous to the one that contains the *flou* by providing form. Rather, the object has always been there, even if the imaginary object is an ontological construct, the information for which comes from the outside, as is the case for the novel. Theorizing about masturbation brings the relation between writing and masturbation to the fore. Writing, both given and received, is the aesthetic metaphor for masturbation, intrinsically linked to it. The homotext is the means of bridging the gap, of forming the *flou*, and thus of providing the epistemological basis for knowledge, plot, character, and theme in writing. But it is the theorized relation between masturbatory activity and writing that furnishes writing with its ontological base.

Intrinsic to the theory of masturbation is the concept of representation as an ever-changing series of possibilities: representation is always metaphoric. As the hand can be various tools and various systems of inscription, the hand repeats all these as it mimics the role of a sexual organ during masturbation:

> The brain furnishes an imaginary object to the sexual organ. It is incumbent upon the hand to embody this object. The hand is an actor, plays at being this or that. At will it becomes tongs, hammer, visor, whistle, comb, reckoning system for primitives, alphabet for deaf-mutes, etc. but its masterwork is masturbation. There, it becomes a penis or vagina at will. (*Mét* 88)

The hand is a double repetition: it substitutes for the other and it inscribes differences within itself as it is a tool, a writing implement, and a sexual organ. Its masterpiece is the act of sexuality that is the metaphoric inscription of writing. In that, it inscribes two kinds of difference: absence and absolute difference. The hand involved in the masturbatory act is the singular organ that *naturally* recapitulates writing as it goes about its activity. Since the differences represented by the hand frame it and prefigure its functions, that is to say, its inscription within writing, writing is given a natural basis: it is normalized and made organic, and its basic difference subsumed within the recuperative metaphor. Like masturbation, writing is a natural function, *the* natural function of the hand.

For Tournier, writing and masturbation require the absence of the real object; desire is invested in the imaginary object formed within the interchangeable writing and masturbatory fantasies. There is a self-sufficiency to masturbation for which the external object or the other is accidental, superfluous, or unnecessary. In fact, the real object itself is an inconvenient imposition that forms a writer's block:

> The sexual object furnished by the brain and embodied by the hand can vie with the same object—real this time—and outclass it. The man who is masturbating, dreaming of a [*un*] partner, will be bothered [*sera gêné*] by the untimely arrival of this partner, and will prefer to return to his dreams, cheating on him [the partner] with the partner's own image.

Even as Tournier is developing a theorization of self-sufficient, autonomous identity, the theory falls apart, for it depends not on an expulsion, as in a heterotextual model, but on an absence. The autonomous model of sexuality and writing is a communicational model with distance; the masturbatory act or model thus refigures the act of writing anew. If verbal and physical presence determine storytelling and homo- or heterosexual intercourse, the question of the writing project, with its distance between writer and reader, is quite different. Like masturbation, the writing project relies on the marking and bridging of an additional absence between sender and receiver, masturbator and dedicatee, or writer and reader (*Mét* 89).

The matter of the textual fetish relates to the figuration of the absent object of desire and the representation of that object; the fetish is thus a textual figure as well. Ultimately, the fetishized object is *any* object to be represented in the text. The absence of this fetishized object keeps the act of representation in control; description occurs in a regular, orderly, and progressive way. The sudden pressure and presence of the object engages the confrontation between the imaginary and the real, and a textual upheaval ensues. The amount of description increases and the processes of fiction making are interrupted; such is the case with the description of Eustache (*Mét* 240–41) in which the presence of the body as the object disrupts the flow of text. The movement toward sex is arrested as a *loquèle* emerges and the text itself becomes a *coup sec*. Just as the masturbatory hand fulfills several functions by reinscribing two kinds of absence, the fetishized object is inscribed as a figuration of an absent set of male genitals: "the arm is a little leg" (*Mét* 241).

Most of the time, however, the insistence on a textual fetish is a mise-en-abyme of the author's procedure. In a process that mimics the author attacking his object, the rats that attack Daniel's body destroy the nape of the neck and the genitals. The latter, however, are set apart, as his belly becomes "a bloody wound" (304). Fetishistic writing allows Tournier repeatedly to inscribe points of power, focal points, textual tools, writing implements, and writing mechanisms that are figures of male genitals. He proposes creating a garbage truck with a trunk (*benne à trompe*), but the trunk must "take on the shape of a penis" (*Mét* 137). More than Freudian phallic symbols, male genitals represent an animation of the fetishized object for Tournier. They are the means of realizing the masturbatory fantasy. Ultimately, they are the way of providing closure to the homotext that now fulfills, completes, and effects both desire and representation. For Alexandre, God is "a hard penis standing above the base of its two testicles . . . an idol with a trunk hung in the exact center of the human body" (*Mét* 123). Though deprived of its transcendental aspects in Alexandre's version, Thomas's theory of the word made flesh finally finds its appropriate place in the novel's complex of theoretical positions.

Despite the pivotal role assumed by theories about interpretation and about the relation between sexuality and textuality, Tournier provides an escape mechanism: an aesthetic system distinct from the homotext, a countermeasure that protects against the failure of the project as a whole—for the project that depends on a perfect organization of the imaginary around a few nodal points is doomed to fail. Writing is always occurring along a *clinamen*; there is always a decline away from the bridged gap; the only truly autonomous text is a silent, autistic one. So despite its strength for producing a singular novel in which sexuality and textuality are the interchangeable, or perhaps the indistinct, signs of one another, the homotext cannot wholly succeed. For that reason, Alexandre must die a relatively ignoble and anonymous death, the negation of the singularity of his homotextuality. The nonnegotiable otherness of some form of heterotextuality always surfaces sooner or later. That is precisely the point: no matter how recuperative homotextuality might be of difference, it too performs an exclusion, the exclusion of heterosexual exclusion, and excluded exclusion or repressed repression will always return.

Tournier's final strategic position is to develop an aesthetic theory that takes into account this necessary, irrevocable decline. The complete homotext in which all difference is accounted for through writing and which can posit an autochthonous origin for itself is aesthetically impossible for Tournier. His theory of imitation, the ersatz, and the fake, announced as such, provides the escape valve. Within the text, this aesthetic accounts for and exposes difference and thereby lets it remain difference. It accounts for whatever does not ring true; it is the theory for the novel as travesty. He says, in fact, that he has "a weakness for food in drag" (*Mét* 95–96); this includes "mushrooms, vegetables disguised as meat; lamb's brains, meat disguised as fruit pulp; avocados, with their buttery flesh. Above all, I like fish, false flesh that is nothing, as they say, without sauce." Difference is not integrated into a homotext or into a masturbatory fantasy; rather, it speaks volumes for itself. In any aesthetic, Alexandre is interested only in imitations because they are the original "pin-pointed, possessed, integrated, eventually multiplied, in short, spiritualized" (101).

Finally, the *dandy des gadoues* posits another creative activity, the process of production and consumption, the repetition of the same, endlessly reinscribed. It still produces a set of fragmentary differences that is the antithesis of the pure aesthetic object; this set is the garbage dump but it is also the *disjecta membra* of the novel, where these copies upon copies lie scattered pell-mell (*Mét* 103). By inscribing an antiaesthetics within an equally valid aesthetics, Tournier allows his own novel to have a safe and sure posterity, at least in a specular fashion. Whether it is an object of mass consumption to be used and thrown away, a copy of some real aesthetic object, or the real thing, its position is already inscribed within the novel's own theorization of itself.

White elephant, elephant graveyard, object remembered in an elephantine memory, pink elephant, elephant joke, Ganesha, the elephant god (*Mét* 51), symptom of elephantiasis: *Les Météores* is an amalgam of all these. Surin, city of elephants, contains multitudes of these strange beasts, gigantic cattle with serpentine parts. The elephantine novel is an attempt to straighten out the masturbatory fantasy closed in upon itself—"the emblem being the snake swallowing its own tail" (*Mét* 89)—without a retreat into the pitfalls or commonplaces of romantic and realist narrative fiction. Those genres are themselves symbolized in the scattered reappearances of real objects in Alexandre's text and especially in the frequent intrusions of a banal version of reality in the last third of the book where elephantiasis has set up a stronghold. Of course, if absolute priority is given to the intentions of the author, if the twins, and not Alexandre, are seen as the subject of the novel, the last third of the novel fits; unfortunately the first two-thirds make less sense. This safer path is the one often chosen by critics, such as Merllié, who feels Alexandre's death is good riddance since Alexandre threatened to take over the text and divert it from its theme of twinning. One way or another, the novel must be seen as lopsided; that is the only manner of engaging its singularity.

Having wanted to write a text in Aeolian, the special language of the twins, Tournier finds Aeolus instead. The work ends with a meteorological figure that still leaves a door open for a successful Aeolian harp the next time. It is a wish for complete sublimation and for the sublime as well:

> Yet the snow layer gets thinner in the fields, and clumps of tilled black earth appear. The sun is strong and provokes the evaporation of the snow *without a thaw*. Above the hard and intact masses of snow vibrates a transparent, iridescent fog. The snow becomes vapor without melting, flowing, or softening.
>
> That is called: sublimation. (*Mét* 625)

Like an elephant, the homotext is incontrovertibly present. It may, like a juggernaut, destroy everything in its path or it may make everything turn into an iridescent *ruach* in an act in which reality and textual difference are completely sublimated. But in any case, if an elephant graveyard—that wasteland or junk pile that no one can remark or sublimate—remains potential but undiscovered, the elephantine novel of the homotext, be it gray, white, or pink, still remains.

Bibliography

Adams, J. N. *The Latin Sexual Vocabulary*. Baltimore: Johns Hopkins University Press, 1982.

Apter, Emily. *André Gide and the Codes of Homotextuality*. Saratoga, Calif.: Anima Libri (Stanford French and Italian Studies), 1987.

Baetens, Jan. *Les Mesures de l'excès. Essai sur Renaud Camus*. Paris: Impressions Nouvelles, 1992.

Balzac, Honoré de. *Le Père Goriot*. In *La Comédie humaine*, vol. 2. Paris: Seuil [Intégrale], 1965

Bannet, Eve Tavor. *Structuralism and the Logic of Dissent: Barthes, Derrida, Foucault, Lacan*. Urbana: University of Illinois Press, 1989.

Barthes, Roland. *L'Aventure sémiologique*. Paris: Seuil, 1985.

———. *Le Bruissement de la langue. Essais critiques IV*. Paris: Seuil, 1984.

———. *La Chambre claire. Note sur la photographie*. Paris: Editions de l'Etoile. Cahiers du Cinéma. Gallimard. Seuil, 1980.

———. *Le Degré zéro de l'écriture suivi de Nouveaux Essais critiques*. Paris: Seuil [Points], 1953 and 1972.

———. *Fragments d'un discours amoureux*. Paris: Seuil, 1977.

———. *Incidents*. Paris: Seuil, 1987.

———. *Leçon*. Paris: Seuil, 1978.

———. "Masculin, féminin, neutre." In *Echanges et communications: Mélanges offerts à Claude Lévi-Strauss à l'occasion de son 60ème anniversaire*. Ed. Jean Pouillon and Pierre Maranda. 2 vols. The Hague: Mouton, 1970, 2:893–907.

———. *Mythologies*. Paris: Seuil, 1957.

———. *Le Plaisir du texte*. Paris: Seuil, 1973.

———. *Roland Barthes*. Paris: Seuil [Ecrivains de Toujours], 1975.

———. *Sade. Fourier. Loyola*. Paris: Seuil, 1971.

———. *Sur Racine*. Paris: Seuil, 1963.

———. *S/Z*. Paris: Seuil, 1970.

Bataille, Georges. *L'Histoire de l'érotisme*. In *Oeuvres Complètes*, vol. 8. Paris: Gallimard, 1976.

Beaujour, Michel. *Miroirs d'encre. Rhétorique de l'autoportrait*. Paris: Seuil, 1980.

Beaver, Harold. "Homosexual Signs (*In Memory of Roland Barthes*)." *Critical Inquiry* 8.1 (1981): 99–119.

Bensmaïa, Réda. *The Barthes Effect: The Essay as Reflective Text*. Trans. Pat Fedkiew. Minneapolis: University of Minnesota Press, 1987.

———. "Du fragment au détail." *Poétique* 47 (1981): 355–70.

Benveniste, Emile. *Problèmes de linguistique générale*, vol. 1. Paris: Gallimard [TEL], 1966.

Bergman, David. *Gaiety Transfigured: Gay Self-Representation in American Literature*. Madison: University of Wisconsin Press, 1991.

Bernheimer, Charles. *Figures of Ill Repute: Representing Prostitution in Nineteenth-Century France*. Cambridge, Mass.: Harvard University Press, 1989.

Bersani, Leo. *The Culture of Redemption*. Cambridge, Mass.: Harvard University Press, 1990.

Blanchot, Maurice. *L'Entretien infini*. Paris: Gallimard, 1969.

Borges, Jorge Luís. *Other Inquisitions 1937–1952*. Trans. Ruth L. C. Simms. New York: Simon and Schuster, 1965.

Bougnoux, Daniel. "Des métaphores à la phorie." *Critique* 28 (1972), 527–43.

Bouloumié, Arlette. *Michel Tournier. Le Roman Mythologique suivi de questions à Michel Tournier*. Paris: José Corti, 1988.

Brown, Andrew. *Roland Barthes: The Figures of Writing*. Oxford: Oxford University Press [Clarendon], 1992.

Butler, Judith. *Gender Trouble: Feminism and the Subversion of Identity*. New York: Routledge, 1990.

Calvet, Louis-Jean. *Roland Barthes*. Paris: Flammarion, 1990.

Camus, Renaud. *Aguets. Journal 1988*. Paris: P.O.L., 1990.

———. *Buena Vista Park*. Paris: Hachette/P.O.L., 1980.

———. *Chroniques achriennes*. Paris: P.O.L., 1984.

———. *Elégies pour quelques-uns*. Paris: P.O.L., 1988.

———. *Esthétique de la solitude*. Paris: P.O.L., 1990.

———. *Fendre l'air. Journal 1989*. Paris: P.O.L., 1991.

———. *Journal romain, 1985–1986*. Paris: P.O.L., 1987.

———. *Notes achriennes*. Paris: Hachette/P.O.L., 1982.

———. *Notes sur les manières du temps*. Paris: P.O.L., 1985.

———. *Roman furieux*. Paris: P.O.L., 1987.

———. *Roman roi*. Paris: P.O.L., 1983.

———. *Tricks*. Preface by Roland Barthes. Paris: Persona, 1982.

———. *Vigiles. Journal 1987*. Paris: P.O.L., 1989.

Camus, Renaud, and Tony Duparc. *Travers*. Paris: Hachette/P.O.L., 1978.

Chambers, Ross. *Meaning and Meaningfulness: Studies in the Analysis and Interpretation of Texts*. Lexington, Ky.: French Forum, 1979.

Comment, Bernard. *Roland Barthes, vers le neutre*. Paris: Christian Bourgois, 1991.

Compagnon, Antoine. *Proust entre deux siècles*. Paris: Seuil, 1989.

———, ed. *Prétexte: Roland Barthes. Colloque de Cerisy*. Paris: U.G.E. [10/18], 1978.

Corbin, Alain. *Le Miasme et la jonquille: L'odorat et l'imaginaire social XVIII*^{e}*–XIX*^{e} *siècles*. Paris: Champs-Flammarion, 1982 [rpt. 1986].

Culler, Jonathan. *Structuralist Poetics: Structuralism, Linguistics, and the Study of Literature*. Ithaca, N.Y.: Cornell University Press, 1975.

de la Croix, Arnaud. *Barthes, pour une éthique des signes*. Brussels: De Boeck-Wesmael, 1987.

Deleuze, Gilles. *Foucault*. Paris: Minuit, 1986.

———. *Pourparlers*. Paris: Minuit, 1990.

———. *Proust et les signes*, 4th ed. Paris: Presses Universitaires de France, 1976.

Deleuze, Gilles, and Félix Guattari. *L'Anti-Oedipe. Capitalisme et schizophrénie*. Paris: Editions de Minuit, 1972.

Deleuze, Gilles, and Claire Parnet. *Dialogues*. Paris: Flammarion, 1977.

de Man, Paul. *Allegories of Reading: Figural Language in Rousseau, Nietzsche, Rilke, and Proust*. New Haven: Yale University Press, 1979.

Derrida, Jacques. *L'Autre Cap*. Paris: Minuit, 1991.

———. *De la grammatologie*. Paris: Minuit, 1967.

———. *La Dissémination*. Paris: Seuil, 1972.

———. *L'Ecriture et la différence*. Paris: Seuil, 1967.

———. *Marges de la philosophie*. Paris: Minuit, 1972.

———. *Positions*. Paris: Minuit, 1971.

———. *La Vérité en peinture*. Paris: Champs-Flammarion, 1978.

Descombes, Vincent. *Proust. Philosophie du roman*. Paris: Editions de Minuit, 1987.

Dreyfus, Hubert L., and Paul Rabinow. *Michel Foucault: Beyond Structuralism and Hermeneutics*. Chicago: University of Chicago Press, 1982.

Duvert, Tony. *L'Enfant au masculin. Essais, livre premier*. Paris: Editions de Minuit, 1980.

Ellis, Havelock. *Studies in the Psychology of Sex*. 4 vols. New York: Random House, 1936.

Fernandez, Dominique. *Le Rapt de Ganymède*. Paris: Grasset, 1989.

Force, Pierre, and Dominique Jullien. "Renaud Camus." In *After the Age of Suspicion: The French Novel Today*. Ed. Charles A. Porter. *Yale French Studies* (special issue), (1988): 285–90.

Foster, Jeannette H. *Sex Variant Women in Literature*. New York: Vantage Press, 1956 [rpt. Tallahassee: Naiad Press, 1985].

Foucault, Michel. *Les Mots et les choses. Une archéologie des sciences humaines*. Paris: Gallimard, 1966.

———. *Politics, Philosophy, Culture: Interviews and Other Writings, 1977–1984*. Ed. Lawrence D. Kritzman. New York: Routledge, Chapman & Hall, 1988.

———. *Le Souci de soi. Histoire de la sexualité 3*. Paris: Gallimard, 1984.

———. *La Volonté de savoir. Histoire de la sexualité 1*. Paris: Gallimard, 1976.

Fuss, Diana. *Inside/Out: Lesbian Theories, Gay Theories*. New York: Routledge, 1991.

Gallop, Jane. *Thinking Through the Body*. New York: Columbia University Press, 1988.

Genette, Gérard. *Figures III*. Paris: Seuil, 1972.

Gide, André. *Corydon*. Paris: Gallimard, 1924.

———. *Journal 1889–1939*. Paris: Gallimard [Pléiade], 1951.

———. *Romans. Récits et Sorties. Oeuvres lyriques*. Paris: Gallimard [Pléiade], 1958.

———. *Si le grain ne meurt*. Paris: Gallimard [Pléiade], 1955.

Girard, René. *Le Bouc émissaire*. Paris: Grasset, 1982.

———. *Des choses cachées depuis la fondation du monde*. Paris: Grasset, 1978.

———. *La Violence et le sacré*. Paris: Grasset, 1972.

Gloaguen, Philippe, and Pierre Josse. *Le Guide du routard. Asie du Sud-Est*. Paris: Hachette, 1987.

Grahn, Judy. *Another Mother Tongue: Gay Words, Gay Worlds*. Boston: Beacon Press, 1984.

Gray, Margaret E. *Postmodern Proust*. Philadelphia: University of Pennsylvania, 1992.

Grevisse, Maurice. *Le Bon Usage. Grammaire Française avec des remarques sur la langue française d'aujourd'hui*. Gembloux, Belgium: Editions J. Duculot, 1969.

Hegel, G. W. F. *Phänomenologie des Geistes*. In *Werke*, Bd. 3. Frankfurt: Suhrkamp Verlag, 1970.

Hueston, Penny. "An Interview with Michel Tournier." *Meanjin* 38.3: (1979), 400–405.

Jay, Salim. *Idriss, Michel Tournier et les autres*. Paris: Editions de la Différence, 1986.

Johnson, Barbara. *The Critical Difference: Essays in the Contemporary Rhetoric of Reading*. Baltimore: Johns Hopkins University Press, 1980.

Jouve, Vincent. *La Littérature selon Barthes*. Paris: Editions de Minuit, 1986.

Koestenbaum, Wayne. *Double Talk: The Erotics of Male Literary Collaboration*. New York: Routledge, 1989.

Kojève, Alexandre. *Introduction à la lecture de Hegel*. 2nd ed. Paris: Gallimard, 1947.

Kuroda, S. Y. "Réflexions sur les fondements de la théorie de la narration." In *Langue, discours, société. Pour Emile Benveniste*. Ed. Julia Kristeva, Jean-Claude Milner, Nicolas Ruwet. Paris: Seuil, 1975. 260–93.

Lacan, Jacques. *Ecrits*. Paris: Seuil, 1966.

Lang, Candace D. *Irony/Humor: Critical Paradigms*. Baltimore: Johns Hopkins University Press, 1988.

Laplanche, Jean, and J.-B. Pontalis. *Vocabulaire de la psychanalyse*. 5th ed. Paris: Presses Universitaires de France, 1976.

Lévi-Strauss, Claude. *La Potière jalouse*. Paris: Plon, 1985.

Lombardo, Patrizia. *The Three Paradoxes of Roland Barthes*. Athens: University of Georgia Press, 1989.

Lyotard, Jean-François. *Le Postmoderne expliqué aux enfants*. Paris: Galilée, 1986.

Marin, Louis. *Utopiques: Jeux d'espaces*. Paris: Gallimard, 1973.

Marty, Eric. *André Gide: Qui êtes-vous? avec les entretiens André Gide–Jean Amrouche*. Lyon: La Manufacture, 1987.

Marx, Karl, and Friedrich Engels. *Ausgewählte Werke*. 6 vols. plus index. Berlin: Dietz Verlag, 1981–83.

Mehlman, Jeffrey. *A Structural Study of Autobiography: Proust, Leiris, Sartre, Lévi-Strauss*. Ithaca, N.Y.: Cornell University Press, 1974.

Melkonian, Martin. *Le Corps couché de Roland Barthes*. Paris: Librairie Séguier, 1989.

Merllié, Françoise. *Michel Tournier*. Paris: Belfond, 1988.

Michel, François-Bernard. *Le Souffle coupé. Respirer et écrire*. Paris: Gallimard, 1984.

Miller, D. A. *Bringing Out Roland Barthes*. Berkeley: University of California Press, 1992.

Miller, James. *The Passion of Michel Foucault*. New York: Simon and Schuster, 1993.

Mishima, Yukio. *Confessions of a Mask*. Trans. Meredith Weatherby. New York: New Directions, 1958.

Mohr, Richard D. *Gay Ideas: Outing and Other Controversies*. Boston: Beacon Press, 1992.

———. *Gays/Justice: A Study of Ethics, Society, and Law*. New York: Columbia University Press, 1988.

Nancy, Jean-Luc. "Larvatus Pro Deo." Trans. Daniel A. Brewer. *GLYPH* 2 (1977), 14–36.

Paglia, Camille. *Sex, Art, and American Culture*. New York: Vintage, 1992.

Pavel, Thomas. *Fictional Worlds*. Cambridge, Mass.: Harvard University Press, 1986.

Penrose, Roger. *The Emperor's New Mind: Concerning Computers, Minds, and the Laws of Physics*. New York: Oxford, 1989.

Pleasants, Henry. *The Great Singers: From the Dawn of Opera to Our Own Time*. New York: Simon and Schuster, 1966.

Pollard, Patrick. *André Gide: Homosexual Moralist*. New Haven, Conn.: Yale University Press, 1991.

Poster, Mark. *Critical Theory and Poststructuralism: In Search of a Context*. Ithaca, N.Y.: Cornell University Press, 1989.

Prince, Gerald. *A Dictionary of Narratology*. Lincoln: University of Nebraska Press, 1987.

Proust, Marcel. *A la recherche du temps perdu*. Ed. Jean-Yves Tadié et al. 4 vols. Paris: Gallimard [Pléiade], 1987–89.

Purdy, Anthony. "*Les Météores* de Michel Tournier: une perspective hétérologique." *Littérature* 40 (1980): 32–43.

Racevskis, Karlis. *Michel Foucault and the Subversion of Intellect*. Ithaca, N.Y.: Cornell University Press, 1983.

Rajchman, John. *Michel Foucault: The Freedom of Philosophy*. New York: Columbia University Press, 1985.

Ricardou, Jean. *Nouveaux problèmes du roman*. Paris: Seuil, 1978.

Riffaterre, Michael. *Fictional Truth*. Baltimore: Johns Hopkins University Press, 1990.

Rivers, J. E. *Proust and the Art of Love: The Aesthetics of Sexuality in the Life, Times, and Art of Marcel Proust*. New York: Columbia University Press, 1980.

Roger, Philippe. *Roland Barthes, roman*. Paris: Grasset, 1986.

Rosello, Mireille. *L'In-différence chez Michel Tournier*. Paris: José Corti, 1990.

Sartre, Jean-Paul. *L'Etre et le néant. Essai d'ontologie phénoménologique*. Paris: Gallimard [TEL], 1943 [rpt. 1977].

Saylor, Douglas B. *The Sadomasochistic Homotext: Readings in Sade, Balzac, and Proust*. New York: Peter Lang, 1992.

Schehr, Lawrence R. *Alcibiades at the Door: Gay Discourses in French Literature*. Stanford, Calif.: Stanford University Press, 1995.

———. "A Chronicle of Production: The Creation of an Enunciative Framework in *Le Rouge et le Noir*." *Australian Journal of French Studies* 22.1 (1985): 43–59.

———. *Flaubert and Sons: Readings of Flaubert, Zola and Proust*. New York: Peter Lang, 1986.

———. "The Homotext of Tournier's *Les Météores*," *SubStance* 58 (1989): 35–50.

———. "Renaud Camus' Roman Columns," *SubStance* 67 (1992): 111–28.

———. "Tournier's Theoretical Pretext Works Like a Charm," *Studies in Twentieth-Century Literature* 12.2 (1988): 221–38.

Schor, Naomi. *Reading in Detail: Aesthetics and the Feminine*. New York: Methuen, 1987.

———. "Dreaming Dissymmetry: Barthes, Foucault, and Sexual Difference." In *Men in Feminism*. Ed. Alice Jardine and Paul Smith. New York: Methuen, 1987. 98–110.

Sedgwick, Eve Kosofsky. *Between Men*. New York: Columbia University Press, 1985.

———. *Epistemology of the Closet*. Berkeley: University of California Press, 1990.

Serres, Michel. *Feux et signaux de brume. Zola*. Paris: Grasset, 1975.

———. *Hermès I. La Communication*. Paris: Minuit, 1968.

———. *Hermès III. La Traduction*. Paris: Minuit, 1974.

———. *Le Parasite*. Paris: Grasset, 1980.

Shapiro, Gary, and Alan Sica, eds. *Hermeneutics: Questions and Prospects*. Amherst: University of Massachusetts Press, 1984.

Sichère, Bernard. *Eloge du sujet. Du retard de la pensée sur les corps*. Paris: Grasset, 1990.

Silverman, Kaja. *Male Subjectivity at the Margins*. New York: Routledge, 1992.

———. *The Subject of Semiotics*. New York: Oxford University Press, 1983.

Sontag, Susan. *Under the Sign of Saturn*. New York: Farrar, Straus, & Giroux, 1980.

Stambolian, George, and Elaine Marks, eds. *Homosexualities and French Literature: Cultural Contexts/Critical Texts*. Ithaca, N.Y.: Cornell University Press, 1979.

Stanton, Domna C. "The Mater of the Text: Barthesian Displacement and Its Limits." *L'Esprit Créateur* 25.2 (1985): 57–72.

Stendhal [Marie-Henri Beyle]. *Romans et nouvelles*. Vol. 1. Ed. Henri Martineau. Paris: Gallimard [Pléiade], 1952.

Thomas, Jean-Jacques. "Sensationalism." *Studies in Twentieth-Century Literature* 5.2 (1981): 205–17.

Tournier, Michel. *Gaspard, Melchior & Balthazar*. Paris: Gallimard, 1980.

———. *La Goutte d'or*. Paris: Gallimard, 1985.

———. *Journal de voyage au Canada*. Photographs by Edouard Bouabat. Paris: Robert Laffont, 1984.

———. *Les Météores*. Paris: Gallimard [Folio], 1975.

———. *Le Roi des aulnes*. Paris: Gallimard [Folio], 1975.

———. *Vendredi ou les limbes du Pacifique*. Paris: Gallimard [Folio], 1972.

———. *Le Vent Paraclet*. Paris: Gallimard, 1977.

———. *Le Vol du vampire*. Paris: Mercure de France, 1981.

Tournier, Michel, and Jean-Max Toubeau. *Le Vagabond immobile*. Paris: Gallimard, 1984.

Ulmer, Gregory. *Teletheory: Grammatology in the Age of Video*. New York: Routledge, Chapman & Hall, 1989.

Ungar, Steven. *Roland Barthes: The Professor of Desire*. Lincoln: University of Nebraska Press, 1983.

Vernant, Jean-Pierre. *Myth and Thought Among the Greeks*, trans. anon. London: Routledge & Kegan Paul, 1983.

Warminski, Andrzej. *Readings in Interpretation*. Minneapolis: University of Minnesota Press, 1987.

White, Hayden. *Metahistory: The Historical Imagination in Nineteenth-Century Europe*. Baltimore: Johns Hopkins University Press, 1973.

———. "Writing in the Middle Voice." *Stanford Literature Review* 9.2 (1992): 179–87.

Wiseman, Mary Bittner. *The Ecstasies of Roland Barthes*. London: Routledge, 1989.

Wittig, Monique. *The Straight Mind and Other Essays*. Boston: Beacon, 1992.

Yingling, Thomas E. *Hart Crane and the Homosexual Text: New Thresholds, New Anatomies*. Chicago: University of Chicago Press, 1990.

Index

Library of Congress Cataloging-in-Publication Data
Schehr, Lawrence R.
The shock of men : homosexual hermeneutics in French writing / Lawrence R. Schehr.
p. cm.
Includes bibliographical references and index.
ISBN 0-8047-2417-2
1. French literature—20th century—History and criticism.
2. Homosexuality and literature—France—History—20th century.
3. French literature—Men authors—History and criticism. 4. Gay men's writings, French—History and criticism. 5. Gay men—France—Intellectual life. 6. Gay men in literature. 7. Hermeneutics. I. Title.
PQ307.H6S34 1995
840.9'353—dc20 94-40433
CIP